2-6-93

To the Women's
Health Center,

Keep up the good
work

Alice Zand

Men, Women, and Infertility

Intervention and Treatment Strategies

Aline P. Zoldbrod

LEXINGTON BOOKS
An Imprint of Macmillan, Inc.
New York

Maxwell Macmillan Canada
Toronto

Maxwell Macmillan International
New York   Oxford   Singapore   Sydney

Library of Congress Cataloging-in-Publication Data

Zoldbrod, Aline P.
  Men, women, and infertility: intervention and treatment strategies/Aline P. Zoldbrod.
    p.   cm.
  Includes bibliographical references.
  ISBN 0-669-27270-1
  1. Infertility—Patients—Counseling of.   2. Infertility—Psychological aspects.   I. Title.
  [DNLM: 1. Counseling—methods.   2. Infertility—psychology.   3. Infertility—
therapy.   WP 570 Z86m]
  RC889.Z65   1993
  616.692′0019—dc20
  DNLM/DLC
  for Library of Congress   92-49301
                                                                                      CIP

Lexington Books
An Imprint of Macmillan, Inc.
866 Third Avenue, New York, N.Y. 10022

Maxwell Macmillan Canada, Inc.
1200 Eglinton Avenue East
Suite 200
Don Mills, Ontario M3C 3N1

Macmillan, Inc. is part of the Maxwell Communication
Group of Companies.

Printed in the United States of America

printing number
1   2   3   4   5   6   7   8   9   10

This book is dedicated to the memory of my warm and loving parents, Monya Greenstein Zoldbrod and Lewis Zoldbrod

Contents

Part 4   Appendixes

List of Figures

Preface

My intention in writing this book is to raise some important questions and issues about infertility and to share, in a practical and down-to-earth way, what I believe to be some useful techniques. This book is aimed at trained therapists who don't specialize in infertility. I hope it will enable them to understand the infertility experience as if they had undergone it. I believe that *Men, Women, and Infertility* also offers some new techniques to even the most seasoned infertility clinicians.

In addition, I hope that this book will be accessible to a wide range of health providers—not just psychologists, psychiatrists, and social workers, but also nurses and physicians. I suspect some patients may take a look at it as well.

This book is not encyclopedic. It does not contain a scholarly review of all of the research literature. It doesn't focus on dynamics, on the how-to's of making various choices, or on ethics. It does not focus on the process of helping with grief or on how to be empathic. If you are just beginning to learn about how to help infertility patients, this is not the book to begin with.

Inevitably, readers will wish that I had covered some topics that are not included here. I am not going to review or repeat all of the excellent work that has already been done on infertility (e.g., Mazor, 1978, 1984; Menning, 1977; Salzer, 1986) or on working with grief (e.g., John Bowlby's masterpiece, *Loss*, 1980). The reader will be directed toward the sources. Useful references can be found in the list at the back of the book.

This book arises out of over two decades of clinical work as a psychologist, out of my long-standing interest in medical psychology, and out of my own three years of experience with infertility. I do not have to dig very deep to bump up against the memories of my own despair, helplessness, and rage during the period of time when I didn't know if I would ever give birth to a child.

My biggest fear is that what I say will be misinterpreted, and that psychotherapists and others reading *Men, Women, and Infertility* will use behavioral interventions to cut off important feelings *instead* of beginning with empathy and sitting with the patients' awful feelings. Those who know my clinical work know I don't work that way. I can tolerate innumerable hours of grief and sadness.

But I also know that empathy is not enough to offer patients who are in a chronic struggle with their infertility. No one can stand year after year of not knowing what the future will bring. The techniques described here can work wonders, and I want to share them.

Some readers will be bothered by the theoretical eclecticism in these pages. From chapter to chapter, I bounce freely between the perspectives of feminism, behavioral medical psychology, psychoanalytically oriented psychotherapy, and multimodal therapy (MMT). So be it. This is how I operate clinically, too. I consider a number of precious women and men my mentors, and their voices have all been internalized (and sometimes have arguments!).

Infertility is undoubtedly a couples issue, and it may seem curious that most of the ongoing therapeutic work described here is individual work done with women. This happened for a variety of reasons, all quite logical. Research (reviewed in Chapter 2) has found women to be more profoundly disturbed by infertility than men, to feel more personally inadequate because of it, to take more responsibility for planning treatment, to have an easier time talking about it, and to feel more comfortable seeking emotional support for it. Frequently, women want individual treatment with a woman therapist. They want to have a special place where they can be understood, can grieve, and can learn some coping strategies—all in order to feel more in control, so that they will then feel more in harmony with their seemingly less upset husbands. This book documents the work I have done, which has been mostly individual psychotherapy with women.

Language presented a peculiar sort of challenge, and I am not certain that I have adequately met it. I have chosen to use the terms *she* and *the patient* frequently, rather than *he or she* or *the couple*. Even though the person with the medical problem is the male at least 30 percent of the time, research and clinical experience have shown that it is most frequently the woman who presents herself as the patient for both medical and psychological treatment.

In general, I discuss interventions made with a relatively health group of white, middle-class, married patients. (For patients who are more seriously disturbed, the therapist should use caution and her best judgment.) One of my great regrets is that I was not able to write about how infertility affects people from diverse racial, ethnic, and class backgrounds.

In a way, I have been writing this book for my whole life. My mother, Monya Zoldbrod, is gone now, but this book reminds me of her. Besides being an unusually empathic and warm person, she was a medical social worker who liked to fight for patients' rights. She believed in the healing power of feeling in control in medical situations thirty-five years ago. She used to send her clinic patients at Montefiore Hospital in Pittsburgh back into the clinic armed with a written list of their questions and concerns to ask their physicians. She told them that it was their right to ask questions until they had all the answers that they needed. My mother was an unusual, wonderful person.

She also had the good sense to marry my father, Lewis Zoldbrod. It is only after delving so deeply into other people's families that I could truly understand how unusually lucky I was in having not just a mother but also a father who took me seriously and respected as well as loved me. My dad also gave me the gift of the writing gene.

I guess that one could consider this a second-generation story of infertility. My parents, who married when they were thirty and forty, respectively, had difficulty conceiving me. Later, my mother wanted to adopt; my father didn't. He couldn't be swayed. That left me an only child, thanks to infertility. My husband and I had difficulty, too. After several years of misery, we wound up with two wonderful children, Monya and Lev.

It has been an interesting few years, writing this book while living in the suburbs, seeing patients, and taking care of two small children. The book took so long—over three years—that Monya and Lev aren't so small anymore. But there were times when I wasn't able to write anything at all for months as, one after the other, they got rounds of illness, were quarantined sequentially, and so on.

I could not have survived these years and written anything without our baby-sitter and grandmother-substitute, Mrs. Joan Kelly Arena. She has loved my children so much, and they have loved her so much, that I never felt guilty, believe it or not. That's a gift. Joan, I could never thank you enough!

This book also could not have come into being without the support and assistance of the wonderful librarians at the Cary Memorial Library in Lexington, Massachusetts, particularly Cynthia Johnson Whealler, and also Wikje Feteris, Jane Eastman, Julie Triessl, and Judy Adams. They got so used to my putting in interlibrary loan requests over the last several years that they thought something was wrong if they didn't have a stack of requests from me. They did some things that were quite above and beyond the call of duty, and they provided both warmth and expert help.

Without the assistance and unflinching support of my husband, Larry Osterweil, this book would have taken thirty years. He nagged me and nagged me to learn to use a word processor when I was in the book-proposal stage, and I finally did. He has bailed me out on innumerable occasions when the computer froze, I gave it the wrong command, or I lost files. He helped compile the citations. He made the book a high priority in his life, too, and his support of my career has made life much more fun.

Throughout this entire process, I have been amazed at how generous friends and colleagues have been with their time and their critical faculties. Let me ask for forgiveness, in advance, from any people whose names I have inadvertently forgotten to list.

I have met a lot of my colleagues through my years serving on the National

Board of Directors of RESOLVE. Dr. Holly Simons, Ph.D. read the entire manuscript. Isaac Schiff, M.D., has taken the time to write me notes of encouragement after reading many sections of the book. Thanks, too, to RESOLVE friend, Gary Gross, M.D. And, I have treasured Pat Johnston's general wisdom and our conversations about adoption.

Judy Calica's genuine enthusiasm for and support of my work has gladdened my heart. Merle Bombadieri, M.S.W., has been generous in giving her time, writing expertise, and encouragement, too, and she read the entire book and commented. Also, Cathy Romeo, Miriam Mazor, M.D., Shiela Mahrer, Ph.D., and Nancy Jainchill, Ph.D., gave willingly of their time and energy in reading and commenting on these words. Sisterhood still lives, even if it is the 1990s.

Thanks are due to Tom and Cathy Richardson, phone friends from Resolve who let me publish their letter. Thanks, too, to all the Resolve chapters that have sent me their newsletters.

A number of nurses have been very helpful to me, reading what I have written and encouraging me: Vicki MacLean, RNP, Laurea Nugent, RNP, Carol Taylor, RNP, Mimi Clarke Secor, RNP, and Judy Carleo, R. N.. Mary Juneau Norcross, RNP was generous enough to critique the entire manuscript. Cathy A. James, RNC M.S., has been invaluable.

Other nurses have been very supportive of the ideas in this book, as presented to them verbally. I'd especially like to thank: Joan M. Hammond, RN, MSN; Kathy Turner-Tamiyasu, RNC, NP; Stanley S. Grant, RN, BSN; Linda Bailey, RNC, and Sandra J. Hahn, RNC, BSN for their enthusiasm and for engaging in critical dialogue.

Much of my work was inspired by the work of a few other psychologists. Arnold Lazarus, Ph.D., and David Barlow, Ph.D., both took time away from their incredibly busy schedules to read and comment on parts of this book. Their support and their generosity of spirit has meant a lot to me. Dr. Lazarus's sense of humor has been a special treat.

Dr. Judy Silverstein read and commented on much of the manuscript and enriched the chapter on male and female sexuality. I also want to thank Veronica Ravnikar, M.D., Richard Reindollar, M.D., Stuart Pesin, M.D., and Peter Rotolo, M.D., Drs. Pesin, Ravnikar, and Rotolo made concrete contributions to the chapter on anxiety and miscarriage. Abe Morgentaler, M.D., and Robert Oates, M.D., read and critiqued much of what I have written about men's issues. Other people whose encouragement has warmed and fed me are Andre Guay, M.D., Robert Hunt, M.D., Andrew Duncan, Ph.D., Leo Sorger, M.D., Joan Jack, Diane Clapp, R.N., and Damon Blank, M.Ed., and my friends Carolyn and Steve. Thanks, too, to the staff at Lexington Books: especially my editor Margaret Zusky, and to Carol Mayhew and Sara Zobel. My copy editor Margaret Ritchie was quite remarkable. Thanks to my illustrator, Judy Bogart.

Bill Kates, M.D., has been my clinical consultant in years past. Even when I don't see him, he still influences me. Bill read selected parts of what I had written and responded in his characteristic thoughtful, supportive, yet challenging way. Even when I didn't agree with him, the points he made were so cogent that I had to respond to them within the manuscript itself.

My cousin, Martha Tolpin, Ph.D., has cheered me on throughout this project. Her ongoing support has been symbolic of the encouragement I was lucky enough to have throughout life from my extended family, including my three dear aunts who are now deceased: Rae Goldborer, Pauline Tolpin, and Caroline Zolbrod. I wish they were still here to see this book come to fruition.

A note to my patients: I continue to be in awe of the human spirit, and I consider myself very lucky to be able to earn my living doing something I love. As is quite obvious, the biggest debt of all goes to you, for sharing your hopes and dreams, for trusting me, and for going so deeply inside yourselves. You are a very courageous group of people.

I disguised and collapsed the case material. Still, some of you may think you see snatches of yourselves. I hope that you take pleasure in how your journey will help others. I love it when you keep up with me, sending me shapshots of new lives, new kids. Life does go on after infertility, thank God.

One other note. Knowledge is power. RESOLVE, the American non-profit infertility support organization has chapters throughout the United States and is a major resource. RESOLVE has assembled a tremendous amount of consumer-friendly, detailed, up-to-date information that patients can purchase at a nominal fee. Available are bibliographies about infertility and close to thirty medical fact sheets about all aspects of infertility, including semen analysis; pinpointing ovulation; miscarriage—emotional factors; artificial insemination; immunological infertility; laparoscopy—what to expect; T-mycoplasma; prolactin problems; and information on various possible alternatives for resolution. Further, as a member of RESOLVE, the patient is able to call into the national office during a specially designated time and get a personal consultation with a highly trained infertility nurse. There is also access to information through periodic face-to-face informational meetings, an anonymous member-to-member contact system, and the choice to participate in structured support groups. Patients should be told about RESOLVE at the outset of treatment (not just when they are visibly upset) and should be reminded about it periodically. RESOLVE offers a kind of support that no therapist can offer.

Part 1
Background

1
Introduction

M ost people in society assume that they will be able to have children "when the time is right." Yet 12 percent of American couples of childbearing age cannot conceive when they wish to (Mosher & Pratt, 1990). Infertility is an equal-opportunity crisis, touching people from urban, suburban, and rural areas, from all sexual orientations, and from every ethnic, racial, class, and religious background.

However, the loss, or the threatened loss, involved in infertility is different from many other kinds of losses. In unexplained infertility and in many common diagnoses, there is tremendous uncertainty that may last for years. Feelings bounce back and forth between hope and despair from week to week. The "patient" remains healthy, but the future she dreamed of may be dead.

Part of the process is grieving, working through, letting go. But the couple may eventually get pregnant, so the ultimate loss does not, in fact, occur. In many cases, neither the patient, the treating physician, nor the psychotherapist knows whether the couple will finally be able to have a child biologically related to both of them. The therapist's traditional skills of support, empathy, tolerance of awful affect, and help with grieving are crucial but, in many cases, are not sufficient.

When the question of infertility is not resolved quickly, it takes on the quality of a chronic illness. As medical research continues, miracles happen, so having the emotional strength to persevere through the trials and tribulations of treatment increases the potential of giving birth to a biological child. However, the longer there is no resolution, the more stressed the couple becomes (Cooper, 1979; MacNab, 1984; Domar & Seibel, 1990; Zoldbrod, 1988). Thus, a necessary part of the therapist's repertoire must be concrete strategies to help the couple better cope with the ambiguity, with the unpleasant affect engendered by the invasiveness of the medical treatment, and with the overwhelming feeling of being out of control. The importance of supplying coping strategies is one theme that pervades this book.

Infertility patients are marked by grief, fear, anxiety, obsession, depression, envy, isolation and alienation, rage, guilt, and blame (Bierkins, 1975; Lieblum, 1988; Mazor, 1978; Menning, 1977; Woollett, 1985). It is of interest, and

3

puzzling, that some research studies have failed to indicate the depth of pain, dysfunction, and despair that clinicians see every day. One wonders whether patients being psychologically evaluated and studied by the same institutions that are providing them fertility services are covering up, in order to look "healthy enough" to get treatment.

Another group of studies has found that couples do have a high level of emotional distress. Harrison et al (1981) compared twenty-two couples with unexplained infertility with ten control couples with normal fertility and found that the infertile patients had higher mean anxiety scores for all emotional factors. In another study, Lalos, Lalos, Jacobsson, and von Schoultz (1985) interviewed twenty-four infertile couples one month before and two years after reconstructive tubal surgery. The authors found that, over the two years, both the husbands' and the wives' feelings had become significantly more negative. In addition, there was a trend toward deterioration in the marriage.

As has been noted anecdotally for decades, research has proved that women, in particular, become highly aggrieved about infertility (Abbey, Andrews, & Halman, 1991; Cook, 1987; Harrison, et al, 1981; Wright, 1991). Sandelowski and Pollock (1986) interviewed forty-eight women during their medical treatment. They found these patients floundering in their life goals, feeling defective, isolated, and alone. In one study of 200 couples entering an in vitro fertilization (IVF) program, 49 percent of the women reported that they considered their infertility the most upsetting experience of their lives, as compared to only 15 percent of the men (Freeman, Boxer, Rickels, Tureck, & Mastroianni, 1985).

The difference between men's and women's reactions to infertility is an intriguing and well-documented phenomenon, which has been discussed at length in the lay literature (Lasker and Borg, 1987; Liebmann-Smith, 1987; Menning, 1977; Salzer, 1986), along with worthwhile suggestions for improved understanding and communication. Research corroborates that men's immediate reactions are more varied and usually lack the intensity of women's reactions (Abbey et al., 1991; Wright et al., 1991). Indeed, the majority of this book reports on women's reactions to involuntary childlessness.

However, there are some subtleties in men's responses that have been missed in much of what has previously been written. Some evidence shows that there may be variations according to socioeconomic class. With time, many men become shaken by the stresses in their marital relationship (Abbey et al., 1991) and disturbed by their growing awareness of the meaning of never having biological children (MacNab, 1984).

There is a group of men who are quite upset, but they have no safe arena in which to discuss their feelings. Husbands' reactions seem to be related, in part, to their relationship with their own father. In Chapter 2, some additional information about men's reactions is reviewed, and the workings of a men's support group is described. Men are also apt to conceal the effect of the crisis on their sexuality. But a few men reveal their deepest sentiments in Chapter 10. The men struggling with infertility speak with nearly inaudible voices. Hopefully, these chapters will amplify those voices, so that health professionals can become more sensitive to men's varied needs.

The infertility crisis has been called biopsychosocial (Cook, 1987). It affects all areas of life—the psychological, moral and spiritual, social, sexual, sensual, and physical—amplifying any existing problems or areas of weakness. Prior literature has focused on the couple's problems with feelings and relationships. A comprehensive theoretical framework, Arnold Lazarus's multimodal therapy (MMT), has been used here to explore how infertility affects women. The multimodal approach systematically looks at feelings, relationships, behavior, cognitions, imagery, sensations, sexuality, and the patient's physical health. It is particularly helpful in allowing the psychotherapist to disentangle, appraise, and treat all of the different aspects of personality that have been affected. Because theoretical discussion can be difficult to grasp, a case study is used to illustrate the detailed application of MMT with one patient.

The less commonly discussed effects of infertility on women's thoughts and belief systems, imagery, physical health, sensuality, and sexuality are explored. The physical cost of the medical regimen of treatment is underreported, except in feminist writings (which are violently opposed to almost all infertility treatment). Women need our permission to pursue medical treatment, but at the same time, they must listen to and take care of their bodies. Some must be helped to stop pursuing medical alternatives. Research on the longer term effects of infertility on sexuality is absent from the literature. In Chapter 11, case studies of sexual problems in two women after prolonged unsuccessful infertility treatment serve to remind us that, in certain cases, the costs of unsuccessful treatment may be higher than anyone has realized.

Use of Different Theoretical Models

A deep understanding of the grief process is a prerequisite for clinical work with infertility patients. Barbara Menning's classic book, *Infertility* (1977), should be read by all professionals working with involuntarily childless couples. In it, Menning uses a model based on Kübler-Ross's work on death and dying. She describes the various stages of the grieving process, beginning with denial, circling through rage and anger, to bargaining, depression, and, finally, acceptance. Writing about mourning after losing a loved one, Tatelbaum (1984) describes slightly different stages: first, a stage of shock and numbness; a long middle phase of "suffering and disorganization"; and a last phase, a period of "reorganization."

These models provide a valuable theoretical underpinning for the work that goes on during the process of resolving infertility. They may provide the only structure necessary when one is dealing with a condition that, once discovered, clearly determines that the couple will never have a child genetically related to both of them, such as, for example, when the husband is found to have a complete absense of sperm (azoospermia).

Grief models are crucial at the end of unsuccessful treatment, when the couple must "bury" their hopes of a biologically related child, mourn, and, only then, go on to choose one of the other alternatives. Adoption, sperm donation, and other "third-party" methods will build families, and they are good alternatives, but they do not cure the couple's infertility. Choosing to be childless doesn't negate the infertility. The parents first must grieve for the child whom the two of them could not produce together.

Patients who have not yet had to go through the death of a loved one are frequently terrified of the grieving process and need a guide. They're afraid to experience the feelings, and once they have them, they're fearful that the pain will never stop. A therapist who cannot tolerate feelings of sorrow is not well equipped to work with these patients. Empathy involves actually feeling the other person's emotions in one's body, and at the same time knowing that it is their sentiments which one is feeling. Thus the healer must be able to tolerate persistent grief herself to allow the patient to complete mourning.

Yet, a grief model is not sufficient to help the patient through prolonged years of medical attempts at pregnancy and protracted ambiguity. Since 1977, when Barbara Eck Menning first wrote *Infertility*, increasing advances in technology have seduced patients to extend the period of "trying" longer and longer, testing the new medications available, having surgery, and attempting treatments such as in vitro fertilization (IVF) or gamete intrafallopian transfer (GIFT). The longer the uncertainty, the more disorganized life becomes. Ambiguous events are more stressful than predictable ones (Taylor, 1990).

As infertility begins to look more and more like a chronic illness with which people have to cope, rather than a single death knell of a diagnosis, which they have to grieve over, new helping models are needed. Woollett (1985) pointed out the desperate need for clinicians and researchers to provide patients with specific "strategies for coping."

Alternative paradigms prove fruitful here, including the theoretical literature on coping and chronic illness, as well as the research findings from medical psychology. Coping is a complex integration of cognitive, affective, and behavioral processes. Lazarus and Folkman (1984) define it as "the process of managing external or internal demands that are perceived as taxing or exceeding a person's resources". Coping consists of behaviors and intrapsychic responses designed to overcome, reduce, or tolerate these demands.

Moos and Tsu (1977) list seven classes of coping skills used by people adjusting to physical illness, many of which are applicable to infertility patients: (1) denying and minimizing the seriousness of the crisis; (2) seeking relevant information; (3) requesting reassurance and emotional support; (4) learning specific illness-related procedures; (5) setting concrete, limited goals; (6) rehearsing alternative outcomes; and (7) finding a general purpose or pattern of meaning in the course of events.

Coping is a more active, aggressive process than grieving. Consider Cameron and Meichenbaum's cognitive-functional analysis (1982) of the coping process: (1) accurate appraisal of the situation; (2) an adequate response repertoire (i.e., assertiveness, communication skills, and relaxation skills); (3) the actual deployment of adequate skills; and (4) the ability to unwind from a stress-coping episode.

By now, there are a tremendous number of controlled studies on coping with chronic disease, disability, and illness. Reviewed and summarized extensively by Taylor (1990), the research points to the same conclusions: "Life events appraised as negative, uncontrollable, unpredictable or ambiguous are typically experienced as more stressful than those not so appraised. Further, *people who believe that they can do something in response to a stressful event appear to adjust better to those stressful events than those without such feelings of control*" (p. 43; italics in the original).

Active coping techniques are just beginning to show up in the literature on infertility. Self-help behavioral strategies have been described by Zoldbrod (1990), and Domar, Seibel, and Benson (1990) have written about success in using professionally led relaxation groups. Unfortunately, large, controlled studies of the efficacy of active coping strategies in adjustment to infertility do not yet exist. However, the weight of the existing evidence from general health psychology supports the wisdom of continuing to research and develop specific coping strategies for the involuntarily childless.

What helps patients feel more in control? Problem-solving efforts and the regulation of emotions are two separate and valuable kinds of coping strategies (Lazarus & Folkman, 1984). Taylor (1990) notes that, in general, problem-solving efforts work well in the management of controllable stressors, whereas emotional regulation skills are particularly helpful in coping with uncontrollable stressors. In infertility, and in most instances when a person must confront an enormous stress, patients intuitively use both kinds of strategies.

Seeking medical help is, in itself, a way of taking control (Woollett, 1985). Ironically, medical treatment is one of the largest sources of stress. Several writers have suggested that physicians should allow patients a better sense of control during medical procedures (Mazor, 1984; Domar & Seibel, 1990; Zoldbrod, 1988), keeping them fully informed and giving them a sense of inclusion in the planning and timing of the workup and treatment.

Early problem-solving efforts may simply be focused on the patient's hearing and understanding the information that is being presented. Just hearing the word *infertility* or receiving a diagnosis of "sperm antibodies" or "endometriosis" is tremendously taxing. If medical or psychological personnel are not acutely sensitive to the blow that the patient receives from the initial information, and if the patient is treated in a cold and matter-of-fact manner, she may not return. At the very least, she will forget whatever information has been conveyed about the facts in her case and will remember only how cruelly she was informed of the problem.

Each new piece of "bad news" is overwhelming, so that the physician, nurse, or therapist continually needs to ascertain whether the patient is reeling afterward. The clinician can make a major contribution by taking a careful survey of the information that the patient has and of the information she needs, by assessing the coping strategies she uses and shoring up the healthiest ones. Later problem-solving efforts often center on helping the patient choose from among several confusing treatment alternatives. For written resources and information that will help patients problem-solve, the reader is directed to the bibliography, to RESOLVE, and to Appendix 5 of this book.

Much of the time, problem solving isn't the best coping strategy. Patients must regulate their emotions in order to adjust to uncontrollable stressors. The lack of knowing whether or when there will be biological progeny produces the overriding tension. Other everyday pressures include having to go through a dreaded operation or procedure; needing to change physicians; having to go to a christening; needing to seem friendly and well balanced with a birth mother or an adoption agency; and getting through an anxious pregnancy after previous miscarriages. Chapters 3, 4, and 9 describe specific techniques that will help patients regulate their emotions during infertility or precious pregnancies, including relaxation, guided imagery (particularly to rehearse alternatives), models and diagrams, exercises in cognitive restructuring, behavioral rehearsal, and pain control.

Using interventions that may help to control stress is worthwhile on medical grounds, as well, as it may improve pregnancy rates. Domar and Seibel (1990) note that firm evidence is mounting that emotional stress, through the workings of the endocrine system, can directly affect the workings of the sexual and reproductive system.

There are several benefits to disseminating and promoting specific behavioral interventions as part of psychotherapy for infertility. First, the patient can use these techniques at home, increasing her sense of being in control. Experience has shown that infertility patients tend to refuse mental health treatment by professionals, even though it would be beneficial (Bresnick & Taymor, 1979; Rosenfeld & Mitchell, 1979). Also, patients may not be able to afford prolonged psychotherapy even if they want it, as medical treatment and fertility drugs are so costly. Third, patients with infertility are spread throughout the country, including rural areas with few mental health services. Professionals who need to be competent generalists in mental health would be aided by a knowledge of specialized treatment strategies for infertility.

Optimal treatment is a balancing act, requiring tremendous clinical sophistication. Timing is crucial, and the treatment "recipe" varies in every instance. It is inappropriate and harmful to use behavioral interventions to cut off painful feelings, which must be faced and worked through. The therapist must be able to sit (and sit and sit) with the terrifying and awful feelings—the shame, the grief, the envy, the rage—if the patient is to be able to accept them, and herself. The patient probably has nowhere else to do this kind of deep, searing work.

However, experiencing negative affect, over and over and over, is not helpful by definition—not unless the patient is actually at the end of the treatment process and is grieving the death of the child she will never have. Maybe the feared loss won't actually occur. Sometimes the patient simply needs relief from her anxiety. There are times when perseverating over the negative simply makes the situation feel worse, and the therapist's allowing irrationally negative affect just makes the patient feel hopeless and more out of control.

Infertility threatens the patient's sense of mastery over her body and over life in general. The adjustment process is enhanced by techniques that help her feel able to manage the threatening event while she is actively (and appropriately) seeking medical treatment, or when she is tolerating being pregnant after a miscarriage (as in Chapter 9). Besides providing empathy and tolerating her feelings, the therapist must offer her resources and techniques that will bring her relief from the negative thoughts, feelings, and images with which she is flooding herself. It is particularly this aspect of treatment that is the focus of this book.

2

Men, Women, and Infertility

Voices from the consulting room:

Wife 1: I hate disappointing him every month when I get my period. I also feel cheated and scared when he doesn't want to cooperate at ovulation time.

Husband 1: I *am* disappointed, but only because Cindy is so disappointed if we don't have children. I'll be OK, but it's Cindy's only focus right now.

Wife 2: Rick is *not* verbal and has difficulty with not being able to "fix" the situation. He doesn't like me to have to go through the physical procedures and the stress accompanying them. He doesn't know that just "being there" is comforting. It helps when he just acknowledges my anxiety and depression. I realize that he can't fix the situation. It helps when he's empathetic.

Husband 2: Judy often tells me she'd like to get a divorce and let me marry someone who could provide me with children. I explain that I only want to have children with her, and that if we can't have children, then we should get on with our life together. I try to explain to her that I love her regardless of the fact that we may not be able to have a child together. But I feel that whatever I say, even when I try to reassure her, many times, my comments become meaningless or don't seem to help.

Wife 3: It upsets me when Jay doesn't seem to know how to comfort me when I'm upset about someone else getting pregnant. Sometimes he appears insensitive and withdraws. He has difficulty understanding how much this is tied up with my self-concept as a woman.

Husband 3: Actually, the worst part is my frustration over her frustration. I don't know how to comfort her and help her move through the upset quickly.

Wife 4: Mike doesn't seem to react at all sometimes. He's supportive, but I feel like the crazy one, because I react and he doesn't. So I get the message that he's OK and I'm overreacting. I feel the need to talk the situation over (and over and over), and he doesn't. I cry, and he doesn't.

Husband 4: I don't think we fight about the infertility directly. The infertility

10

has created a higher level of stress that is becoming the new normal level for us. Our fights are about everyday, relatively small things. However, because our stress level is consistently elevated, it doesn't take much to set either of us off. Lately, I've started to withdraw and sometimes even leave the scene because I'm so frustrated and angry that I don't know what to say or do.

Jane seems to have a need to talk about it often. I feel caught, because I think it's good for her to do so, but I get frustrated by the amount of time we talk about our infertility.

Wife 5: My husband shows very little reaction to our infertility. He will be supportive, but only when I force him to talk to me. I feel I'm dealing with this problem, "my problem," alone. This is *very* difficult. He appears to accept everything. I look for answers and seem to fight until I find them.

Husband 5: Susan's medical problems seem ever-changing. Each time we think we've solved the problem, a new twist pops up. Surgical adhesions, irregular cycles, and hormone problems have all been tried with no success. The fights have become unpredictable and very frequent. Before, fights centered on her getting her period—another unsuccessful month. Now, the fights can occur at any time.

Wife 6: We fight because he tells me that the only thing I talk about is having a baby, and I should be talking and thinking about other things.

Husband 6: I love my wife very much. She is what is important to me, not a possible child. If and when we have a child, she will still be the most important person in my life. If we don't have any children, I still plan on leading a full life.

Wife 7 (doing artificial insemination by her husband because of sperm antibodies): He gets extremely upset about having to take off work, given the type of job he has. On our good days, Ted is usually cooperative, but I still feel it's a struggle. Sex is minimal and mechanical. Ted rarely, if at all, initiates conversations about the infertility or adoption.

The dissimilarities between men and women's reactions to infertility are legion and have been well documented in the literature for at least three decades (Abbey et al., 1991; Bierkins, 1975; Bresnick & Taymor, 1979; Kirk, 1964; Liebmann-Smith, 1987; Menning, 1977; Salzer, 1986; Simons, 1988; Wright et al., 1991). These differences make it difficult for spouses to understand and support one another. Back in 1964, Kirk wrote that men seem to feel less bereft by involuntary childlessness because it is "probably more readily compensated for by occupational activity." He also noted that, when the wife initiates discussion of infertility, the "husband often feels overwhelmed and withdraws."

A number of writers have asserted that men do not have any significant emotional reactions to infertility (Bresnick & Taymor, 1979; Denber, 1978; Drake & Tredway, 1978). It is true that no research to date has found men to be more distressed than women, according to Wright et al. (1991), who did a meta-analysis of thirty-eight previous investigations of involuntarily childless couples.

In a carefully crafted new study of the psychosocial responses of 449 couples just entering an infertility clinic, Wright et al. (1991) found that "women appear to experience significantly more . . . distress than their partners (p. 104), with wives showing higher depression, anxiety, cognitive disturbance, and hostility. In addition, wives had lower self-esteem.

A study by Abbey et al. (1991) also looked at couples who were in the early stages of the infertility process. These authors surveyed 185 infertile couples and 90 presumed fertile couples and came to the same conclusions about male–female differences. Among their interesting findings were that (1) both men and women tended to see the wife as more responsible for the infertility, even when the husband was the diagnosed source of the problem, and (2) husbands perceived chance factors as more responsible for their fertility problems than did women, that is, the women felt more guilty. One of Abbey et al.'s contributions is a superb review of the recent literature on the gender gap in couples' reactions.

Just recapping what we now know about how men and women respond, it is clear that many involuntarily childless couples are in for some rocky times until their crisis is resolved. Infertile women have been found to be more depressed, anxious, guilt-ridden, frustrated, and isolated than infertile men (Bresnick & Taymor, 1979; Daniels, 1989; Daniluk, 1988; Lalos, Lalos, Jacobsson, & von Schoultz, 1985a). Wives experience lower self-esteem than their husbands (Bernstein, Potts, & Mattox, 1985; McGrade & Tolor, 1981) and are less interested in (nonprocreational) sex (Daniluk, 1988; Lalos et al., 1985b). Husbands are more likely than their wives to be satisfied with the meaning they find in the infertility and feel that they have learned more from the experience (Abbey et al., 1991).

Women more often take the initiative to obtain treatment and make decisions, and they take all the responsibility for carrying out the treatment protocols (Greil, Leitko, & Porter, 1988; McGrade & Tolor, 1981). Greil et al. (1988) interviewed twenty-two women and found that 27 percent were annoyed that their husbands were not more involved in the treatment; some of the husbands thought the wives were overreacting. About 30 percent of the couples in McGrade and Tolor's 1981 study found themselves arguing about their fertility problem.

Half the women in one study viewed infertility as the most upsetting experience in their lives, as compared to only 15 percent of the men (Freeman et al., 1985). Several authors have found that husbands are less disappointed by the likelihood of a life without children than are wives (Abbey et al., 1991; Greil et al., 1988; Van Keep & Schmidt-Elmendorff, 1975).

Harriet Simons's 1988 dissertation looked at couples who were in RE-SOLVE support groups. She found that 23 percent of the men reported that they would consider child-free living as compared with only 11 percent of the women. One man who rejected child-free living explained that his wife had wanted children since she was very young.

The men in Simons's study did not see themselves as in need of help regarding the infertility; instead, they viewed themselves as being in the role of supporting their wives in their distress. Some of the husbands expressed their perception of RESOLVE as a woman-oriented organization that served as "therapy" for the wife (p. 184). Simons found the men in her sample to be significantly less likely than the women to have counseling (23 percent vs. 53 percent), a fact that may reflect both men's smaller investment in infertility and their greater reluctance to seek help.

The Differences in Male and Female Socialization

When one thinks about it, these results are predictable because of several differences in the way boys and girls are socialized. First, men have been socialized to think of parenthood as one possible ingredient in their sense of being grown up. In contrast, girls are told that the achievement of motherhood is absolutely necessary to their identity as adult women.

Russo (1976) made a strong case that motherhood is a mandatory identity, and that no other activity can substitute for it. She showed that other aspects of feminine identity can be interchanged. For instance, women are supposed to be pretty. But it is acceptable not to be pretty if you are sweet enough and a good enough mother. However, there is nothing a woman can do or be that is an adequate substitute for motherhood. Women's children are their credentials. Women *correctly* perceive a threat to their ability to become mothers as a threat to their ability to be seen as legitimate adult females in society. For many men, the potential loss of the role of the father is not as threatening. One can be an adult man without children if one is strong, aggressive, and successful financially.

Also, sons and daughters are treated differently by mothers and fathers, so that sons and daughters have different memories and images of the parent–child relationship. Because females are allowed to be dependent, girl children are allowed to have the pleasurable experience of having their emotional needs satisfied by their mothers, who may be frequently present, and also by their fathers when they are available.

Girls are allowed to cry when hurt, they are allowed to be comforted when afraid, and they are allowed to be embraced and touched lovingly throughout their lives. Many girls grow up being especially close to their mothers, sharing thoughts and feelings and developing empathy. Without their thinking about it, their internal images of motherhood involve replaying these pleasurable scenes of love. But this time, they will be the loving mother to their own small children.

In contrast, conventional fathers only allow boys to be dependent when they are very small. They are soon taught not to cry when they are hurt and instead to act like "little men." By the time they are five or six, they are encouraged to leave the soft world of their mothers and go into the masculine world of sports and competition. For boys, the range of acceptable feelings is quite restricted. According to Pleck and Sawyer's *Men and Masculinity* (1974) some of the "rules of masculinity" are the following:

Low Self Disclosure of All Emotions (Except Possibly Strength, Confidence, Anger)

Under No Circumstances Show Weakness

Be Strong and Silent

Be Autonomous. Only Sissies Depend on Others

Be Competitive

Compete Well and Be Successful

Perform Well Sexually

Be Athletic

Be Successful in Work

Of course, the orthodox view is that in order to teach one's son how to be a man, it is necessary not to kiss him, hold him, or nurture him too much, because that kind of behavior is not appropriate for men (or between men). It may even lead to homosexuality! What tenderness the son needs, the mother will supply.

Many men had fathers whom they perceived to be aloof, unavailable, competitive, or rejecting. Many of these fathers loved their sons dearly, but they believed their main task was to toughen their sons up, to make them independent, unfeminine, brave, and strong. For many men, consequently, there are few internalized images of tender moments between father and son.

Hartley (1974) commented:

In addition to the effect of the relative absence of fathers from boy's experience, we also have evidence that the relationship between boys and their fathers tend to be less good than those between girls and their mothers or fathers. Since identification is affected by the quality of relationships existing between the child and the identification model, this diminishes still further the boy's chance to define his sex-roles easily and naturally by using his male parent as a model. Boys . . . often report their fathers as the punishing agents, their mothers as protectors. Fathers in general seem to be perceived as punishing or controlling agents. (p. 8)

Lowenthal, Thurnher, and Chiraboga's research, *The Four Stages of Life: A Comparative Study of Women and Men Facing Transitions* (1975), lends weight to this hypothesis:

> In general, portrayals of mothers were more positive than those of fathers— partly, perhaps because the concept of a "good mother" is more clearly and narrowly defined than is that of a "good father." Thus, respondents tended to evaluate mothers in terms of nurturance, caring and understanding, and generally to see them as meeting these expectations.
>
> Fathers, on the other hand, were appraised in terms of their occupational competence and performance as family providers, as well as their mood and personality and their capacity to relate to others. . . . Mother–child relations were seen as smoother than father–child relations.
>
> When asked which member of their family of origin they felt closest to, men and women of every life stage mentioned mother almost twice as often as they did father, the sense of closeness often transcending negative appraisals or reports of functioning in the relationship. (p. 42)

So, whereas most women grow up wanting children and are immediately attuned to some of the important losses represented by infertility, the notion that parenthood may elude them does not come initially as a terrible shock or blow to many men. They don't have good feelings about the father–son bond; they do not feel they are in danger of losing anything valuable.

Even men who had loving fathers may not tell us how they feel about infertility. After all, male socialization discourages men from expressing their feelings of sadness, distress, or "weakness" in general.

Men are taught not to break down and show any vulnerable feelings in life. Even in dramatic tragedies, men stay cool in front of others. Diane Cole, in an article in *Psychology Today* entitled "Grief's Lessons: His and Hers" (1988), cited research showing that, although men may feel equal amounts of pain, they are less forthcoming than women about their feelings when discussing the death of their child, a miscarriage, or the loss of their spouse. Men fear losing control in front of other people.

In a follow-up of subjects who refused to participate, one study of men and grief found that the men who had not taken part were more depressed than those who had agreed to participate (1988, p. 60). It may be that the men most in need of help are the least likely to go out and look for it.

Socialization may also account for gender differences in the metaphors men and women use when speaking and thinking about loss. Recent theoretical work has focused on women's growth coming through a sense of being connected to others, whereas the male model focuses on separating emotionally and being independent and autonomous (Stiver & Jordan, 1991). Cole (1988) cited Phillis R. Silverman, Director of the Child Bereavement Study at Massachusetts

General Hospital, who commented that the "male model" of loss includes learning to break away from the past, to "get on with life" (p. 61). In mourning many kinds of losses, men tend to prefer to get quickly involved in work or other activities.

In a longitudinal study of fifty-two involuntarily childless men, Snarey (1988) found that all of them chose to throw themselves into activities to substitute for parenting and to help them through the wait-and-see period. Sixty-three percent substituted involvement with a nonhuman object on which they lavished their feelings (for example, a car, their house, or a dog). A few (12 percent) substituted themselves, becoming involved with personal health, body building, or "macho sexuality" (including affairs). Only 25 percent chose to cope with the pain of infertility through connectedness with other people's children. Interestingly, Snarey found that the men's choices in the process of "getting on with life" colored the rest of their adult development. Men who had gotten involved with other children were the most successful in their marriages, tended to adopt, or finally had children. Further, when the men reached age forty-seven, Snarey looked for evidence of generativity, that is, Erik Erikson's concept of showing concern for the next generation. Those men who had coped by connecting with other people's children were the most likely to have reached the generative stage.

Are these differences between the sexes changing? Are the youth of today more "liberated"? Even though there seems to have been a loosening up of male and female gender roles, research indicates that the major distinctions still hold. These traditional male–female sex-role patterns—in which men are associated with power, and women are invested in relationships and emotions—still appear to be consistent across the world. For example, in the United States, the emotional life of teens is quite different for boys and girls. Tina Alder (1989) reported on a study by Stapley and Havilland of 262 mostly white public-school students in the fifth, seventh, ninth, and eleventh grades, Stapley and Havilland, found that the boys were much more likely to deny ever having emotional experiences, although they clearly did have them, and not to tell others how they were feeling. Further, when they did admit to depression, the boys tended to blame their depression on concerns about performing well; the girls tended to cite interpersonal problems. According to a second study, of nearly six thousand adolescents from ten nations (Atkinson, 1988), "boys appeared to be more self-centered, even self-indulgent, while girls appeared more other-oriented and more emotionally open" (p. 26).

These differences account for the difficulties that infertile couples often encounter. After all, empathy is the ability to allow oneself to feel what another person is feeling. Because men have been trained not to let themselves experience painful or vulnerable feelings, they will not let themselves feel what their wives are feeling during infertility. Husbands are threatened by their wives' pain and push them away, as the following case vignettes illustrate:

Patsy, twenty-nine, came into individual psychotherapy for help with depression. Her severe and long-standing endometriosis caused her constant physical pain. She was being treated by a top-rate specialist, but she was deeply saddened by her inability to get pregnant.

It immediately became clear that Patsy felt no emotional support from her contractor husband, Barry, even though she felt that he did love her. Patsy was asked to bring Barry to future meetings.

Barry, thirty, a burly guy in a plaid flannel shirt, entered the consulting room warily but warmed up after a short while and stopped answering questions with "yes" or "no" answers. He was the essence of a logical fellow. He confessed to withdrawing from Patsy out of sheer frustration.

"I can't stand the roller coaster of her feelings," he said. "This famous doctor tells her she has only a 40 percent chance of getting pregnant because of the endometriosis. So why does she get bent out of shape each month, since she can possibly, at best, get pregnant only in one out of three? So why doesn't she just tell herself, on two-thirds of the cycles, that there is *no* chance of pregnancy and only get upset if pregnancy doesn't occur during the third, and let the other two pass her by?"

Sally came in with her husband, Jeff, an engineer. She reported that Jeff had been "mostly wonderfully supportive," but she thought that he didn't understand her and could use some support of his own.

Jeff came from a quiet home. Emotions weren't shown. His own father was an engineer, too, a shy and steady man. Sally's family had been more open about feelings.

Sally was devastated by her infertility and envious of her pregnant friends. In church together, at the last friend's child's christening, she had whispered to Jeff, "I'm so furious at God that I'd like to break every window in the church!"

Jeff confessed that, although he felt very loving toward Sally and wanted to take care of her, he found her envy "very hard to take." He was afraid of her anger and thought that maybe Sally was so out of control that she should be in a mental hospital.

Men like Barry and Jeff need help in understanding and tolerating their wives' feelings. Barry avoided Patsy and his own feelings about childlessness by supervising the builders on their new house. This activity made him feel powerful and feel that he was doing something concrete toward creating a better future for them. He needed to understand that his own feelings of fear of feeling out of control were making him avoid his wife. He agreed to spend ten minutes three times a week holding her and listening to her sadness.

Jeff needed to hear that Sally's envy was normal, which was illustrated to him by numerous examples of other envious women. And he had to realize that he would not allow himself to feel anger before he could understand why he was so frightened by Sally's murderous rage. Both of these men needed some in-depth help in looking at their own feelings of loss at potentially not being able to father.

Subtleties and Differences in Men's Reactions to Infertility

Professionals who want to learn about how wives feel, or about the dynamics between the typical infertile husband and wife, or about strategies for couples counseling, have a wealth of material from which to choose (Menning, 1977; Osherson, 1986; Salzer, 1986). However, although it may appear that we understand how men feel about infertility, that is quite untrue. What we know about is how men feel compared to women. We don't know much about differences between men. We don't know about distinctions between men who have been diagnosed as the infertile partner and men whose wives have the medical problem. We don't understand class differences. And we don't know much about how men's feelings change over time.

What does being a father mean to a man? John Ross's theoretical work (1979) is among the most satisfying sources. Ross stated, "Professionals have largely ignored . . . the matter of a man's fatherhood" (p. 74). He described paternal identity as a "sense of self as the masculine procreator, producer, caretaker". Parenthood is a way of bringing adult love to fruition, of experiencing love in new ways. It also allows a man to fantasize about creating a better version of himself, or to imagine an idealized form of child raising. Particularly for men, there are conflicting feelings about the overwhelming sense of responsibility and the loss of personal freedom and privacy.

Professionals' interest in male development and the reproductive role is just beginning to deepen. Men and their problems with infertility, in particular, have not received much scientific attention, (MacNab, 1984, p. 25; Osherson, 1986). In part, infertile men have frustrated researchers by being uncooperative (Wright, 1991, p. 101) and unavailable (MacNab, 1984).

Although professionals may not have focused on the connection between fatherhood and adult male status, the link is evident to others. In Jamison, Franzini, and Kaplan's study (1979) of students' views of voluntarily child-free men and women, a hypothetical, voluntarily child-free man was judged even more harshly than voluntarily child-free women, as "selfish, atypical, unfulfilled, less well-adjusted, and less sensitive and loving" (p. 273) than a man described identically but, in addition, as the father of two. And a study by Humphrey (1977) found that men, especially childless men, do associate fatherhood and masculinity.

As descriptive and research studies have increased and become more sophisticated, it has become evident that men are distressed. Wright et al (1991) found that, early in the treatment process, men in infertile couples scored higher than same-sexed population norms on measures of psychiatric symptomatology. Harriet Simons (1988) commented, "the fact that more than half of the males report depression suggests that the extent of the impact of infertility on males may have been underestimated" (p. 182). Abbey et al. (1991) discovered that wives found infertility more stressful than did their husbands but that infertile husbands experienced more home-life stresses and lower home-life performance than did their wives.

One revealing body of writing comes from psychologist Sam Osherson's intense account of his personal journey through infertility in his book *Finding Our Fathers* (1986). Unlike some men, Osherson desperately wanted children. As a psychologist, he divulged some sides of men's feelings that are too dangerous for others to expose. When his wife was being invaded and hurt by medical instruments, he talked about feeling powerlessness, "when instead you should be able to protect her"; terror and insecurity, because you fear that she may be injured or even die; and relief, at times, that she had to endure the pain and he didn't. In addition, he felt guilty, as if he were causing her the pain. Osherson admitted to being angry at his wife for being too depleted herself to take care of him. Last, he confessed to having fantasies of being with a woman "with a young womb, unsullied by doctors and needles" (p. 139).

Tracy MacNab (1984) completed research that gives us the best look to date at men's distress over infertility. MacNab used structured questionnaires, interviews, and psychological testing to investigate how recent or past infertility had affected the lives of thirty white upper-middle and middle-class men in the Boston area. A measure of the difficulty of doing research on men and infertility (and of how threatening this question is for men) is that it took him one and a half years and the distribution of four hundred questionnaires to get his study group of thirty men.

As in many other studies, these husbands felt that their wives had had a harder time than they had. And taken as a group, they showed more variation in reaction than would a group of women; that is, a few were not affected at all. But MacNab's research unearthed some very interesting findings: Most men are distressed by infertility, but only after several years. It takes three years of treatment for men to give up their position of "hopefulness." At that point, they feel most of the same feelings that their wives have been feeling for years: out of control, depressed, and isolated.

Until then, many of the men had used various defenses to avoid feeling pain or panic, such as having tremendous faith in the wonders of medical technology, denying that they wanted a child, or throwing themselves into work and avoiding the issue. Some of the men in MacNab's study looked back on their defensive actions with chagrin. One confessed that he used to say to his wife when she was extremely upset in the morning, "Well, it's your problem. I'm going to *work!*"

MacNab's men recounted how others had given them the message that men *shouldn't* be upset, that "men are not involved in such matters." One reported that, after his wife's surgery, everyone asked about how his wife was, but "expectations were that I would be strong, get on with business, et cetera." This man went on to say:

> And I did. I didn't deal with my feelings for a long time. I bottled them up while I took care of her after surgery [and] went back to work. When I finally did start dealing with them, the impact was very severe. I suffered a 2–3 month severe depression because of issues directly and indirectly connected with infertility. In a way [my wife] was much more fortunate, because she was forced to take time off to physically recover, and she used that time to emotionally recover, too. I had no such time.
>
> It's tough not to play "macho man" when that is what your environment reinforces. But when it comes to dealing with infertility, playing macho man just tears you apart. (p. 144)

MacNab (1984) gathered the bulk of his qualitative findings by interviewing ten men: five whose infertility had gone on less than three years and five whose infertility had had a duration of three or more years. In the group were three men with male-factor infertility, four with mixed-factor, and three with female-factor. Four were waiting for adoption, four had adopted, and two finally had biological children.

The themes that developed from these interviews showed quite clearly that the infertility had become a major crisis after three years of active infertility struggle. Many of the upsetting feelings that their wives had been experiencing all along suddenly became understandable. Their lives began to feel out of control in general. Their self-esteem was damaged. They were distressed by the medical interventions performed on their wives' bodies. Recurrent cycles of hope and despair were experienced as various medical solutions did not work. It became painful to be around children. They resented the pressure and intrusiveness of family and friends about their plans for children. They felt socially isolated, as if they were "different from others," and afraid to talk about the infertility because others would think they were impotent. They began to grieve for the loss of their genetic line.

Some men had begun to look for a higher order of meaning or spoke of the "forced examination of values" that infertility had brought about. It had taught some of them some new things about themselves. They explored their motivations for parenthood. They felt more philosophical, older, wiser, and more able to tolerate and talk about feelings (p. 114).

Several of the men stressed the need for a forum for men to discuss their feelings about infertility, but they acknowledged how difficult it is for men to publicly address intimacy and sexuality. Many of these same themes were found by Osherson (1986).

Potential Class Differences

We need to be on the lookout for huge generalizations about how men feel about having children and about infertility. Such oversimplifications obscure the subtle differences between men and make medical and mental health personnel less sensitive to them. For instance, there seem to be class differences in initial attitudes toward having children. The men in Simons's and MacNab's studies were predominantly middle class. But David Owens's descriptive research (1982) of British working-class men whose wives were being seen at an infertility clinic sheds some light on the possible effects of class on men's attitudes. In this group, having children was seen as "natural." The men could barely talk about why they wanted children because having them seemed preordained. However, they were able to say that they saw children as being "fun," as providing companionship, and as bestowing the prestige of adulthood: "Motherhood, in particular, was perceived as a highly valued status to which the wives should aspire, a fulfilling and all embracing career, and children were seen as central to [women's] lives" (p. 82). The vast majority of Owens's respondents denied that infertility was a threat to their virility (although their wives felt that it was) or to their self-concept as men. Instead, the infertility was seen as a threat to their role as *husbands*. They felt "guilty" or "to blame" that they would be "letting their wives down." They did not necessarily feel personally or psychologically inadequate, but they were failing to meet marital expectation.

Lowenthal, et al. (1975) did a study of adult development using lower-class and lower-middle-class subjects instead of the middle-class and upper-class subjects usually found in infertility research. They found that young lower-class and lower-middle-class newlyweds, both male and female, looked forward to the natural progression from marriage to parenthood.

However, there is no research whatsoever on attitudes toward infertility among men from nonwhite ethnic groups. Clearly, we have a lot to learn on this topic.

The Influence of the Past Father–Son Bond on Reactions to Infertility

A man's relationship to his father seems to be a major determining factor in how powerfully he is affected by infertility during the first few years of treatment. As we have seen, some fathers have been distant or competitive with their sons, in an attempt to socialize them to be adequately masculine. In such cases, there may be only a sad, lonely image of the father–son relationship, and unconsciously, there is a wish not to replay inner pictures of the father–child dyad. Men with difficult or distant relationships with their fathers are likely to avoid thinking about fatherhood or to deny wanting to become fathers.

In addition, if the medical problem is the husband's, a strong and warm father–son bond may predispose a him toward the acceptance of donor insemination. Some case vignettes are used to illustrate:

Evan, thirty-four, was the oldest child of four siblings and seemed to be his father's favorite. He came from a warm, close family and loved his siblings and both his parents. The next two children were girls, and the last was a boy much, much younger than Evan.

Charles, Evan's father, was a successful businessman, an avid skier, and an aviator. When Evan was a little boy, his father got in the habit of taking him out, almost every Sunday, in Charles's plane for half-day or whole-day jaunts. They had quite an adventurous time together. Charles even pretended to let Evan steer. Evan was a bright and delightful boy, and clearly Charles was proud of him.

Gloria, Evan's mother, usually a very competent woman, was afraid of the plane. When the little girls were born, they picked up on their mom's fright, so Evan had an extended period—about ten years—of having his father to himself on Sundays. During the rest of the week, and on Sundays when flying was not safe, life was pretty good, too, with a lot of family fun. Evan loved all of the younger kids and took a fathering role toward them, as Charles worked very hard and was gone long hours.

When Evan married Diane, they both looked forward to having children. After graduation, when Diane had trouble conceiving, with no known cause, Evan was every bit as upset as she was. He went to all the doctor's appointments with her, and he was so upset that he talked to his parents about their problem. After four years, they finally got pregnant. During that entire time, they weathered the stress together. They never fought about the infertility because Evan was every bit as clear about wanting to be a father as Diane was about wanting to be a mother.

Tad, tall and funny, and Adina, short and warm, were meant for each other. Adina was from an overprotective home and had been well loved. Tad's life had been much more challenging. His father had abandoned him when he was small. His mother loved him devotedly and had made sacrifices for him. Although she wasn't well physically, his mother worked all her life doing relatively menial labor to make sure that he got a college education. But life had been precarious. When Tad graduated, his mother was tremendously proud. He got a good job. Then, when Tad was twenty-three, his mother got ill and died.

Tad met Adina shortly after. Besides being attractive, she was very maternal. They got married and had years when their lives centered on one another. Adina wanted children much before Tad did, but he gave in eventually. He couldn't picture himself as a father at all, but he could easily picture her as a mother. He couldn't stand watching the process and going through the pain and the ups and downs, and they fought quite a bit.

Unfortunately, Adina tried years of treatments with no success. Tad was extremely frustrated by the fact that Adina's whole personality had changed. He felt that he had lost her. He didn't particularly want children; he wanted his wife back. When Adina wanted to adopt, he put his foot down, saying, "I don't want to take the risk. I just don't think I can bear any more disappointment in my life." Adina loved Tad so much—and understood him so well—that she decided that they would not have children at all.

Jack grew up in a large, religious Irish Catholic family. He was the third son; all of the sons were athletic. When they were kids, life had been a struggle financially, but there was a closeness in the family that money couldn't buy. John, the father, worked hard, but he played hard, too. He didn't talk much, but he spent a lot of time with his kids. They had ritualized sports activities on the weekends, changing with the seasons, and Jody, the mother took a lot of pleasure in being the cook and cheerleader for her crew. John encouraged the boys to go to college and supported them, although Jack's education was mostly paid for by a sports scholarship. He married Maureen when he was twenty-six.

His was such a masculine background that Jack was astounded to find out that his sperm count was zero. The urologist felt that his problem had been caused by a bad case of the mumps. Maureen was devastated.

Shortly after Jack received the diagnosis, the couple came in to discuss donor insemination. Jack felt absolutely clear that he wanted to do it. He didn't care what the pope thought. He couldn't imagine not being a father, and he loved Maureen and wanted to be a father to a child who was biologically related to her. He felt so close to his parents that he thought he would tell them about the inseminations, and he thought that his father loved him so much that he would accept it.

Peter had come from an abusive home. His mother was an alcoholic. His father drank, too, and was a physically and emotionally abusive man whether drinking or sober. He told Peter he was a bum and wouldn't amount to anything.

Peter ran away from home when he was eighteen. He met Virginia while working at a crafts fair in Berkeley. She came from a large, warm family who accepted him with open arms.

Peter and Virginia got married. After several years of unprotected intercourse and no children, they began to investigate. Peter's sperm count was zero. A biopsy showed that the prognosis was hopeless. It looked as if his parents' negligence during a childhood episode of high fever may have been to blame.

Peter was absolutely devastated. He loved Virginia and had wanted to have a child with her. His inability to father reminded him of the awful relationship he had had with his own father, and of his father's low opinion of him. Virginia wanted to do donor insemination, but Peter refused. He felt that the child who would be produced would always be a reminder of his inadequacy.

Hal was six-one, 220 pounds, and an inner-city fireman. His father was distant, critical, and authoritarian. Hal didn't think about his father much, as with his father, "It was always a losing battle." He and his wife had been trying to have a child for two years. The only medical problem that could be found was the fact that Hal's sperm had antibodies. Tammy was being treated with intrauterine inseminations with washed sperm. She was constantly upset and depressed by their lack of success. Hal paid attention only when having to provide the sperm sample created problems in his work schedule. Then he complained to Tammy, which infuriated her. He didn't know what the big deal was for Tammy and would just as soon forget the whole thing and maybe adopt.

Of course, sometimes the correlation doesn't hold true, and a man who doesn't have an especially strong father–son bond still develops the idea of himself as a future father early in life. These men, too, are strongly affected by infertility:

Sid and Joan came in to discuss donor insemination. Sid was thirty-one; Joan, thirty-four. They had been married for eight years and had been trying to get pregnant for most of that time. They had found out a year before that Sid's sperm count was zero.

Joan said that Sid had "cried for days" when he heard.

"He's very sensitive," she noted. "He is the only one of his brothers and sisters who cried when his grandmother died."

Sid declared that he had always known that he wanted to have children.

Sid was the youngest of four kids. He said he hadn't felt very close to his father growing up because his father had been out working most of the time. However, he felt close to his father now. He had a lot of contact with his nieces and nephews, and he loved the children and said they loved him.

During the workup, the urologist did a biopsy, which proved that nothing could help. At that point, the physician mentioned adoption but said nothing about donor insemination. Sid was excited, later, when he heard about the idea of donor insemination, because he wanted to create a child with Joan and had already fantasized about what their child would look like. He thought of using a cousin's sperm but then decided against it.

Currently, he was getting evaluated in order to participate in a program at a medical clinic.

Joan said that Sid was so excited about her getting pregnant by donor insemination that he had called her at work at three to tell her to leave work early, just to make sure that they'd be on time for their clinic appointment at five-thirty.

Men who are in touch with wanting to father stay "in synch" with their wives throughout the crisis, whereas other men may take years to "catch up" to their wives' feelings. It is ironic that men who lacked a close father–son bond often initially reject the opportunity to become fathers themselves, because parenthood offers them an opportunity to repair this relational gap.

When couples come to therapy because of the husband's lack of investment in pursuing pregnancy and parenthood (and also when men have to decide whether or not to bank sperm in cases of testicular cancer, where treatment will cause infertility), the therapist should carefully explore the man's relationship with his father. Men with distant or unsatisfying father–son bonds need to explore the importance of the relationship. Many need help in grieving over the lack of a loving, giving father in order to understand the true meaning of infertility to them.

The Workings of an All-Men's Support Group

Reviewing what is now known about infertility and men, we can arrive at some tentative conclusions. First of all, there is wider variation in reaction among men than among women. Men are not unaffected, as had previously been believed (Abbey, et al. 1991; Kedem et al, 1990; Wright, et al. 1991), but they aren't as upset as women. An individual man's reactions may depend on his relationship with his own father (Zoldbrod, 1991), and some men are quite distraught over the possibility of not being fathers. These sensitive men remain isolated and hidden, ashamed to talk about their feelings.

Second, most men believe that their wives are more distressed about infertility than they are. They get the message that society thinks this balance is appropriate (MacNab, 1984), that "men don't care about such things," and that they will be seen as "wimps" if they do care deeply about having children. It follows then, that most men avoid or deny their sad feelings for quite a while, sometimes for several years (MacNab, 1984), whereas women may feel threatened and upset at the first signs of infertility.

Last, once men do realize that they are having problems with infertility, their lives are deeply affected, particularly in the areas of their self-esteem and their sense of mastery (MacNab, 1984).

How many themes heard in Osherson's self-chronicle (1986) and MacNab's descriptive research (1984) might be found among men struggling with infertility? Could men support each other in going through the infertility experience? How might professionals be able to help? A few preliminary answers to these questions can be found in this report of the workings of a men's group.

Osherson (1986) gave an implicit plea for men's groups when he spoke of his isolation from other men and his fervent desire to talk to them about the "confusing mix of vulnerability, hope and disappointment that infertility brings with it" (p. 130). On the other hand, he felt that perhaps talking to other men wouldn't be safe, that "the link to sexuality may raise competition or embarrassment among men" (p. 129) and, further, that "being taken seriously emotionally by another man means that you feel less manly for feeling so deeply about an event" (p. 138).

What follows is a report on a nine-month-long, once-monthly Boston-based men's group for dealing with feelings about long-term infertility. In September 1988, I organized a one-shot workshop through advertisements in the Massachusetts State RESOLVE newsletter and notices in physician's offices. After a long wait, calls began to trickle in. Several inquiries were made by wives! When all was said and done, we had a group of six (only five committed to an on going group), a herculean accomplishment.

These were middle-class men in their thirties and early forties, one African-American and the rest white.. After several years of struggle, they were "unresolved" and trying desperately to get to a final decision: Either they would finally have a biological child, probably by one of the "high-tech" means, or they would decide, with their wives, to live child-free or to adopt.

Naturally, no claim is being made that all men with long-term infertility would agree with the themes expressed by this group. It was a highly self-selected set. But the case material that follows is indicative of the real-life, day-to-day feelings about infertility that more men might allow themselves to feel if the environment did not relegate concerns about children to the category of women's work and did not ignore the important role that fatherhood plays in men's adult development.

These men had something important to tell us. They weren't answering structured interview questions. They were not rational and dispassionate, and they were not looking back at the process from a distance (as were some of MacNab's respondents). They weren't mental health professionals who were more in touch with their feelings than other men. What they had to say will be instructive to the other men in the world who are full of deep, painful feelings about possibly not being able to father their own biological child.

The workshop was held in a homelike, nonclinical atmosphere, with coffee and food and candy available. Because this was to be a one-time, three-hour workshop, the leader thought that, after some initial shyness, the men would open up to each other much more readily than one would expect in a longer term mixed-sex group. (They did not have weeks for a "getting-to-know-you" stage, and they all had exactly the same agenda.)

But nothing was adequate preparation for the extraordinary way in which these men related to each other. They were prepared to tell the truth, to reveal their secrets. They were altogether accepting of each other and totally empathetic. There was no competition for time or space in the group. They spoke from the heart, and to the heart, evidencing, just as Osherson and MacNab predicted, "a deep hunger for a connection with other men." They wanted to be somewhere where infertility was defined as a men's issue.

At the end of the workshop, which was three and a half hours of uninterrupted talking, all but one of the men wanted the group to continue. Given the way in which they were relating, I suggested that they might want to make it a leaderless group. That way, they could have the experience of being nurtured by other men.

But they would have none of it. They said that I had created a special space for them physically (with the nonclinical environment) and emotionally (with my comments and questions). Most important, they felt that having a woman present was a sign to them that it was all right to talk about their feelings this way. They all wanted me to participate and lead.

Remarkably, they said that, if the same group of men got together again, having shared as they did, knowing that they all had the infertility in common, but they were sitting in a traditional male setting like a bar, they would sit around and talk about sports and politics—business as usual! We decided to meet once monthly for as long as it made sense.

Discussion Topics

One of the first topics was the relief of not having to appear to be the strong one of an infertile couple. Several of the members had already participated in mixed-sex infertility support groups. They felt that, in the mixed setting, the men all unconsciously conspired and hid behind the stance that within their couple, the wife was hurting the most. This unspoken expectation made it difficult for individual men to admit weakness and their own need for support. And it evoked their socialized competitive feelings toward the other men: "If John is saying that he is much less upset than Cindy, how can I admit that I am at least as upset as, if not more upset than, Mary?" By discussing this topic first, the men defused their own competitive feelings. One by one, they revealed their deep vulnerability.

One of the most powerful forces squelching self-revelation to men outside this group was an intense fear of other men's competitive barbs or scorn about sexual prowess. When women discuss infertility, other people do not cast doubts on their sexual abilities. But this threat looms large among men.

John said that he had tried to discuss his infertility experience with a close friend, and his friend had been speechless. John had felt ashamed about opening up and had also felt abandoned. As they free-associated, the other members vividly recalled feeling like losers in past competitions with other men, and they could imagine the humiliation of some fellow's saying to them, "What's the matter? Can't get it up?" or "What's the problem? Shooting blanks?"

None of these men had any serious problems with their potency, and several had adequate sperm. But they all felt that, until another man somehow proved that he was sensitive to these issues—and hardly any were—isolation was preferable to potential mortification.

Revealing Secrets

Because of the intense competitiveness for power and status among men, including comparisons of genital size and sexual prowess, for the men who are the impaired marital partner, revealing their problem in the group and being accepted and praised by the other men *was* magical. In the first three-hour meeting, Joe, a lawyer, revealed that he had had a child by donor insemination and that he and his wife were trying to have another. Often, when an important secret is revealed in a group, the members are stunned and remain silent. In this group, each of the members must have anticipated that some of the others had problems with their sperm. After Joe's revelation, there was no silence. Each of the members chimed in with a comment or question. There was a long discussion of the social versus the genetic origins of fatherhood. They all said that they respected Joe for making this choice. They asked him to talk about how he felt about his little girl and were happy to hear how much he loved her. Stan complemented Joe for his "bravery" in using the donor sperm and wondered if he himself would "have the guts" to do the same thing in a similar situation.

Here, we see masculinity redefined as having the strength to be giving to one's wife and generative in life, even if the choice breaks all the macho rules. Over the months, this issue resurfaced many times, as all of the men struggled with the possibility of adoption. It helped them immeasurably to witness Joe's profound love of his child.

For his part, Joe expressed extreme pleasure in having been able to share his dark secret, previously known only to his wife and his therapist. He and his wife felt that it was not safe to be honest with their families, as certain relatives had been very damning of donor insemination after hearing it discussed on a TV show. When his secret was accepted by other men, Joe felt he had truly been seen. He felt liberated.

Life Out of Control, Full of Obsession

As MacNab (1984) found, when men finally begin to stop denying, they find themselves caught up in a whirlwind of painful feelings. Even though men go off to work every day, a job or career does not necessarily offer protection from the feeling that life is out of control. The feelings of disappointment, inadequacy, and frustration totally pervade their lives.

It is well known that women's mood swings during infertility are intimately tied to where they are in their menstrual cycle. Some husbands just tune out, paying no attention, but other men are closely attuned to their wives' cycles of optimism and disappointment. They are the silent partners, frightened of and embarrassed by their own mood swings.

One of my patients, an adopted child himself, was desperately hoping to have a biological heir. In one session, he blurted out that he "just couldn't stand the up and down of it all. I don't think I can bear any more disappointment in my life."

One group member had a wife who was undergoing in vitro fertilization (IVF) as an outpatient in a large Boston hospital. He reported that he was trying extremely hard to stay on an even keel, to modulate himself between irrational hope and cynicism, obsessing every moment while he was at work. He said:

> "No one understands this. Obsessed. That's what I am. Obsessed. Finally, I can't stand it anymore. I can't stand not knowing. Right about noon, I have to call her at home, have to find out what the results are. Is she still in the program, or was she canceled? After I find out, and she is still in the program, I can relax. Well, at least for that day. But no one knows what this feels like. It's like being on a tightrope, on a tightrope with your damned eyes blindfolded!"

The other group members understood his feelings exactly.

Not feeling understood was another major theme. The members abhorred the fact that men do not talk honestly about any tough feelings, not only about infertility.

Several have discussed their own use of withdrawal from other people as a defense, particularly at work. But unlike some of MacNab's subjects, who used work as a peaceful oasis, several members withdrew unhappily into their own shells because they felt so wounded and vulnerable that they could no longer make the normal and necessary small talk at their jobs. So they retreated — behind office doors, behind stacks of reports, and behind computers. They simply could not concentrate. They honestly could not function at work. At the same time, of course, they had some anxiety that their careers might be in jeopardy if someone found out what a "mess" they truly were.

The literature talks a lot about men escaping from the pain of infertility into their work role. Some men may be able to do this, particularly in the early years of infertility, but the men of the group, many of whom had been struggling with infertility for several years, were describing an entirely different way of being at work: feeling insulated, alone, isolated from other men, and cut off from the entire human race.

George, who looks as if he should be playing for the National Football League, tearfully talked about how upset he got when people in his office came around looking for contributions for baby gifts for fertile coworkers. He talked about being "angry, resentful, tearful," and about how he needed to hide these terrible, unmanly emotions. He was so afraid that his feelings would show on his face that he would go into one of the cubicles of the men's bathroom, cry if he had to, and "pull himself together" by putting on what he called his "mask of strength." Several of the other men chimed in, feeling the same way.

One of the members described the false, jocular front he needed to put on with all of his coworkers. He hated himself for being such a phony, but he couldn't risk telling anyone about his day-to-day obsession with what was happening to his wife, as he and she underwent various intrusive, high-tech diagnostic tests and treatments.

The men in this group certainly did not expect support from their coworkers, and they felt that it was unmanly even to ask their wives for support. The wives were their loving companions who obviously knew about the problem, but the men were in terrible conflict about admitting to their wives that they felt needy, as they felt that they should be the strong ones and their wives should be the weak ones. This conflict was compounded by the fact that none of these men had to undergo any painful tests or treatments (e.g., had no testicular biopsies and no varicocele surgery), so there were no situations in which they could legitimately act like the patient.

There is irony in this situation. These men felt many of the same things that their wives felt: anger at siblings for giving birth to children seemingly effortlessly; feelings of being defective; feelings of being out of control; and desires to avoid social situations with small children and pregnant women. Yet, because it is seen as unmanly to be weak, they could not reveal themselves to their wives. Further, they noticed that, when their wives' feelings got too close to home, they cut themselves off and withdrew. Some of them even got angry at their wives for being so irrational or so weepy.

They saw the irony. They talked about how constricted they felt by their socialization to reject all things feminine. Stan said that he wished that he could be more like George, who cried during the first meeting. They felt helpless. They hoped that society would be restructured so that they had permission to feel. They saw that their macho behavior isolated them at work and in their relationships. But it was too dangerous to stop playing the role.

Anger at One's Wife

> When my wife was canceled from this last cycle of IVF, we were so disappointed, and she was just heartbroken, but—I hate to say this, it sounds so awful—but I was just *furious* at her. Just *furious*. I really hated her. It is irrational, but I just wanted to find someone else, some fertile "chick" and take her to bed—to get away, to get out of this whole horrible, bad dream.

As pained as John was in stammering these words, he knew that other members of the group would not be shocked because three other members had voiced the identical sentiments in previous weeks. He was lucky: he knew that his emotions toward his wife were "normal" in this extremely difficult situation. He knew other men had coped with such feelings and survived.

At different times, four of the group members shared their rage at their wives. In some cases, guilt because of this anger contributed to an emotional distance from their wives: If they couldn't share all of their feelings honestly, they didn't feel able to share at all. Because the group provided an arena for the feelings toward their wives of anger and deep disappointment, their loving feelings ultimately resurfaced.

The men talked about how irrational their feelings were when their wives had the medical impairment. Clearly, the wives didn't want to be infertile, so how could the husbands possibly be so angry about something out of their wives' control? But it hurt the fertile men to the quick to come to grips with the fact that their "accidental" choice of a wife would probably doom them to a life without a biological heir. This loss was so great for several of the men that they could stand to face it only sporadically. They shared their grief, and they shared their escape fantasies.

And fantasies of escape abounded. Stan talked about walking down the street, looking at a strange woman, and thinking, "My, she looks fertile!" The other group members laughed at how ridiculous this reaction actually was because, by now, they all knew that nothing in life is what it seems to be. They turned over in their minds how different their lives would be if they left their wives and found new, fertile partners.

They talked about having affairs. Men with professional wives reassured themselves that, because their wives were so highly educated, "If I left her, thank God, she would be OK. She could take care of herself." Naturally, these feelings were secrets they had from their wives. None of these men actually wound up leaving his wife. However, their thoughts seem to add weight to the hypothesis that men are more likely to think of beginning life anew as a way of dealing with loss, whereas women are more focused on intimacy and keeping their connections. Wives think briefly of discarding infertile husbands but then feel too drawn to keeping the relationship to consider this alternative seriously.

Men may need an opportunity for a full examination of the possibility of leaving their wives and for a conscious decision not to do so before they can recommit themselves to the marriage and to the likelihood of adoption, third-party pregnancy, or child-free living. Ultimately, most of the subjects in MacNab's research (1984) felt that going through the infertility experience had strengthened their marriage and had added to the amount of love and respect they had for their wives. My men's support group seems to have made going through the painful process of examination and recommitment less lonely. The men all understood the duality of their feelings toward their wives. Yes, infertility had stirred up feelings of hate, but each felt strong feelings of love, too. I asked them whether they were fighting with their wives. Because most men in this group had been dealing with infertility for several years, this question elicited a lot of comments about what kind of "jerks" they used to be. Several described how, at the beginning of the process, they hadn't been able to stand their wives' being so upset. But, they said, now that they were upset themselves, they felt closer to their wives than ever.

They talked from time to time about the horrors of the medical treatments and tests to which their wives had to submit. A large part of one session was spent commiserating with each other about how awful it was to give one's wife shots of medication, to have to cause her pain, and, on top of it, to have to act calm so that she would not get more upset. Several of the men were anxious about being able to give the shots correctly, without injuring the women they loved.

Stan, who was a veteran, having gone through two cycles of in vitro fertilization, guided the rest of the men through the process. He shared how sick and weak his wife had become from the anesthesia and how frightened he had felt. Other members talked about their understanding of how painful certain tests had been for their wives. It was evident that they were concerned about their wives. But actually, they spent little of the group talking about how bad their wives felt. They knew that this was the only space available to ask for the support they needed as men.

Loss of the Genetic Line

The potential loss of one's genetic line was a topic brought up at almost every group meeting. In this group, there was wonderful dialogue at different times between two men who were not able to father children themselves and three men who presumably would have been able to father biologically if their wives were not impaired.

Matthew, an engineer, had found out about his extremely low sperm count and was not terribly disturbed about it. He explained that he had never liked or felt close to his father, and so not continuing what he perceived to be his father's genetic line did not feel like much of a loss. Instead, the goal was to be a good father, and adoption immediately seemed like a fine alternative. Paul, whose sperm count had been compromised by a bout with a childhood illness, had initially felt negative about the possibility of using donor sperm, but he had accepted this as a solution by the time he came to the group.

There were times when the members with unimpaired fertility were awestruck that their infertile friends—whom they cared about, admired, and thought of as strong, wise, and manly—could be so accepting of having a nonbiologically related child. At the initial workshop, Stan asked Paul, who was talking about donor insemination, why he did not insist on having his own sperm treated first. Paul matter-of-factly said that his sperm "were not good enough." Paul went on to say that his own genetic line was quite mixed ethnically and that, when he imagined it, he didn't think of it as a pure strain that was being interrupted by the donor's genetic line; he felt instead that the donor's genes were simply being added to a genetic mishmash.

Surprised, Stan, who had a high sperm count, talked passionately about how important it was to him that his sperm were viable. He came from a large, dysfunctional, alcholic family. Stan had little respect for his father and felt that his father's sole accomplishment had been to sire children. The fact that Stan couldn't sire a child because of his wife's medical condition frustrated him and made him feel inferior to his father. He told of feeling shattered one time, during the in vitro fertilization process, when eggs were retrieved from his wife, but his sperm failed to fertilize them. Stan's sperm were then scrutinized for whether they could penetrate a specially prepared hamster egg. Stan felt tremendously relieved when his sperm passed the hamster-egg test. Later, his sperm successfully fertilized one of his wife's eggs during the in vitro process. The fertilized egg, however, did not implant in his wife. Stan said he didn't know what he would have done had his sperm been found inadequate.

Stan's father image from his childhood was of an irresponsible, angry, unnurturant, critical drunk. The only respectable masculine trait his father possessed was champion sperm. I pointed out to him that he was competing with his father, which he had not realized. Because he honestly felt quite confident of his superiority to his father in many realms, he was able to ease up slightly on his sense that he must produce a biological child to be OK.

John, too, had found that he might be prevented from fathering a child by his wife's medical condition, and he felt much the same as Stan. Even though he was functioning well sexually and making good money and had an excellent sperm count, the fact that he and his wife might not succeed in reproducing themselves biologically made him feel, "I'm just not sure I am still a man." As John talked about it, he admitted, "I don't know if I will ever be able to feel whole again if I have to adopt." Again, as we explored, John's internalized equation of masculinity with his father's kind of masculinity came through. Like Stan's father, John's father had produced many offspring, including a few sons. He had taken great pride in his kids, particularly the boys. Although John had achieved much more than his father professionally, and even though rationally he liked his model of manhood better than his father's model, he did not feel he was his father's equal. Like Stan's, John's definition of male adulthood meant equaling or surpassing his father's ability to produce a child (and probably a son).

George was a man who talked about fathering his own children with great feeling. He was praying that the attempts at in vitro fertilization would work so that he could carry on the family tradition of being a wonderful parent that his own father had begun. George had the most moving, adoring, unabashedly positive memories of his relationship with his father of all of the group members. George's father had been warm and available. They had spent a lot of time together, riding bikes, reading, playing ball, and talking. As a small child, he had dreamed, "When I grow up, I am going to be a father, like my daddy!"

George had almost a visual image of the genetic chain of continuity between his father, himself, and his child. He had planned to relive his cherished memories of his father, now dead, through his loving, giving relationship with his own children. This time, he would take the father role, he would become The Father, the giver of support and love. Although he had an adopted brother whom he loved, he felt that if he could not live out his lifelong dream of biological fatherhood, a part of him would die.

Not surprisingly, George was the most tuned in to his own grief. He cried in the group, reported feeling isolated from other men at work and socially, and felt tremendous jealousy of fertile siblings and coworkers, pregnant women, and couples with small children. George's feelings were probably far from the realm of what most men consciously feel about fatherhood, because most don't have a father image like George's. The group offered him a place where other men might—and did—admit to being jealous of pregnant women. In one exchange, George and Stan talked about what a terrible feeling envy is, how horrible it is to begrudge other people their happiness. They each said that envy made them feel small. The group heard the confession of what George and Stan genuinely felt was a sinful, ugly feeling, and of course, the group absolved them by understanding and accepting the feeling. George helped his fellow group members by providing a passionate, sensitive portrait of masculinity with which all of the other members could identify.

Men: Forming a Small Support Group in the Real World

Women naturally form support groups around emotional issues, and this ability prevents them from feeling lonely. Little support groups spontaneously spring up among the women who are going through the various phases of IVF treatment together, sitting in the waiting rooms, waiting for the results of their bloodwork or ultrasound results.

No such opportunities exist for men. Even when husbands are present in the waiting room, they are outnumbered by women, so that the group that forms is a women's group. But John and Joe wound up with a support dyad outside the group at one point, when they met each other accidentally several times in the treatment setting during IVF. Tom felt overjoyed to see a friendly male face and couldn't wait to introduce his friend to his wife. At first, John felt shy. In some way, he felt that having to answer questions about how he knew Tom might make him compromise some confidential information. Women are used to keeping important secrets about friends' feelings. Men don't have as much practice. (Or it is possible that John wanted to keep his men's group separate from his wife, so that it felt like his special place?)

At any rate, as the two couples progressed through the rigors of the IVF program's ups and downs, both the men began to appreciate their relationship.

Each one felt that the other was going through the process "with" him. Each thought of the other between group meetings. John and Tom's relationship gave each of them a way to have a male experience of IVF. When they met at the group each month, there was a rush to trade and review experiences, and there was a lot of affection.

The Fatherhood Mandate

Contrary to what most people may assume, women are not the only sex to feel the mandate to have children. The group talked a lot about the pressure to have kids, agreeing that other people assume that you are a bad or immature person if you are not a father. As John said, "Having kids is the only option for being an OK human being." Also, having biological children was the only future that all but one of the men had ever considered.

As the group matured and the individual members passed down the road of their journey, there was a lot of talk about the uncertainty of the future. None of the men wanted not to have children. Because the group gave each of them a chance to explore in depth his own sense of sadness, outrage, frustration, and loss, the effect of the infertility became more real to each man. All of them completely stopped projecting their feelings onto their wives. This outcome led to a deepening of sadness and allowed them to speak the unspeakable: fears that they would never, in fact, be able to "get through" the process, come to resolution, "feel whole," and love an adopted child.

Stan dropped out of the group when he and his wife didn't succeed in IVF, and he felt too depleted and heartbroken to consider adoption immediately. He couldn't stand to hear of the other members' struggles when he was putting his own infertility "on hold." (This pattern may be related to sex role. Women have learned that in having close friendships, you open yourself up to your friends' pain. Stan hadn't learned this yet and didn't want his hard-won feeling of being temporarily at peace with infertility to be interrupted by his sad feelings for a friend.)

The remaining members continued to talk meaningfully about their fathers, about their deprived childhoods, about whether or not they would be able to give enough emotionally to be good fathers, and about the frustration and humiliation of the adoption process. They spoke with pleasure about the links to other men that they had in the group. Each of them knew that he had been able to be sensitive and nurturant to the other men. For each of them, a new sense of himself as loving, generous, and empathetic contributed to an identity as a "whole," "adult," "real" man. This sense of themselves as givers and nurturers may have been the greatest benefit of the group. Eventually, the remaining members either began to resolve the problem and to feel good about making a choice or went "on vacation" from treatment, and we decided it was time to end the group.

Discussion and Conclusion

The answer to the question of what men feel about infertility will probably depend on the man to whom we are speaking, on when in the infertility process we ask him, and on the cues he gets from other men in the environment. Menning (1977), MacNab (1984), and Osherson (1986) have all shown that men are actively discouraged from expressing and exploring their feelings of distress by family, friends, and medical personnel.

Some professionals in the field, clinicians and researchers, take the fact that men do not reveal their feelings about infertility to mean that men have no feelings about it. Abbey et al. (1991) made the common suggestion that men need to understand the unique stressors facing women undergoing infertility treatment. Who is going to advocate that the rest of us look at the unique stressors facing men?

Two of the members of my group had wives who were undergoing IVF at a large Boston teaching hospital. When they asked the social worker if there were any support services or support groups for the husbands, she replied that there were none "because there is not enough interest." One urologist with whom I spoke said that he couldn't imagine referring men to an all-men's support group, because by the time men came to him for a repeat sperm analysis for azoospermia or oligospermia, "They already suspect that there is something wrong, so they aren't all that upset. Their wives cry, but they don't." Many of us seem to confuse how men act with how they feel.

There is an interesting semantic issue in all of this discussion about how men handle feelings that has implications for how we work with men. Sometimes, we clinicians use the word *denial* in describing what men do with their upset emotions. Ron Levant, a psychologist whose work has focused on men's issues, objects to this usage: "Denial is more rigid. What men have is a trained incapacity to experience feelings. Men are educable; the problem is susceptible to intervention. If you give men some practice in empathy, they are off and running" (personal communication, September 26, 1991). The group processes described above offers support for Levant's position and shows that men can gain pleasure from becoming more conversant in the language of feelings.

Clinics have a responsibility to offer specific services for men, even if most men do not take advantage of them. Just the acknowledgment of need is an important intervention. In general, MacNab's suggestion (1984) that services be provided for those men who have already struggled with infertility for several years makes practical sense, as these men would be more likely to accept help. However, in a more ideal world, men who are "out of synch" with their wives and out of touch with the threat of not being a father after a year of medical treatment would be encouraged to look more closely at their relationship with their own dad.

The process of the men's group described here indicates how men who are in touch with the loss act with one another. Common themes were (1) feelings of resentment about societal expectations that they be strong; (2) immediate connection and empathy, as well as tremendous relief at being able to share vulnerable feelings with other men; (3) extremely nurturant, uncompetitive behavior; (4) sharing angry fantasies of leaving their wives for a more fertile woman; (5) revelations of angry and jealous feelings about others' pregnancies; (6) intense support for men with no or low sperm counts; (7) isolation at work, from friends, and from wives; (8) disturbing feelings of not measuring up as men because of the inability to reproduce; and (9) competitive feelings with their fathers.

Future studies on how men react to infertility should look at men at different times during the infertility struggle, including after several years. Ethnic, class, and cultural differences also should be explored.

In the section that follows, multimodal therapy (MMT) is used to describe the impact of infertility on the typical therapy patient, a woman. Although husbands need encouragement to get in touch with (or amplify) their feelings of distress about involuntary childlessness, wives may need different strategies: periodic interventions to contain or manage negative cognitions, behavior, imagery, and feelings.

Part 2
Losses across the Personality: Taking a Multimodal Perspective on Infertility

3

Using Multimodal Therapy with Infertility Patients: Cognitive and Behavioral Interventions

C linicians who are just beginning to work in the field or those who have not experienced fertility problems may not be aware of how profoundly all aspects of one's personality and life are affected. Using a "multimodal" perspective, the chapters that follow are an overview of the plethora of losses that infertility may entail for each patient. Because the greatest body of my work has been with female patients, and because women react differently from men, unless specified, my remarks are about how fertility problems affect women's lives.

The term *multimodal* belongs to Arnold Lazarus, one of the most famous and well-respected modern-day psychological thinkers. Lazarus (1981) created multimodal therapy (MMT), a systematic and comprehensive approach to psychotherapy that integrates the behavioral, affective, sensory, imaginal, cognitive, interpersonal, and biological modalities of personality (which Lazarus calls the "BASIC ID").

Much of what has been written so far about infertility focuses on its effect on the patient's feelings and relationships. MMT is a tool that allows us to take a new and more comprehensive look at how we may intervene in other realms of patients' functioning, particularly their cognitions, behavior, and imagery. Because MMT is grounded in learning theory and has a large behavioral component, it can be used to design psychotherapeutic interventions. Realizing that they have the choice and the ability to target and change thoughts, behavior, and imagery related to infertility helps many people feel more in control of life.

Each individual or couple who enters treatment fills out Lazarus's general MMT questionnaire (see Appendix 1), a lengthy interview form that gathers historical data as well as data on behavior, affect, sensation, imagery, cognitions, interpersonal relationships, and health and health behaviors.

Lazarus's interview contains one subtest that identifies favored mode(s) of operating. One patient may exist mostly in the world of thoughts. Another may tend to act before she thinks. Still another tends to process events by using feelings and imagery. The MMT therapist discovers the patient's preferred

41

modalities and plans to intervene by concentrating on them, thus speaking each patient's special "language."

Every patient and partner also completes a questionnaire on the effects of infertility (see Appendix 2) based on MMT, which focuses on how each experiences the problem in the various modalities, clarifies the dynamics of the marriage system, and indicates how each partner feels the infertility has affected the marriage.

The material in these MMT chapters is based on data collected from this questionnaire on the effects of infertility. In many cases, the MMT "profile" of how infertility has affected separate lives is strikingly similar.

The Cognitive Modality: Thoughts and Belief Systems

The cognitive area is of great importance in understanding and healing patients' distress. The thought process is involved in an accurate appraisal of a situation. During a crisis, adequate coping cannot occur without accurate appraisal (Cameron & Meichenbaum, 1982). Frequently, the patient's appraisal of a situation is flawed or inaccurate, so that it is difficult for her to develop a constructive plan of action.

The losses of infertility are huge. Fully grieving their losses is imperative before patients who cannot have a biological child can choose an alternative. But the grieving process can be distorted or negatively prolonged by irrational beliefs.

The most deeply melancholic infertility patients are the ones who have the largest number and the most persistent set of negative or erroneous beliefs— about what their infertility means about them, about their relationship with their spouse, about how medical caregivers should treat them, about what the future will bring, about their ability to cope with the other choices available to them if they cannot have a biological child, and about their relationship to God, their families, and others. Their beliefs make their sadness unbearable and intractable. An ancient Greek saying sums up the process: "It isn't the events themselves that are significant, but the meaning that we ascribe to events."

Cognitive therapy was introduced by Aaron Beck in 1963. It postulates that irrational thoughts and fantasies are the cause of distress. Beck suggested that each disorder has its own set of distinctive ideations, which contribute to the subjective distress of the client. For example, depressed patients devalue themselves, have a negative view of life experiences, and are pessimistic about the future; anxious patients focus primarily on thoughts of danger.

Beck categorized irrational thought processes such as selective attention to failures, the magnification of negative outcomes, or the minimizing of positive outcomes. The cognitive therapist teaches the patient that negative and irrational thoughts are the precursors of unpleasant feeling states, helps the client discover that a particular thought pattern is maladaptive, and trains the client to assay her ideas through hypothesis-testing procedures. This chapter discusses some of the common negative beliefs that occur during infertility, along with strategies that challenge them.

Patients report "feelings" to us that are in reality a mixture of feelings and thoughts and beliefs. For example, one woman wrote on her questionnaire on the effects of infertility in the "feelings" section, "I feel bad about myself that I am not good enough because I cannot get pregnant." There is no news here: the infertility patient's sense of being defective is well known. Nevertheless, once the therapist and the patient have a good working alliance (that is to say, the patient knows that the therapist cares about her and takes the grief of infertility quite seriously), no such statement should be left unopposed. All the different components of this feeling/thought should be teased out and contested.

The implication of this patient's statement is that only people who are "good enough" get pregnant, and that people who aren't "good enough" don't. Whenever a patient makes such a statement, it should be lovingly yet logically questioned and refuted: Good enough for what? Are thieves and murderers plagued with infertility? Doesn't she know anyone marvelous who is infertile? If she is in a support group with other women or couples, are they all awful people? (If you make your patient laugh at herself, give yourself a pat on the back.)

The patient should be taught to pay attention to her irrational thoughts herself, to keep track of them by writing them down in a notebook daily when they occur, and to stop them by refuting them with logical ideas in her head and in the notebook. The patient soon recognizes many of her negative and irrational thoughts, as the same ones tend to occur again and again. (David Burn's book *Feeling Good,* 1980, is helpful to patients.)

If the patient is deeply depressed, as some infertile women are, she may not be functioning normally cognitively. As her therapist, you must supply the logical thought. Research studies have begun to show that depressives, as well as schizophrenics, have impaired thought processes (Burns, 1980), as the following case illustrates:

Ruth, a very bright woman of forty, had miscarried for the second time a few weeks previously. She was completely devastated and was certain that this was happening for a reason, that she was being punished. Ruth was unusual in that she did not have any past life events over which she felt consciously guilty—no abortions, very little premarital sex, no affairs, and so on. After we spent some time articulating and then refuting her irrational beliefs, she finally got to the point where she could empathize with herself instead of blaming herself for imagined wrongdoing. She was simply crying, which was a very normal and reasonable response to her loss.

After she had cried for some time, she began to talk about how much she wanted someone to take care of her, how exhausted she felt. I softly asked her what might be some pleasurable things she could give to herself, or what nice things her husband or friends might do for her? She drew a complete blank. Sitting in my office for ten minutes, she could not think of a single thing that might give her pleasure. She herself was amazed at her inability to think adequately in the midst of feeling so sad.

On one hand, what I have just described is a normal response to intense grief and a concrete loss. On the other hand, for patients who have been struggling with long-term infertility and its monthly cycle of hope and despair, or with serial pregnancy loss, this incapacity to think, this inability to imagine any pleasure, now or in the future, becomes the everyday, "normal" mode of thinking. As therapists, we need to lend patients our clearer ideas, our creativity, and our vision of possible futures.

Paying Attention to the Tracking Order

Beck (1979) wrote about negative thoughts as "precursors" to bad feelings. Albert Ellis noted the A-B-C phenomenon: There is an Activating event, Beliefs that follow, and Consequences of those beliefs, often bad feelings. Lazarus (1981) had a similar concept, that he called the "tracking order," the interaction between the modalities of personality. Thoughts, images, and sensations, one leading to another in some sequence, *cause* behavior and feelings. Awareness of her typical tracking order can help a patient cut off feelings of depression or anxiety before they become full blown:

> Sara, an infertile woman of thirty-eight, reported that she was depressed by seeing a pregnant woman near her house. "That pregnant woman made me feel sad," she exclaimed.
>
> However, as we explored her train of associations, it was her thought on seeing the image of a pregnant woman:—"I'm afraid that that will never be me"—that actually caused her to feel sad. The exploration that followed helped Sara to believe that if she didn't ever get pregnant, she and Ned would still be parents, through adoption.
>
> We decided that the next time she saw a pregnant woman, she would think to herself: "I hope I get pregnant, that's for sure. But no matter what happens, I am going to be a mother to a baby." Despite a spring season brimming with other full bellies in parks and at parties, Sara was less vulnerable to sad feelings after this point.

Patients tend to have different tracking orders. One patient may begin with a thought and end up with a sad feeling; another may lean toward creating a whole chain based on a visual image. Women who have previously miscarried have horrible thoughts and feelings based on physical sensations. (see Chapter 9). It is up to the therapist to point out that, much to the patient's surprise, feelings do not spring out of nowhere; they are caused by events, beliefs, sensations, or images that are linked, one leading to another.

Common Negative Beliefs of People Who Are Infertile

Certain cognitive changes occur during the infertility crisis that are normal responses to any kind of catastrophe, such as coping with an acute or chronic illness, violence, a natural disaster, or the loss of a loved one. (Taylor, Wood, & Lichtman, 1983). People who reach adulthood without being touched by calamity often believe that they are invulnerable, or at least less vulnerable than other people. This belief is demolished when tragedy of any kind strikes.

It is largely the psychological loss of one's cherished beliefs that forms the common thread among all forms of victimization. Experiencing tragedy affects our beliefs in personal invulnerability, our perceptions that the world is meaningful, and our positive self-views (Taylor, 1983). For victims who were cautious and good people, the world now seems to lack meaning. Victims view themselves as weak, needy, frightened, and out of control (Horowitz, Wilner, Marmar, & Krupnick, 1980). Markus and Nurius (1986) posited that after this change in self-image, victims may need to re-create an image of themselves as healthy, active, or strong in order to regain a convincing sense of control.

A great deal of the cognitive activity that occurs in the midst of any tragedy involves attempts to understand the cause of the outcome, to judge whether or not the outcome was inevitable, and to create alternative scenarios for how things might have gone differently (Taylor, 1983). In a second cognitive process during times of catastrophe, people typically create some distortions (or illusions) in their sense of reality that are adaptive and help them bear the pain (Taylor, 1983; Taylor & Brown, 1988). Often, these are beliefs that the tragedy served some greater purpose, or that other people are worse off than they, the victims, are.

The infertility patient's continual struggle to understand "Why me?" has been well documented in the literature (Mazor, 1978; Menning, 1977; Woollett, 1985). However, unlike other victims of tragedy, infertility patients seem less likely to create protective illusions to help themselves cope. Infertile women are profoundly pessimistic, sometimes unrealistically so. Their pessimism and tendency not to use illusion as a coping mechanism have implications for their interpersonal relationships, discussed in Chapter 6.

Patients' problem beliefs about infertility are ascertained by the following questions from the questionnaire on the effects of infertility:

Are there any beliefs you have about the infertility that you wish you didn't have?

Are there any beliefs about the infertility you don't have but wish you did?

Are there any beliefs or thoughts about infertility that actually make you feel worse?

Are there any beliefs you have about infertility that make you feel better?

Unlike victims of other tragedies, infertility patients see no hidden blessings in the dark cloud of their infertility and usually write "no" in response to the question "Are there any beliefs you have about infertility that make you feel better?" If patients do have thoughts that soothe them, these thoughts should be encouraged.

Unpleasant, upsetting, sometimes irrational thoughts abound. Answers to the question about upsetting beliefs included, "I believe that I will never be a parent, and I can't stand that thought"; "I don't think I will ever be able to be happy without a child of our own"; and "I believe that we will never have a child to love, and we would be terrific parents." The general sentiment is "Life is empty, a waste. There is nothing to look forward to." For the most part, these patients are unaware of their pernicious, irrational beliefs and need guidance from a therapist to identify and dispute them.

Sins and Guilt

Guilt, remorse, and shame are ubiquitous: "I think that this infertility is my fault, and I'm undeserving of having a baby"; "I am being punished for my affair"; "I believe I am being punished for my abortion"; or "I think that maybe I don't deserve what I want."

Many of these patients, however, do recognize the destructiveness of one of their belief systems. When asked which thoughts are making things worse, they answer, "The wrong thoughts, that I have sinned", or "The wrong thinking, that God is punishing me."

Often, a patient's convictions about her involuntary childlessness are the major obstacle that she must surmount in order to overcome her depression, anger, obsession, or jealousy, or to get on with the process of resolution.

Religious beliefs are particularly common factors in patients' continuing depression and jealousy. The therapist can be extremely helpful to the patient by teasing out upsetting positions, getting the patient to articulate her reasoning thoroughly, and challenging the patient to modify her views.

Some patients believe that God has infinite powers, and that He sees and approves of everything that occurs to every mortal on earth at every moment. At the same time, there is the conviction that God is kind and just and inflicts pain and punishment only on people who have been evil, that "everyone gets what he or she deserves."

When a patient has this view, two things cause problems. First, she is enraged by the number of "undeserving" women who get pregnant. Every time someone she knows becomes pregnant, she compares herself with that person and determines either that the pregnant woman is less "good" than she is, which makes her furious and bitter toward the woman, or that she is not as "good" as the pregnant woman, which just makes her more miserable and self-hating. Second, just when she most needs to find comfort in God, she loses faith: "How could God be so unfair?"

When caught in this belief system, women become trapped in computing an ongoing accounting of every person's "moral bank balance":

Ann, a devout Catholic, became physically ill over her promiscuous first cousin's illegitimate pregnancy. This cousin was happy to be having her baby, even if it was out of wedlock, and the whole family rallied around her, planning a baby shower.

Ann railed on about the hypocrisy of her Catholic family's acting happy about her cousin's pregnancy and, encouraged to talk more, began to cry. It seemed that she had been trying to figure out why God would let this particularly unwholesome cousin become pregnant, and in the course of her moral accounting, she had dug up a whole list of major and minor sins that she herself had committed.

As we explored her thinking, I asked Ann what she thought about bad luck. She said that she never used it as an explanation for anything. I then asked her what she thought when something bad happened to anyone else. For example, when she was out shopping, what did she think when she saw someone who was badly crippled? Did she think that the disability meant the person was being punished by God? Ann reported that, in fact, when something awful happened to someone else, it never occurred to her that that person must have deserved it but instead she just felt sorry about the person's pain.

But when it came to looking at her own life, Ann firmly held onto the concept that sad events happened as a punishment for sin. Therefore, she felt that she *had* to go on with the unsuccessful and highly stressful medical treatments that she had undertaken for the last several years because it would be possible for her to see herself as forgiven by God only if He allowed her to have a biological child.

In the course of this discussion, Ann saw the trap that she had dug for herself in her belief system and considered a few alternative ways of thinking about God and infertility. It made some sense to her that God knew something about her that she didn't, for instance, that her back, which was weak from a congenital abnormality, may in fact not have been able to support a pregnancy. She also thought that perhaps God's plan for her was that she would adopt a special child who would flourish in the care of her and her husband. Finally, she began to be able to imagine a God who did not direct every minute event that happened to every person on earth. She began to be able to let go of the thought that her infertility was her punishment for wrongdoing.

When she challenged this set of notions about how God works on earth, Ann began to be free to live her life more fully. She felt much less hostile toward her cousin, was more able to take part in family events, and, most important, began to take steps toward giving up her long, unproductive medical treatment. (A case description of Ann's treatment is contained in Chapter 8.)

The "why me" syndrome is classic among infertility patients (Mazor, 1978; Menning, 1977); just as it is among other victims of tragedy. Even among people who staunchly reject religion, infertility is often attributed to some wrongdoing on their part (De Brovner & Shubin-Stein, 1975). The struggle to find something that makes the infertility understandable, that makes it make sense (Woolett, 1985), is almost inevitable. As no one is perfect, most people have something to feel guilty about. At its worst, though, attributing one's infertility to something "bad" leads to intense feelings of shame.

Karen: Guilt over an affair:

Karen, a teacher in her early forties, was happily married for the second time. She was unusually shamed by her infertility. In her unhappy first marriage, she had had an affair. She was now plagued by the belief that her ectopic pregnancies were caused by an infection that she had contracted from her illicit lover. Despite my attention to working on it, she was never able to banish her belief that her infertility was punishment for her wrongdoing.

Mary Kay: Guilt over an abortion and help by priestly absolution:

Mary Kay, in her late thirties, was a practicing Catholic. Early in psychotherapy, she began to talk about her guilt over a abortion eight years before and her fear that her inability to conceive now was God's punishment for her wrongdoing.

We discussed the issue in psychotherapy, but it was clear to me that, as a layperson, I was not powerful enough to help her. She needed to be absolved by a priest. I asked her to think of a priest who might be sympathetic about her problem. She named one right away, but she resisted talking to him because she still felt guilty and ashamed about the abortion. Her guilt and the infertility-as-punishment theme persisted through the months ahead.

One day, almost a year later, she came into therapy looking more relaxed than usual. I asked her what had happened. It turned out that she had taken my advice. She had gone to see the priest who she had thought would be sympathetic.

The priest was moved by her story. He told her that, because of all the suffering she had done over the abortion for the past several years, she was already forgiven. In fact, he added that, if she had any other sins she had forgotten, he was forgiving her for them, too! From then on, she made no mention of guilt.

For religious patients, talking to a member of the clergy may help. For patients who would respond well to a rational, secular approach, excellent cognitive strategies to help patients overcome regret are contained in Freeman and DeWolf's *Woulda, Coulda, Shoulda* (1989).

Isolation

One client found herself feeling quite isolated from others. When she explored this isolation with me, she found that she was telling herself, "You have to have a child to be a family, or to understand those with children."

Magical Thoughts That Intrude on Happiness

The stress of infertility is so intense that it can throw people into magical or obsessive thought patterns:

Martha, an in vitro fertilization (IVF) patient, tried to master her anxiety by convincing herself that if she controlled all of her own behavior perfectly, conception would definitely occur. This belief made her life a living hell. She thought she had to be in excellent physical condition, that she had to eat only completely healthy foods, and that she had to be in the "right frame of mind" every second of the day.

She came in complaining of headaches and depression. Then we uncovered her belief that perfection on her part would guarantee success in

IVF. She detailed her minute-by-minute attempts at perfection and expressed relief that she was agreeing to give up her rituals.

By the next week's session, she was feeling much better. She was ready to talk about the reality that, statistically, the odds of her achieving pregnancy from IVF were only 15 percent. Although she was still sad about the possibility that she might not create a child with her husband, her headaches had disappeared, and some of the tension arising in her marriage because of her obsessive behavior was gone.

Cognitive Distortions in Looking at Parenthood

Couples often discuss the pros and cons of parenthood in a realistic and balanced manner during the courtship period and in the early years of their marriage. The stresses of the parental role are acknowledged, along with the very real sacrifices of the parents' privacy, energy, sexual relationship, sleep, and finances.

Partners regard the children around them, noticing which children are a pleasure to encounter and which ones are difficult. Hopes of having good, easy, healthy children ("like that darling girl we saw in the park and my sister's son Mark") are played off against the bad fantasies of producing offspring who cause trouble or who have traits deemed undesirable ("like cousin Sally's son Billy. Boy, he really ruined their life!" or "Eeek! What if she's a nice kid but she gets your brother's nose?"). The indisputable costs are weighed against the equally real pleasures of having children in one's life. Eventually, a decision about whether to have children is reached.

After a significant period of experiencing infertility, cognitions about what life is like parenting an infant or a small child are affected, so that pregnancy and parenthood are idealized. In addition, for some couples, fantasies about how wonderful and perfect one's own biological offspring would be are contrasted with negative pictures of what an adopted child might be like.

Misunderstanding the Love Bonds in Adopted Families

Patients and therapists alike may misunderstand the kinds of love bonds that exist, under the best of circumstances, in adoptive families (Kirk, 1964). Some believe that, in adopting, they must forever forgo the kind of "real" love that exists only in biological families. David Kirk tells the awful story of a woman who met Kirk's wife waiting anxiously in the family room of the hospital after their adopted daughter had surgery.

"Isn't that sweet?" the woman commented. "Just like a *real* mother."

A similar story was told during the 1991 Open Door Conference in Millis, Massachusetts, by a lovely and articulate woman who was on a panel of adult adoptees. She was a Korean woman who was the eldest of five children adopted by a Caucasian family in Seattle. She loved both of her parents very much. At twenty-six, after she had been married and had a two-year-old, her father died. At the funeral, a long-time friend of the family, who had known her for most of her life and who knew how close the family was, came up to her and said, "Well, Anna, at least this isn't so bad for you. You have another father."

Anna was stunned. This was the only father she had ever known, and the only one she wanted to know. She said that she now felt as if she had had two losses, as she no longer felt this "friend" understood anything about her.

Beliefs about the Medical Care System

The patient's beliefs about physicians and the medical care system can also make medical treatment more or less stressful. Certainly, we would all hope that all physicians and clinics will be sensitive to their patients. However, the patient who expects that this will usually be, or should be, the case is bound to be frustrated and disappointed.

Good (1989) described beautifully how the medical student's idealistic notion of helping and caring for patients is transformed by the medical education process until "the abstraction of 'helping people' becomes 'invading the other,' and relationships with people become objective rather than empathic" (p. 305). Even though physicians do have some psychosocial training in medical school, Good's study indicates that the thrust of this education is superseded by their biological instruction.

Good (personal conversation, 15 May 1989) feels that we can help patients feel less vulnerable to the medical care system by training them to see physicians as "biomechanical specialists," and to expect them to be only as empathetic as auto mechanics. As Good commented, "You wouldn't expect auto mechanics to listen to your whole tale of woe of how your car broke down three hundred miles from home and needed to be towed. You would just depend on them to fix the car."

Beliefs That Create Trouble between Husbands and Wives

Once a couple become distressed, their perceptions of each other become distorted. Research studies have shown that, although such couples may be reasonably objective in the motives they attribute to other couples, they inaccurately attribute negative motives to their own spouses (Fincham, 1985;

Holtzworth-Monroe and Jacobson, 1985; Jacobson, et al., 1985, Noller, 1980). Aaron Beck's *Love Is Never Enough* (1988) is highly recommended for couples in conflict.

Sometimes one partner, usually the wife, believes the infertility to be the direct fault of the other. Such a belief adds immeasurably to the resentment, hurt, and even hate that she is harboring. It dramatically raises the tension level, implying that one partner has consciously set out to do something to deny the other a child. A major part of therapy, then, is refuting this belief.

One familiar story concerns the wife who was ready for a child many years before the husband (because women are so programmed to have children, this situation occurs quite frequently). The wife has literally had to fight to try to get pregnant, and when she finally has her husband's "permission" to begin trying, she is already behind in her own internal schedule of child rearing. That is, she is already angry at him.

If either of them turns out to have infertility problems, the wife deems it the husband's fault that "time is running out." She becomes panicked that her fertility has been impaired with every passed-up month, or that they should have pursued adoption, donor insemination, or some other alternative earlier in their lives, when their "chances were better." Occasionally, one runs across couples in which the husband and wife appear to be so full of hatred and in such poor communication that one wonders how they ever thought they loved each other enough to want to produce a child together. However, on exploration, it turns out that one of them is harboring this kind of grudge.

This negative situation is maintained as follows: Suppose that the wife gets stuck on the idea that her husband's postponing the pregnancy *caused* the infertility. Each time that he is less than perfect in the relationship or lets her down in some way during the infertility process, she repeats this idea to herself: "And it's all his fault, anyway. If it hadn't been for him, we'd have a child already!"

As she repeats this thought over and over, it becomes gospel. Her feelings of hate for her husband grow, and she distorts the fact that she was simply the loser in a power struggle over when to start their family. She begins to think of the infertility as something her husband did to her, on purpose.

The therapist's job is to get the wife to examine the irrationality of her thoughts. Yes, there was a power struggle in the marriage over when to have children, but there are plenty of power struggles in marriage (and granted, men have superior power and may win more than their share of these struggles). But had she got pregnant quickly after they agreed to begin to try, she would have been perfectly happy with her husband.

The husband could not see the infertility lurking in the future. Probably, he was intimidated by the huge financial and emotional commitment represented in having children, so he tried to postpone it until he felt more solvent financially or more grown up. The infertility was certainly not something that he intentionally caused.

In a situation like this, the wife is asked to monitor her thoughts. When she catches herself bringing up the old feelings of resentment about the initial decision of when to begin trying for kids, she is to stop herself and remind herself of the reasons she loved her husband to begin with. Many women are surprised to find that they have been thinking these abominable thoughts about their husbands quite regularly, several times a day. When they interrupt this negative process, they find the old feelings of love returning. Needless to say, husbands respond well to renewed expressions of love and interest on the part of their wives. Future pregnancy is not guaranteed, of course, but the partners can again begin to take pleasure in the marriage.

Another common belief that causes marital problems is this: Wives simply cannot understand and accept the fact that, often, their husbands are less upset about the infertility than they are. Although I empathize deeply with wives who feel alone in their distress, the societal forces that have put many men so out of touch with the need to create and parent a child are stronger than any one woman. When a wife gets caught up in the belief "He *must* feel as awful about this infertility as I do; otherwise, he can't support me and doesn't love me," she is wasting her energy. And she may be nagging her husband in ways that do make him less available to her emotionally.

It is helpful to explain to both partners the reasons why men and women feel so differently, and to reassure the wife that her husband's behavior is typical. It doesn't mean that he is a terrible person or that another husband would necessarily be more in tune with her in her distress. A thought that helps is "My husband can be less upset than I am about this situation and still support and love me."

The flip side of the woman's beliefs is her husband's frustration at the loss of the relationship and the obsessive focus on pregnancy: "All she cares about is getting pregnant. I feel as if I'm being used" or "I feel like a damn sperm machine. At this point, I'm so fed up with all of this medical stuff that I'd like to quit. But she really doesn't care about how I feel now. She just wants a baby." Intervene with the husband in a parallel way, explaining how socialization affects men and women and showing him that his wife's behavior is normal. The soothing thought for the husband is "She's just like most women who get to her age. She still loves me, but women are just trained to want to have kids."

Sometimes one partner second-guesses whether the other partner will ultimately be happy with the alternative on which they have agreed. Even after having professional help as a couple coming to grips with the implications of a particular choice, the partner who first desired it and pushed for it is fearful that her spouse will regret it "too late."

Susan, thirty-two, was drained after five years of invasive treatments. She wanted a child desperately. The marriage was secure, but it had been a long time since there had been laughter in the air at the Schwartz house. Jack and Susan both felt that they had neared the end, medically. Jack spoke longingly of the days when Susan seemed carefree and relaxed, and he wanted them to adopt. Mostly, he said, he wanted a child because one would make her happy.

Susan wanted to adopt, too. But she was bothered by a persistent idea: Jack was five years younger than she. Maybe she and Jack would go on to adopt, and then, in five or ten years, Jack would decide that he wanted a biological child and leave her for another woman.

She firmly believed that Jack didn't know his own mind and that, in years to come, he would get in touch with a "deep longing for a biological child." Armed with this fear, she found it difficult to stop trying for a biological child.

In my assessment, Jack felt positive about adoption. I finally helped Susan dispute her belief that he would regret the choice by having her talk to a few adoptive fathers about their feelings about their children, their wives, and themselves. Not only did these men feel secure and complete in their love of their children, but several of them recalled that they hadn't been as enthusiastic as their wives about parenthood to begin with. Susan began to trust Jack's feelings more and felt it safe to let go of medical treatments and pursue adoption.

Pushing one's spouse toward any potentially life-altering course is a big responsibility. The therapist can help by having a separate interview with the previously recalcitrant partner, using imagery to help him project himself into various future scenarios and see how he feels about the alternative to which he has agreed. If the partner's choice is, indeed, made thoughtfully and willingly, the therapist's go-ahead can free the couple to act.

Confronting Cognitive Errors in the Grieving Process

The potential loss that infertility entails is so great that patients are overwhelmed and not able to think logically. They make certain cognitive errors when evaluating the possibility that they may not ever get pregnant, anticipating deprivations that will occur if they cannot get pregnant together biologically. However, in the midst of their terror and pain, they get mired in grief, mourning losses that may not occur. We will explore this phenomenon by looking at helping patients contemplate adoption. The same principles can be applied to considering other alternatives, such as donor insemination or egg donation.

Adoption is a potential route to parenthood, and a good one for many couples. However, patients lose total, or periodic, sight of the fact that adoption, and thus parenthood, is possible:

A woman stood up to ask a question during one of my lectures on stress control during infertility. She wanted to know how to handle a single friend of hers who was envious of her marriage and of her material success. As she was talking, she stated that she and her husband were planning to adopt if she didn't become pregnant. She went back to talking about her friend's envy of her large new house and the beautiful room that would be a nursery.

Then, feeling momentarily disheartened and depressed about her infertility, she said dejectedly, "Well, maybe it will be an exercise room." I asked, "would you adopt, or not?" She said, "Yes." I said, "Well, then it will be the nursery." She brightened up, smiled, and said, "Right!"

It is fascinating that, when momentarily facing the profound sadness of not having a biological child, this woman lost touch with what was her *conscious* alternative life plan: "If we don't get pregnant, we'll adopt." This is a powerful negative thought pattern found frequently among couples.

I do not mean to say that adoption is some kind of "easy cure" for infertility. Pat Johnston (1984), a well-respected and well-known adoption educator and advocate, spelled out the most tangible losses that occur for a couple who cannot conceive biologically:

1. The loss of individual genetic continuity and an unbroken family bloodline.
2. The loss of the dream of a jointly conceived child.
3. The loss of the gratification of the pregnancy and birth experience.
4. The loss of the emotional satisfaction of the in-utero bonding, the mythical goal of bonding at birth, and the probable loss of the breastfeeding experience.
5. The loss of the opportunity to parent.
6. The loss of control.

Johnston added the patient's loss of her sense of self-esteem and self-worth as factors that make it difficult to sort through her feelings. Others have further described subtle losses that are significant (e.g., Mazor, 1979, 1980). For instance, the loss of the image of being a man or a woman *biologically*, like our fathers or mothers. (Changes in idealized body images are treated in Chapter 10.)

A related loss is the sense of *psychological* continuity. Our parents created us. Ideally, we, in turn, become adults and create our children with the partner we have chosen. If this doesn't happen, the chain of psychological continuity is disturbed.

Adoption addresses and solves only Item 5, the loss of the ability to parent. Johnston (1984) made the point that different losses are significant to each couple and must be consciously mourned. Giving the example of a man who mourned his genetic continuity, she pointed out that a person or couple may *not be willing* to accept a particular loss (p. 26). Adoption would be a poor choice in such a case, leading to future unhappiness for both parents and adopted child. Johnston worried about adoption's being offered as a panacea to all infertility patients.

Johnston's warning is wise. Each of the privations must be processed and grieved before any couple is *actually* ready to adopt. This mourning is part of the task in psychotherapy when biological parenthood (for both or either partner) is not possible. Grieving may be part of future psychotherapy, too, because the couple will continue to have to deal with these deprivaltions at various times in their lives after they adopt. But people differ markedly in their ability to process and come to terms with all of these losses.

Adoption is absolutely objectionable to some patients and forever remains unacceptable. For the sake of brevity, we can call them *adoption-negative*. Often, these patients are quite clear about how they feel early in the process of psychotherapy. As one woman said to me, "I'm just one of those people who really wants to mother her own children. I've thought about it, and I just know adoption isn't for me. If I can't get pregnant, I'm not having kids." For this woman, the loss of the biological connection was too great to bear.

Others can adjust to all of the losses. Most patients have had experience in living through great dissatisfactions in life and finding pleasure again. A parent dies. We're badly injured. We don't get the job we wanted. We lose our youthful looks. Many people are able to adjust to disappointment repeatedly throughout their lives. Many couples who cannot conceive go on to adopt, with great joy and satisfaction.

Early in the process of infertility, many of these couples believe on the *unconscious* level, that adoption would be a good possibility for them. They are *adoption-positive*. They have *preexisting positive ideas and imagery about adoption* (although they may not be aware of their adoption-positive views). Some of them have thought about having a family of biological and adopted children since they themselves have been children. Some of them feel positively about adoption out of idealism or for political reasons. Some of them knew and liked or loved adopted children when they were growing up, so that adoption doesn't feel mysterious, or foreign, or dangerous.

And there is a third group of people who are *adoption-neutral*. They do not have good ideas or images about adoption, but they are not opposed to adoption. When adoption-neutral people cannot get pregnant, some of them go on to adopt happily after a period of grieving.

Yet the shock of feeling betrayed by their bodies, the shock of not getting to choose how to have children, floods all of these couples, adoption-positive and adoption-neutral couples included, with thoughts of a childless future and bleak beliefs about the lives of childless people (e.g., "The thought that I'll never be a mother is unbearable," or "I feel left out, because I don't think people without children have anything to say to people with children"). These thoughts are a significant source of depression because they make images of the future unbearable. So adoption-positive and adoption-neutral couples at the beginning of an infertility crisis tend to overwhelm themselves with thoughts of future losses that will not occur if they do, in fact, adopt. Many of their dreams of parenthood can come true:

1. They can have the pleasure of loving a child, and of being loved.
2. They can have the pleasure of watching a child grow up, of teaching the child and participating in the child's life.
3. They can have the pleasure of being in a relationship with the child throughout life, and the pleasure of taking care of that relationship.
4. They can have the pleasure of seeing themselves in the parental role.
5. They can get to relive their childhood through their children, if they allow themselves to identify with them.
6. They can have the richness a child brings to a couple's life, and the interesting challenges of raising a child who isn't genetically related.
7. They can have the sense of really being an adult, responsible for a new generation, for the future.
8. If their parents are alive and accept adoption, they can have the pleasure of watching their parents love and interact with their children.
9. They will have someone to whom to leave an inheritance.

Early in the psychotherapy process, even while patients are in a state of panic and confusion about what is happening to them, the therapist should help them assess which losses are the most salient and which can and cannot be tolerated. What alternatives will be acceptable, finally?

Teach patients who are adoption-positive or adoption-neutral to monitor their negative thoughts, so that they are grieving only the losses that may occur. Do not allow them to flood themselves, constantly, with thoughts of heart-wrenching losses that will not occur if they follow their ultimate plan. Such thoughts lead to deeper depression, making attempts to cope less effective.

One exercise that helps patients focus on how they feel about various alternatives is an imagery exercise I call the *crystal ball,* which is discussed at greater length in the section on imagery in Chapter 4. The directions are:

Close your eyes and get relaxed. Imagine a magical being, with supernatural powers. She has a crystal ball and can see the future. When she looks at your future, she sees that no matter what you do, no matter what medical treatments you try, and no matter what high technology interventions are developed in the future, you will never have a biological child.

Now, keeping your eyes closed, picture it. What will your future look like? (Zoldbrod, 1990, p. 19)

Many couples are startled to find out that they would be able to deal with the finality of knowing absolutely that they can't create a baby together. Some picture enjoying living as a family of two. Others can picture loving a child created by donor insemination. Still others are amazed at the vivid, concrete internal images they have of the child they would adopt.

Again, we'll use the example of adoption. In Chapter 8, the case of Ann and Joseph is described. The crystal-ball exercise was the most important intervention in Ann's treatment. Ann was feeling disgusted with herself, stuck in her long and unproductive treatment, and angry at the world. However, unbeknownst to her, she was quite adoption-positive. The crystal-ball exercise produced proadoption imagery that was so powerful that she decided to stop medical treatment within six weeks after doing it, much to her adoption-positive husband's relief. She stopped picturing them in the future as "childless people who lead selfish lives," or as "a couple who should have children but don't." Instead, she saw herself and Joe as future parents. No longer believing that "life is a waste," she felt much more empowered and optimistic. The knowledge that, no matter what, they would parent a child soothed her. Ann and Joseph immediately began to pursue adoption, and she and her husband now have an adopted son.

This exercise achieves a powerful cognitive restructuring early in psychotherapy with some patients. The knowledge that, "come hell or high water," they will parent a child is soothing. If they succeed in getting pregnant, that is wonderful. But in the meantime, their experience of the present is not so bleak, and the future looks gratifying.

Other clients may resist discussing adoption or other alternatives at the beginning of their medical treatment. They are in the midst of processing what may be a tremendous future loss, bouncing back and forth from minute to minute between denial of their infertility, hope about the next medical treatment, and the depths of despair. They do not feel in any way ready to anticipate that they may not succeed in becoming pregnant.

The mention of the word adoption took Katya's breath away. No, she said, in a whisper. "Please don't talk to me about that yet. I'm just not ready. I can't even stand to think about it. I'm still young . . . maybe in three or four years I'll think about it, not now. I can still try in-vitro fertilization (IVF), I can try gamete intra-fallopian transfer (GIFT)." Needless to say, I did not pursue the topic with Katya at this time. (But you can see that she was open to the idea of adoption in the future.)

Sometimes, there is magical thinking going on when a patient rejects discussing the issue of adoption. She believes something like, "If the Gods of the

Universe know that I see that I can be happy adopting, they won't bother to help me try to become pregnant anymore."

Patients need to be reminded that simply considering adoption or another alternative positively does not mean that one must pursue it, immediately or ever. It simply means that one can give up thoughts that one will be forced to live a life without children.

> Felice came to one of my couples experiential workshops on stress control. She had been struggling with infertility for years. She was so visibly depressed about her infertility that the whole group noticed it. We did the crystal-ball exercise near the beginning of our time together, and afterward she commented that she just wasn't ready to think about adoption yet (although the exercise had produced some positive adoption imagery for her).
>
> After spending only two hours in the group examining her thought patterns and her imagery about infertility, Felice spoke up and said that she now could see and understand that allowing herself her positive thoughts about adoption as a possible alternative had helped.
>
> Because she had seemed so depressed initially, I checked in with her twice during the next six months. She reported that she had maintained the gains that she had made in the group, had kept reminding herself that she could adopt, and had felt less depressed.

When patients cooperate, use the crystal ball to achieve some cognitive restructuring and to lessen despair early in psychotherapy. Later, if medical interventions prove unsuccessful, help the patient consider the practical, lifelong consequences of building a family by adoption (Johnston, 1984; Kirk, 1981), donor insemination, egg donation, or surrogacy (Glazer, 1990). Families created in these new ways have differences from biologically built families, and such differences must be explored before a patient is ready actually to pursue them. Techniques for further exploration can be found in Chapter 4.

Other Cognitive-Behavioral Techniques

As we have seen, each patient has her own list of irrational thoughts, some of which are idiosyncratic. Along with the various approaches that have been discussed already, one useful general technique is *thought stopping.*

After identifying her important negative cognitions with the patient, the therapist can teach her to scan her thoughts consciously. When she catches herself thinking negatively, she says, "Stop, stop, stop!" loudly to herself. Some people even like to wear a rubber band on the wrist and to snap it as they say, "Stop." After the patient has stopped the bad thought, she should replace it with a more positive belief or image.

Another technique to use along with thought stopping is *behavioral rehearsal* (Meichenbaum, (1977). When a patient is troubled about how to handle a difficult social situation, the therapist encourages her to think about and imagine what might occur and to rehearse how she will handle the interaction gracefully. A useful way to describe the process is to tell the patient to "run a movie in your head of what will happen. Analyze the movie, frame by frame. For each bad event or interaction that you think will occur, come up with a way to handle it successfully."

Often, at first, the patient imagines behavior that acts out how she feels: "OK, when she asks me, 'What's new?' I'll kick her! And when Trudy shows me the baby pictures again, I'll rip them up!"

The point, however, is to create a plan for behaving in a way that makes the patient feel more competent and more in control. All the worst-case scenarios are played out, over and over, until there is a behavioral solution, or even a script, for each difficult encounter.

One of my patients, Marie, was distraught after a miscarriage. She lived in a lower-middle-class suburb where many women had children young and didn't work outside the home. Marie felt that there was an unspoken pressure always to be friendly. The women on her street were, one by one, having children and parading outside with their new babies in carriages.

Some of the women even walked with swollen bellies at the same time that they pushed small children in strollers, a situation that Marie found intolerable. As the weather got warmer, more and more women went outside with their new offspring.

Marie felt ashamed that she could not walk up to each new mother, smile, say something really gushy about the new baby, and tell her how happy she was for her. She began to believe that these women were talking about how rude she was in not congratulating them. Marie got so upset that she couldn't even sleep through the night without dreaming about bumping into one of the new mothers and bursting into tears, embarrassing herself to death.

We went through many role plays. Marie took this opportunity to say all of the hateful things she felt to me/her neighbors, because it felt good to her to get the venom out. She then felt free to talk to me about each of the women's decent qualities.

We took this opportunity to write down some of her thoughts on each neighbor. Marie decided to buy a card for each woman, write all the nice, heartfelt thoughts on the cards, and mail them. As she rehearsed the situation, she realized that, once she had done the correct thing, she felt better about herself and felt "off the hook." From that point on, she could just wave when she saw the women and their children, or she could stop very briefly and simply comment on how big the baby or child had grown. She did just that, and she felt much less vulnerable on her street.

Marie was in touch with her wish to avoid painful social situations. But other patients are deluged with imagery about life being out of control because they are trying too hard to be nice, rational, normal people while they are in the throes of great misery brought about by their infertility. Patients dread going to baby showers, but they do go because they "should." It "isn't nice not to go to Cousin Sally's baby shower." It is "babyish" and "self-indulgent" to spare themselves the trauma of going to their tenth high school or college reunion, where everyone will be sporting pictures of their children. Such patients may need permission to protect themselves.

A useful piece of behavioral jargon is *stimulus control*. Certain stimuli (e.g., a shower or a christening) tend to increase the frequency of certain negative feelings, images, and behaviors. To control the unwanted outcome (jealousy, depression, or discomfort), it is responsible to try to control the stimulus. (This approach is similar to not keeping cookies and chocolate in the house when you intend to go on a diet.)

Stimulus control is not a permanent strategy. The patient will resolve her infertility eventually, and from that point onward, she will do her utmost to live up to her social responsibilities. She can explain herself to friends and family so that she is not seen as cruelly rejecting them. Using the technical term *stimulus control,* though, the therapist can give the patient very scientific-sounding permission to avoid the problem situation now. Therapists beware: When the dreaded event is occurring on the husband's side of the family, it is [Cespecially important to explain the rationale of stimulus control to the husband.

Many infertile women intuitively decide to use stimulus control and to avoid highly painful child-centered activities. However, with no high-sounding rationale, this choice is judged as being very selfish by many who do not understand how difficult it is to confront the fertile world. Betsy, aged twenty-six, told me this story after hearing my lecture on why men and women fight during an infertility crisis:

Betsy is an occupational therapist married to a carpenter, Matt. They live in the South. Over the last several years, they have become close friends of two other couples and have been getting together at least once a month, alternating dinner at each other's houses. Not only are the women in this group of six friends, but the men are close, too.

Betsy began trying to get pregnant even before she met the others, for four long years. Recently, Betsy had been getting more and more depressed. Then she suffered a miscarriage at four weeks. The miscarriage put her "over the edge," as she described it.

Meanwhile, one of her friends got pregnant. Now the second one is pregnant and is beginning to show. In her pain, Betsy began to withdraw from social contact. She got to the point where she told Matt that she simply couldn't stand to watch the others get bigger, month by month. She wanted to explain herself to them and tell that that she loved them and would connect with them in some other way or at a later time, but she wanted to cancel plans to have a dinner party to which both couples were invited.

Matt was infuriated by her "selfishness" in breaking up this treasured friendship. They had an enormous fight, with Matt screaming and Betsy crying. He stormed out of the house and slammed the door. She heard him banging around outside the door, but she didn't think much of it.

He eventually came back inside when it got dark, but he still wouldn't talk to her. The next day, she went outside to go to work. As she backed out of the driveway, she glanced at the house. She was startled to see that Matt had painted a huge red X across the front door. Underneath the X, he had painted, "No fertile people allowed!"

Not all professionals understand how stimulus control can be helpful. A member of RESOLVE of Montana reported the following story:

There are not a lot of professionals in Montana with experience in treating the emotional aspects of infertility. So one infertile women called up a talk-show radio psychologist to get some help. She told him that her best friend was pregnant and she couldn't stand to go to the shower. He said to her, "Well, shame on you! How could you begrudge her her happiness? You just get yourself to that shower!"

Needless to say, after that professional advice, the woman felt even more ashamed of herself. This is unfortunate because both behavioral rehearsal and stimulus control (avoidance) are useful strategies for coping with envy of others' pregnancies.

A Note on Groupwork and Cognitive Interventions

Cognitive interventions can be taught and practiced quite successfully in a group format. In brief, one-meeting stress-control workshops for involuntarily childless couples, I teach participants to recognize cognitive errors through a series of exercises. This format is fun and far from boring because in a group of people there are many disparate illogical belief systems and cognitive errors. These groups of "strangers" are empathetic and bond together quickly because of their shared infertility. With good humor and compassion, they take great pleasure in pointing out the irrationality of their fellow members' thoughts about infertility.

In an exercise designed to focus people on some sources of pleasure, the group made an "enjoyable activities list." In this group, it contained quilting, crafts, biking, hiking, dancing, socializing, Tanglewood (an outdoor music festival), shopping, taking walks, sailing, swimming, and foreign travel. The group had a touching discussion in which they all shared how they felt about the items on the list. Some people realized that there were activities that they loved that they had stopped doing. One couple said that they still did the old activities, but the pleasure was gone.

> One woman, Felice, was able to identify a tracking order that undermined her. Each time Felice found herself enjoying pleasurable activity, she stopped herself with a recurring thought: "This activity would be more fun with a baby." She then began to feel sad. She described several episodes in which she had been interrupted by this thought.
>
> When I asked Felice to look at why she believed this, and why any activity would necessarily be more fun with a baby, other than kid-oriented activities such as baby showers, playgrounds, or amusement parks, she realized that this was an irrational idea that had played a part in keeping her depressed almost all of the time.
>
> As Felice considered her irrational thought, she came up with a related pattern in her thinking that is shared by other infertility patients: When she was in the middle of having fun, she stopped herself. She had thoughts such as, "What's going on here? I'm not supposed to be having fun; I'm depressed," or "What will people think? I'm not supposed to be having fun; I'm defective."

Even though other members had difficulty enjoying themselves as well, they saw that Felice's pattern was totally irrational. They found themselves fascinated by the notion of the distorted, all-or-none thinking in Felice's life and in their own. We talked about the cognitive distortion of always seeing babies as fun.

I encouraged Felice and the others to carry a small notebook around and document episodes in their travels in which small babies and children made life more difficult for the adults around them. At that point, several members of the group spontaneously began sharing tales of times when babies and kids had made themselves unwelcome in restaurants, stores, museums, and so forth.

The group brainstormed and wrote down activities that would probably be more fun without children, or at which children would be unwelcome: "Opera, symphony, ballet, theater, overnight trips, golfing, skiing, good restaurants, water-skiing, good conversations, sex, being spontaneous, splurging money, shopping, sleeping late, and sleeping at all."

One of the men mentioned sailing. Then he commented with a smile, "Of course, Felice would think sailing would be much more fun with an infant tied to the jib!" The group howled, and so did Felice. They were not laughing at Felice, they were laughing at themselves.

I offered a diagram (Figure 1) that I learned from the late Alvin Goldfarb, a geriatric psychiatrist. Goldfarb used it to describe why the mourning process is so painful. But I use it to show people how their obsessive thoughts and avoidance of pleasurable non-baby-related activities make them feel more depressed.

The diagram shows that when a person interacts with a love object who is alive, the energy that is invested in the love object comes back to the person (stage 1).

However, when Person B dies, in the beginning of the mourning process Person A is investing the same amount of energy in Person B. But person B is not there, so the love energy leaving Person A, aimed at the now-gone Person B is no longer returned. As Person A continues to invest energy in Person B, she gets more and more depleted and sad (stage 2).

As the mourning process continues, Person A learns to withdraw love

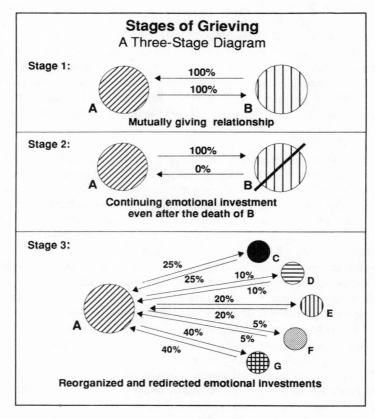

Figure 1

energy from the memory of Person B and to reinvest some of it in other living person(s), Person C, D, E, F, and G. (stage 3).

As I explain using Figure 2, when you sit around and invest your energy in thinking about your infertility or how sad you are that you don't have a baby, you are getting nothing back that "feeds" you, that makes you feel alive. The "return" on your investment is sadness. You are putting energy out and getting nothing good, stimulating, entertaining, thrilling, relaxing, or satisfying back. Because there is no good energy coming back to you, you feel empty and sad. It is similar to mourning a lost love when the person is gone and there is no one to relate back to you, feed you, or love you.

In the lower part of Figure 2, you are investing your energy in sources that bring you pleasure, relaxation, intimacy, excitement, entertainment, or challenge, and you get something back: the thrill of the opera, being stimulated by your job, enjoying the drama of a play, or being involved with friends. You feel more full and more alive than you did before you put your energy into the activity. You are infertile, and you still feel that you have an interesting life. Figure 2 illustrates why it is worthwhile to force yourself to do pleasurable things while you are struggling with infertility. The group used the diagram as a stimulus, and they each committed themselves to doing one pleasurable activity a week in spite of their infertility regimes.

One of the other group members, Crystal, had a different set of irrational thoughts. At forty-one, she was extremely pretty, short, and petite. She

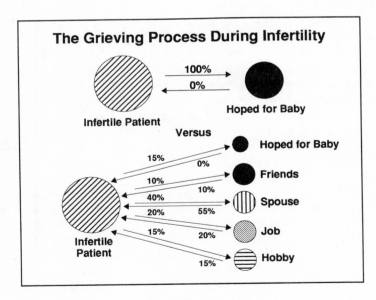

Figure 2

came to the group dressed in tight blue jeans with a very blousy overblouse. Crystal felt that the Pergonal she had been taking for six years had ruined her looks and made her fat, shattering her self-esteem.

Crystal had been trying to get pregnant for eight years and had had several surgeries. She had married early and had not continued her education because she intended to have a family. In the early years of her marriage, she had loved to "party, drink, smoke, and have fun."

"I really don't feel good about myself like this," she complained. "I just can't have any fun, can't feel any pleasure, anymore. I can't smoke or drink because I'm always trying to get pregnant. I used to pride myself on my looks. I used to wear tight clothes and high, high heels all the time. I prided myself on being so tiny and so sexy. I spent all of my time buying sexy clothes. I can't wear high heels anymore, now. My weight gain is giving me knee problems, and so I wear tennis shoes. And I don't buy sexy clothes anymore. All I buy are pregnancy clothes. I have pregnancy clothes for every season of the year."

The group was absolutely astounded. "What weight problem are you talking about?" they all asked. (Crystal couldn't have weighed more than 110 pounds.) "Don't you think you're pretty and sexy now?" As Crystal went on and on about her weight problem, everyone else in the group had their eyes opened wide in astonishment.

They asked Bill, Crystal's husband, how much her body had changed. Bill said that she had gained a tiny bit of weight but that she still looked very much the same as she had. He had tried over and over again, telling her that she looked beautiful, but to no avail.

"It's like anorexia," commented one woman. "That's how distorted her sense of her body is." The group had an "aha!" experience. Everyone, including Felice, noticed how firmly Crystal held to her irrational belief that she was fat and no longer attractive. "If she can believe so firmly that her distortion is the truth, how I am distorting things?" each person asked.

When the group was over, after we had worked with Crystal's problem, each of the ten members filled out an evaluation of what they like the best. The most common answer listed was that they "found it most useful to look at how others distort their thinking because of infertility."

There are many resources to help patients explore their cognitions. Aaron Beck has devoted his career to describing how to intervene in patients' negative and irrational cognitions. Beck's *Love Is Never Enough* (1988), Freeman and DeWolf's *Woulda, Coulda, Shoulda* (1989), and David Burns's *Feeling Good* (1980) are wonderful resources for infertility patients, even though they do not specifically address the distortions common in infertility crises. Beck's works such as *Cognitive Therapy of Depression* (1979) are important readings for the therapist dealing with infertility patients.

Working with the Patient's Behavior

Infertility negatively affects the behavior of both partners in a marriage. Thus, particularly when the marriage is distressed, behavioral intervention with the couple makes therapeutic sense.

Occasionally, women patients feel so wounded by life and so angry at their husbands that they do not want to work on their own behavior. They want individual support from the therapists, and individual therapy may well be the best starting point. However, when the therapeutic alliance is cemented, behavioral assessments and interventions can be included in the therapy.

At other times, it is liberating for patients to be asked which of their behaviors they want to eliminate, and which they want to expand. After all, most voluntary behaviors can be controlled more easily than can infertility.

Here are my patients' observations on their own behavior, taken from their answers on the effects-of-infertility questionnaire: "What behaviors related to infertility do you most want to eliminate? Which behaviors would you most want to increase? Which pleasurable life behaviors and activities have you stopped doing or wish you did more?

Infertile women want to eliminate similar behavior. The most common statement of women patients is that they want to stop complaining about or picking fights with their husbands. For instance, one patient said:

> I get very upset with Jake over an issue unrelated to the infertility, blow it out of all proportion, goad him into fighting. Then, I feel remorse over being so mean and nasty. He rarely engages in the arguments, I do. I tend to pout more, be sarcastic.

Commented another:

> We fight monthly, around the time my period is due, and we go through a difficult time when the early-pregnancy test reveals I'm not pregnant. I also provoke fights when I see blood.

One very high-functioning woman noted:

> I want to lessen the amount of anger, jealousy, withdrawal, and frequent crying.

In a related vein, another wants to

> stop complaining to my husband about how much time he spends at work.

When asked what kinds of behavior they want to increase, many women reply that they wish to be able to reinvest in their husbands emotionally. One woman said she wanted to be "more of a lover to my husband, less of a mother."

Another commented, "I would like to be more excited when my husband plans a trip or gives me a present. This was never a problem before; I was always a 'cheerleader.'"

These comments illustrate the obsessional quality of women's thinking about infertility. They also hint at what happens to the husbands' sense of self-worth in the marriage. Husbands feel that they cannot do anything right. What will soothe their wives? If gifts and trips won't help, what will?

Because he feels confused, helpless, lonely, or frustrated, the husband tends to withdraw. As was described in Chapter 2, wives and husbands often react in drastically different ways to infertility, and on different timetables. MacNab's doctoral work (1984) suggests that husbands are often not in touch with being disturbed until they have had several years of infertility. Wives get distraught much earlier. Consequently, husbands do not understand what wives are feeling and how they can help.

When asked which behaviors they want to increase or decrease, the husbands reply, "Try not to spend so much time at work"; "Try to talk more"; or "I just don't know. Nothing seems to help. Sometimes I'm afraid we'll get divorced."

With couples who are highly distressed, and where communication has shut down, couples therapy including concrete, behavioral interventions seems to help. The less distressed women feel guilty and ashamed of the irrationality of their angry behavior toward their husbands. Their behavior negatively affects their self-esteem, and they look forward to changing it.

Some patients are so caught up in the pain of the infertility that their judgment is impaired, and their sense of the interactions in the marriage is distorted (in their favor). A behavioral assessment in which both partners describe the specific interactions taking place daily protects against this.

Sally and Bill provide a good example of how important it is for couples to be specific in discussing their behavior patterns. Their marital problem and its astoundingly simple resolution also provide an excellent illustration of the complex intermixing of cognitive, affective, and behavioral processes in Sally's assessment of the problem:

Sally and Bill had been married for four years and had been trying to have a child for two years. Sally needed support during the infertility and wanted more closeness with her husband. She was especially disturbed by what she felt were problems in their sex life. Bill wouldn't kiss her. He had never much cared for kissing, even in the years before they discovered the infertility. Sally had felt rejected then, but she had never addressed this feeling directly with him. By now, she had had two miscarriages and her sense of pride in her body had been damaged. Bill's inability to kiss her seemed to her to be proof of his total lack of caring for her and his disgust with her body. Sally's description of Bill centered on his aloofness. She wanted to be with him, whereas he was putting his energy into projects around the house.

Bill described total confusion in dealing with his wife. He never felt that he could make her happy these days, so he had retreated. He gave several behavioral examples of interactions in which he felt that he "couldn't win." For instance, he would come into the kitchen to greet her after work, happy to see her, and immediately be given the cold shoulder. Rationally, he knew that she was upset about the miscarriages, and he tried to forgive her. But inside, he was hurt. He would retreat to his workshop and work on a project that would improve their home. They hoped to sell the house and buy a bigger one, so he felt that he was not selfishly retreating but instead was doing something that would benefit their family. In the therapy sessions, he clearly said that he loved Sally and that he was on her side, but her behavior made it too painful for him to risk trying to be close.

Sally felt that, in fact, he was the rejecting one. She began to talk about how Bill didn't kiss her. This issue had always been so threatening to her that she had avoided discussing it. The tension level in the room was palpable as she raised the issue, and she was weepy.

I then began exploring Bill's lack of enthusiasm for kissing Sally. As it turned out, Bill had terrible allergies almost all year long. He didn't like to kiss because he needed to breathe through his mouth and felt he was suffocating during kissing. This came as total news to Sally.

Bill said that, in fact, he was very attracted to Sally sexually. Sally was glad to hear this but still felt upset because she believed that she needed to be kissed on the mouth to be aroused sexually.

Sally and I brainstormed about other ways that Bill could touch her that would arouse her. She realized that any prolonged, gentle, light touches on the face, mouth, and neck were very pleasant to her. "They would be?" said Bill, quite surprised.

Sally and Bill were sent home to be sensual together (and sexual, if they felt like it). Sally's thoughts about the meaning of Bill's behavior had been modified. She was clearer about how she had been rejecting him. Bill had a new understanding of how he had unwittingly contributed to her sense of being defective. They had an easy piece of new behavior to try, which was a sign to each of them that they wanted to be close together in a new way. Over the weeks to come, their relationship improved.

The therapist must act as a consultant and a detective. The first and often greatest help for the couple is to understand the different ways in which the two sexes react to infertility: She is not the only infertile wife in the world to be obsessed and sad much of the time. He isn't the only husband who withdraws in the face of her distress and who feels totally confident that "medical science will fix it." Each spouse's behavior needs to be reframed and normalized in the light of what we know about gender differences in reactions to infertility. These gender differences come to light immediately in couples groups, and this is one reason that these groups are invaluable.

As the detective, the therapist focuses on getting pleasurable interactions to occur in the marriage. One strategy is to get each partner to make a list of what kinds of behavior are soothing in the midst of the crisis. Lazarus (1981) commented that couples' happiness is based on friendship. This is more true than ever in a situation where sexuality is a problem. Specific traits which constitute friendship are sharing, caring, empathy, complimentarity, concern, self-disclosure, and positive reinforcement (p. 246). Each partner should talk about specific kinds of interactions that would make him or her feel closer to the other. In later weeks, damaging behaviors should be listed as well. Sharing these initial lists in a therapy session can be a potent intervention that starts the process of change. Even if the therapist is forced to do individual psychotherapy for a couple's problem, this behavioral approach still works.

Patients should keep notes on their behavior for a week and create a baseline of positive and negative behavior. The therapist and the patient(s) then create a contract that delineates which behaviors will be increased and which decreased. Charting the behaviors and recontracting become part of the work of the therapy hour each week. Usually, just paying attention to a few small changes changes the climate of the marriage.

Patients who begin this process and do the homework always succeed to some extent because just being sensitive and aware and charting behaviors tend to change behavior in the desired direction. Feeling more in control of feelings, more loving, or like "less of a bitch" helps women begin to repair part of their spoiled self-image. In a similar vein, a man who knows which behaviors will help his wife feel close to him and a little less miserable feels more competent as a man and a husband. For some readings in behaviorally oriented couples therapy, the reader is directed to the work of Neil Jacobson (*Marital Therapy* by Jacobson & Margolin, 1979).

Increasing Positive Behavior

Commonly, patients discover that most pleasurable activities have been discarded in the process of investing all their available energy in the pursuit of pregnancy. One patient of mine who was an Olympic finalist in swimming no longer swam. A woman who was a singer stopped her singing lessons. Another, who loved to work out in a gym, stopped going there. Someone to whom her friends had been very important had withdrawn from them.

> Janice, a patient of mine through four years of infertility treatments, decided to take a break and visit a dear friend in Maine for a few weeks.

While she was there, she did some painting, which she found very rewarding. She returned home feeling renewed, with paintings in hand.

Her husband felt that her work was excellent, and that she should pursue it. She then showed her paintings to an acquaintance who was an art teacher. The art teacher agreed with the husband that the paintings, which had given her such enjoyment, were superb and suggested that she go to art school.

Janice and I were discussing what it would take to rearrange her life and pursue painting in some way. She began to look at the specifics of going out and buying the paint and the easel, and setting up the place and the time to paint. She then began to go through all of the reasons that this couldn't be done: it would be too expensive; she couldn't find the time; the light in the house would not be good enough for painting.

Then she paused and said, "You know, if Dr. Smith or Dr. Brown had said that, if I would paint two hours a day, it would increase my chances of getting pregnant, I know I would rush right out and do it. And if I needed to spend three hundred dollars on blood tests to figure out why I can't conceive, I wouldn't think anything of it. My God, I have *become* my illness."

Sometimes patients don't even realize how completely they have rejected the dependable sources of pleasure still available in their lives. One exercise that

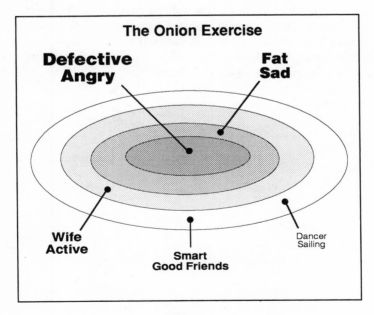

The Onion Exercise

Defective Angry

Fat Sad

Wife Active

Smart Good Friends

Dancer Sailing

Figure 3

helps raise awareness of this rejection is giving patients a homework assignment to diagram their personality using a series of concentric circles, like the layers of an onion (see Figure 3). In the center circle, they are to put the items that are their essence, the qualities closest to their core. In the two or three outer rings, they are to list other characteristics that make them uniquely themselves, arranged to show the current amount of their psychic investment in these items. Where is the infertility on the onion?

This simple exercise yields a lot of data, some of them diagnostic. A client who is dangerously depressed may be shocked and a appalled to find that her core contains only the words *female, infertile, defective, sad, fat, angry,* whereas all of her positive roles, attributes, and valued activities ("swimming, massage, actress, smart, cute, good friend, good student, funny, wife") are relegated to the outermost rings. Sometimes the experience of graphically and concretely facing how her priorities have decimated her life goads a patient into vowing to change her behavior and to include more pleasurable and esteem-building activities.

Often the results of the diagram boost self-esteem and serve as a reminder to the patient to reintegrate her pleasurable roles and activities into her current life. The client can be asked to agree to include one of the fun events in the next week's schedule. The diagram itself can be Xeroxed and hung in several strategic locations in the patient's house.

In summary, behaviorally oriented couples therapy is especially valuable when couples are seriously distressed. It moves the focus from whether or not pregnancy is achieved to looking at whether a given interaction promotes or is detrimental to the couple's overall intimacy. In individual psychotherapy as well, working on behavioral changes can increase self-esteem and the patient's sense of control. Next, we will look at the enormous potential therapeutic impact of working with the patient's imagery.

4

Use of Imagery in Treating the Emotional Aspects of Infertility

The infertility patient is in emotional agony. His or her body is out of control; it simply won't do what it is willed to do. Motile sperm are not produced. Scar tissue forms where one hoped it wouldn't. Eggs that were meticulously harvested and fertilized outside the body refuse to implant in the uterus. Feelings bounce back and forth between anxiety, hope, despair, self-hate, and hope. The marital relationship feels tense.

Most logical problem-solving strategies, such as gathering information and planning activities, seem useless in the face of the tremendous frustration of a body, or two bodies, that will not "work right." Any technique that allows the patient to regulate emotion or feel a sense of control in the face of the chaos of changing and conflicting feelings is valuable indeed. Imagery is such a technique. As a psychologist, I have found imagery to be one of the most powerful tools at my disposal for helping infertile individuals and couples.

Imagery has already been proved to be a powerful healing tool, and for years it has been used in psychotherapy by a small group of psychologists and psychiatrists. Imagery has been used to treat depression (Schultz, 1978), sexual malfunctioning (Singer & Switzer, 1980), chronic pain (Jaffe & Bresler, 1980), and several kinds of phobias and anxieties (Meichenbaum, 1977; Singer, 1974). Systematic desensitization, which uses imagery has been proved to allay anxiety and fear.

Using his multimodal therapy (MMT) approach, Arnold Lazarus routinely explores the usefulness of imagery with all his patients. However, most psychotherapists have not explored imagery as a psychotherapeutic modality.

What Is Imagery?

What do we mean by *imagery?* To put it in the most unscientific terms, imagery involves processing ideas or information and expressing them through pictures, sounds, tastes, textures, or smells. Dachman and Lyons (1990) reminded us not

73

to confuse imagery and imagination: "Imagination, or fantasizing, is often aimless and unfocused. . . . Imagery is much more focused" (p. 42).

We all have the capacity to think in words and concepts, to be logical and linear. The capacity to think in words is governed by the left hemisphere of the brain. However, the capacity to image, which is not a logical process, is governed by the right hemisphere of the brain, the same part of the brain that houses our intuition. The image modality has a sensory, immediate character. This "gutsy" character communicates information in a special way.

Richardson (1969) defined imagery as "all of those quasi-sensory or quasi-perceptual experiences of which we are self-consciously aware, and which exist for us in the absence of those stimulus conditions that are known to produce their genuine sensory or perceptual counterparts."

Dachman and Lyons (1990) wrote, "We can all image, and we all do, every day. Think about how you wince when you hear a car's brakes screech. Think about what a sponge feels like or what a cup of vinegar smells like. Your mind recognizes these images and responds to them, whether or not the car, the sponge, or the vinegar are [sic] really present" (p. 54).

Imagery is one of the three basic modalities of being, thinking, and expressing things in the world (Horowitz, 1978; Sheikh & Jordan, 1983). We can use the *motoric* mode (moving and activity), language (the *linguistic* mode), or *imagery*.

Most of us communicate what we are thinking and feeling in a linear, logical way, using words and concepts—the linguistic mode. Language "integrates extremely diverse phenomena into one . . . label that permits very rapid subsequent retrieval" (Singer & Pope, 1978). As a result, language has typically been the main medium of human communication and the medium for most psychotherapy.

However, there are some problems with language as a instrument of expression, particularly when it comes to conveying strong emotion. Language abstracts experience and takes away its immediacy. The linguistic mode is limiting because it "encourages us to avoid being conscious of the aspects of our experience which we cannot easily describe or characterize" (Sheikh & Jordan, 1983).

Perhaps imagery is especially potent with infertility patients because the loss occasioned by not being able to have children is so vast that it is indescribable by ordinary linguistic means. Also, the imagistic mode allows patients to project themselves into the future, into a time when their infertility will be resolved in one way or another.

Professionals who practice with imagery have differing views about why it has such great powers to heal. Meichenbaum (1978) believes that three psychological processes explain the effectiveness of all imagery-based systems: (1) the feeling of control that the client gains as a result of the monitoring and rehearsing of various images; (2) the modified meaning or changed internal dialogue that precedes, attends, and succeeds examples of maladaptive behavior; and (3) the mental rehearsal of alternative responses that lead to the enhancement of coping skills and to mastery.

Sheikh (1986), who is a master of imagery technique, noted the potency of images as vehicles for learning. He implored us not to ignore the healing power of the "nonconscious, the symbolic, and the magical" (Sheikh & Jordan, 1978), On the simplest level, imagery may work in part because of the novelty of the imagery experience. Just vividly picturing being in a pleasant place can offer a break in the midst of infertility.

One of the ways imagery alleviates emotional distress is that it helps patients have hope. Psychologist C. Rick Snyder has been studying hope as a distinct quality in the human psyche, separate from related factors such as optimism, positive and negative affect, and achievement. Snyder was dissatisfied by the medical model of illness, which focuses on pathology. He wanted to study the factors that account for human strength and resilience.

Snyder defined hope as being made up of two factors: agency and pathways. *Agency* refers to the will or energy to achieve goals. *Pathways* refers to the ability to see many ways of achieving these goals (De Angelis, 1991, p. 18). Snyder uses imagistic techniques to shore up his patients' sense of both agency and pathways.

In his studies, Snyder found that high-hope people see goals as challenges, whereas low-hope people view them as threats. High-hope people choose higher and more difficult goals than low-hope people. However, they don't cling to a goal when the goal becomes obviously unattainable. Instead, high-hope people generate alternative pathways to get to where they want to go.

When the patient's sense of *agency* is weak, Snyder suggests assigning imagery exercises designed to foster a sense of goal-directedness or having the patient listen to tapes or read books about successful people (a clever way to give the patient potent aural or visual pictures of agency). Imagery can be used to expand the sense of pathways as well. Imagery exercises that generate alternative pathways to resolving the fertility crisis are described later in this chapter.

The use of imagery in infertility has not been well explored, with a few exceptions. The first is Cathy Romeo and Claudia Panuthos's excellent book *Ended Beginnings: Healing Childbearing Losses* (1984). Second, Merle Bombadieri's *The Baby Decision* (1981) is rich in guided imagery and is a precious resource for patients who want to explore living without children.

In the past several years, I have been experimenting with using interventions in imagery to help patients regulate their emotions, explore their feelings, and generate alternatives to involuntary childlessness (Zoldbrod, 1990). My work has focused on two major applications of imagery. The first is changing spontaneous negative imagery. During infertility, free-floating, spontaneous, critical self-images are common. Being constantly deluged with such images increases self-contempt, feelings of anxiety, a sense of being out of control, and hopelessness. Spontaneous negative images about the future create fear. Patients are taught to become aware of these unbidden negative images and to work on stopping them and substituting other, positive images.

The second application is guided imagery. Images may be evoked specifically because they are soothing. Other images elicited are intentionally disturbing and tap into the patient's unconscious, get her unblocked, evoke strong feelings, or help her explore alternatives.

In other words, depending on the theme of a particular session or the goal at a particular stage of treatment, imagery can be used differently. The basic principle in using imagery for stress control is to decrease negative images and to increase positive images, but when imagery is being used to explore feelings (for example, to grieve), negative images are educed and explored rather than suppressed.

All patients have some capacity to use imagery because the ability to imagine is an innate potential in all of us. Like all potentials, it is improved by practice. Thus patients who want to become better imagers can do so. In addition to practice, imagery is enhanced by certain conditions, such as by relaxation, by concentration, by talking in the present tense, by imagining things using as many of one's senses as possible, and by taking a supine body position (Sheikh, Sheikh, & Moleski, 1985; Zilbergeld & Lazarus, 1987).

The most important prerequisite for experiencing vivid imagery is that the patient must be deeply relaxed. However, moderate or even mild relaxation may be adequate for a great deal of the work described here. The therapist should be gentle in introducing the topic of relaxation, as the inability to relax is one of the natural concomitants of infertility. To achieve relaxation in a nonthreatening way, the breathing exercises given by Reid Wilson in *Don't Panic* (1986) are superb.

Because people vary tremendously in their ability to see things in their mind's eye, can only "very good imagers" profit from using imagery as a technique during infertility? Some research has indicated that vivid images are necessary in order to effect "deep personality change" (Sheikh et al., 1985) However, even patients who cannot as yet imagine vividly gain a sense of control from trying imagery exercises.

It is beyond the scope of this book to describe fully the process of imaging and imaginal learning. Suggestions for therapists for further readings are contained in the reference section. For lay readers, Zilbergeld and Lazarus wrote the popular book *Mind Power* (1987), which gives detailed instructions on how to become relaxed in order to imagine vividly, and on using imagery to achieve life changes. Patients for whom imagery is an important modality will gain much from reading this book, and all patients can benefit from its discussion of relaxation.

Getting around the Boulder in the Road: Using Imagery to Cope with Fertility Problems (Zoldbrod, 1990) was written specifically as a self-help book for the infertility and miscarriage patient. It contains many of the exercises found in this chapter.

The Imagery of Infertility

Psychiatrist Mardi J. Horowitz (1982) has studied and written about the important role of spontaneous imagery in processing and integrating stressful life events. Horowitz found that, in his subjects, the degree of intrusive spontaneous imagery correlated with the degree of reported stress: the higher the stress, the higher the amount of intrusive imagery. He believes that intrusive imagery during stressful events is a part of the ego attempting to integrate the event:

> Apparently, there is a gradual integration of both memories and associations activated by the incident. The loss or injury presents news that will eventually change inner models. But change is slow. Time is essential for review of the implications of the news and available options for response. The mind continues to process important new information until the situation or the models change, and reality and models of reality reach accord. This important tendency to integrate reality and schemata can be called a completion tendency. (p. 727)

Until completion occurs, the new information and reactions to it are stored in active memory because the topic, or the injury, is so significant to one's sense of self. Because the contents are "strongly coded" in active memory, like an important problem without a solution, they tend to be represented intensely and frequently in the unconscious imagery.

Markus and Nurius (1986) and others (Horowitz et al., 1980) believe that creating images of the self as healthy, active, or strong may be necessary to regain a convincing sense of control after tragedy or victimization has activated negative self-images of the victims as weak, needy, frightened, and out of control.

Obviously, then, intervening and changing the patient's continuing obsession with negative images makes sense from a number of theoretical standpoints. Negative spontaneous imagery is prominent in infertility and often continues for years because of the ever-changing nature of the crisis. There is not just one discrete negative reality to which the couple need to adjust. Perhaps they will have a biological baby, perhaps not. Often this isn't clear for years.

Where patients may draw a blank if the therapist asks them about what sensations or beliefs trouble them, they respond to questions about their troublesome imagery with an abundance of answers. In the effects-of-infertility questionnaire (Appendix 2), patients are asked, "Are there any mental images you are having at this time which you wish to lessen?" Typical responses from women were

"I see myself old and lonely, without children or maybe a husband."

"Empty arms."

"Jealous images of a neighbor who has a baby."

"I hear a friend telling me she is pregnant."

"Going to my college reunion and being the only one who doesn't have a baby or children."

"The image of our marriage failing because we cannot cope with our infertility."

"I picture my eggs as deformed."

"I keep picturing coming around a corner and always bumping into a pregnant woman."

"The yeech of the adoption process."

"I can just see myself at that party, totally alone, hurt, feeling outside of everyone and everything."

"I walk around with my adopted child, whom I love, but I still feel as if I have the 'scarlet I' on my chest: I couldn't do it myself."

Patients are also asked about images that are positive. They have a more difficult time reporting imagery that lowers stress. Images given by women included:

"Living among children and animals, happy with my husband."

"Being at the ocean."

"Nursing my baby."

"Seeing my baby girl's face."

"None."

Men's and women's initial imagery about infertility may or may not be similar. Marital distress, often caused by the differences in the husbands' and wives' perspectives on the fertility problem, may cause distance in the marriage. Then, both husbands and wives see upsetting visions that the marriage itself will be torn apart:

"I wonder if I'll wind up without a baby *and* a husband."

"My wife is so upset that I wonder if she'll ever recover and whether we'll ever get our old relationship back."

In addition, both for men who are the infertile partner and for infertile women, body imagery is changed:

"I see my body, old and ugly."

"I don't see my body as being masculine enough anymore."

"I'm producing Martian sperm."

"I see my sperm, trapped hopelessly, in my wife's mucus."

But early in the infertility, there are typically more differences in men's and women's imagery than there is similarity, undoubtedly stemming from their different socialization. Men's images of their sexual and reproductive powers are tied together, and both are related to the social and psychological portrait of a "proper" male. Activity and strength are central concepts in the definition of masculinity, and most notions of male sexuality also focus on assertiveness and activity.

Men's initial imagery about infertility is frequently focused on *competitive* imagery with other men (Zoldbrod, 1990). In contrast, women's imagery focuses on the loss of the relationship with the child, and also on the potential loss of the relationship with the husband, family members, and friends.

The essence of the man's role in reproduction is to do—to plant the seed in the woman, where it will grow. An inability either to plant the seed or to see it come to fruition may unconsciously become a metaphor for failure. As we found in Chapter 2, even men with adequate or excellent sperm counts may feel vulnerable and helpless, without understanding why, when their wives have fertility problems.

As soon as medical treatment begins, men's sexual imagery may change. Previously pleasurable images of making love may be superseded by images of sex as a public act. Glenn said, "I was making love to my wife, and all of a sudden, I saw her on the doctor's examining table, her legs in stirrups, men in white coats around her." Needless to say, this image interfered with Glenn's ability to feel safe and good about himself during the sexual act.

The cold, clinical, and humiliating aspect of having to masturbate, repeatedly, to produce sperm samples also creeps into men's sexual imagery during this period. For certain men, including some men of color and men from Fundamentalist religions, masturbation is seen as sinful or shameful. Their self-image is disturbed. That is, if "real men" have sex and only sissies masturbate, if I am masturbating because of infertility am I a sissy? A sinner?

Men who have experienced temporary impotence as a result of having to perform one time too many for a postcoital test, a hamster egg test, or an insemination find themselves associating sex with pictures of future failure.

Men who are personally infertile or subfertile may be plagued with pictures of sexual vulnerability left unresolved from adolescence. After getting back the poor results of his sperm count, one patient, who was able to produce vivid images, had a flashback to the sounds, smells, textures, and sights of his high-school locker room. He could feel the steamy heat and hear the sounds of the snapping towels and the teasing words about his genitals. The image remained too painful to share with either his wife or his friends.

The men in my men's group revealed powerful negative pictures of what would happen if and when they talked to other men about their infertility. They could hear the taunts and jokes: "Why don't you let me take care of it for you? Maybe you don't know how to do it." To make matters worse, their worst fears came true in some cases, when the revelation of the couple's infertility was met by a male friend's joking about sex and potency.

Reactions to medical procedures cause other problems in men (Osherson, 1986). Despite feeling that they are supposed to be "strong," most men dread giving their wives injections, and quite a few are bothered by images of blood and pain.

Men with childhood memories of their mothers' falling ill and mysteriously disappearing into strange-smelling hospitals, to return weaker, or not to return at all, are quite vulnerable. This happened to Mark Bates, the husband of one of my patients, Libby.

Libby had severe endometriosis. Three different and well-respected physicians all suggested that the surgery needed would be quite extensive and was impossible to do with a laser. Mark began to get agitated as soon as the surgery was suggested, and he felt adamantly opposed to it.

Libby tried to reason with him, because she saw the surgery as her only chance to get pregnant. She tied his reaction to his childhood experience of feeling abandoned and frightened when his mother went into the hospital for an operation. She had got very depressed afterward, never really returning to her previous self.

Mark had horrible images of seeing Libby weakened, with tubes in her arms, hardly able to speak, and in danger of losing her life. He had equally frightening responses to the physical reality of accompanying her into a large hospital, and he had a reaction when he went with her for a consultation. The sights, and particularly the smells, of the hospital made him feel nauseous. Although Mark tried to be reasonable during the day, he was bothered by flashbacks to his mother's hospitalization. When he went to sleep, he had night terrors. He needed a lot of reassurance that, after surgery, his wife would emerge alive and well, that her body would not be horribly scarred and repulsive to him, and that life would go on as it had in the past.

Often it takes many years for men's imagery to "catch up" to the grief and loss imagery that women feel. As MacNab (1984) found, the men in his study were not able to make an attachment to, or feel the loss of, "the idea of a child" (p. 134). But when men do get upset, their imagery changes from competitive imagery to imagery about the loss of generativity and "feeling weak." At that point, they begin to join their wives in the sadness, to notice cute infants on the street, to feel left out at parties with other young families with children, and to feel not quite masculine because they aren't "family men." And given the fact that fatherhood, past the "planting-the-seed" stage, is not seen as being the essential ingredient of adulthood for males, men feel unsafe discussing their vulnerable feelings, and their confused feelings about parenting. Their new, sad feelings are foreign. They feel vincible and frightened. Later imagery may include fears that their sadness will make them "break down" or cry in public, maybe even at work, or worries that they will "lose hold" and show "uncontrollable anger," images that were cited by several male patients who were not members of my men's group.

Men can picture having bitter conversations with their fathers in which they tell their fathers that biological grandfatherhood is unlikely or impossible. At this point, men may feel much closer to their wives because they have stopped construing the infertility as the wives' issue. But they feel enormously isolated from other men and desperately need a place to discuss their new images and feelings about parenthood.

Women's Spontaneous Imagery

Because mothers have always been the primary nurturers of small children in our society, most women's unconscious sense is that female adulthood equals motherhood. If one asks a small girl what she wants to be when she grows up, she is likely to say, "A mommy, like my mommy."

Because of the intense relationship she is likely to have with her mother, a girl's self-image may well contain powerful memory-based, detailed images of herself as a future mother—acting and being like her own mother. Women have grown up imagining the children they surely will have, carrying the memory pictures of them for decades. Some women who miscarry feel that they already knew the child they have lost. Other infertile women don't feel as if they were never able to have children. They feel as if they had the children, having imagined them so vividly, but the children died. (Zoldbrod, 1990).

Most women, when they fall in love and marry, begin picturing what their children will look like, imagining the mixing of their genes with the idolized genes of their beloved. The wife imagines a darling little girl or boy with her husband's wonderful broad smile, or his beautiful, curly black hair. Infertility brings not just the loss of a child, but the loss of a specific child who has been imagined. Here is a rather typical example of this phenomenon:

The Christoses came in for several sessions to talk about the possibility of doing donor insemination. They were in their twenties and had been married for five years. Jonathan, who was Greek, had no sperm. JoAnn, who was blond, seemed to be perfectly fertile.

When a physician had mentioned donor insemination as a possibility, Jonathan immediately felt that this was a good solution. He was very close to his brother and had even told his brother that he was azoospermic. He felt that his genes would be carried on in the world through his brother's children. That gave him a lot of comfort and made him feel that "the issue of the genetic line has already been covered." Although he was sad that he couldn't have biological heirs, he felt secure in his manhood, and he very much wanted to see JoAnn pregnant, to watch her get bigger day by day, and to have a child to love who carried her genetic material. He had no doubt that he would love the child madly, just as he loved JoAnn.

JoAnn was much more upset than was Jon about the loss of his genetic line. She talked quite a bit about the child she had imagined they would have together, who would have Jon's Mediterranean looks, which she loved. When she was checking through the catalog of donors, her deep feelings of genetic loss surfaced because there were no Greek donors. Her fantasies about their future child, blended from their genes and symbolically embodying their relationship, were much stronger than his. She had to grieve the loss of this specific dark and beautiful child before she was able to go forward with insemination and subsequent pregnancy.

A woman's sense of sexuality, like a man's, is intricately tied to her reproductive abilities. But a woman's sexuality develops differently. For most women, sexual feelings and images have been tied primarily to deep feelings and hopes about current and future relationships, rather than to showing one's prowess and competence.

Women's bodies are put together differently, too, and thus women's imagery differs from men's. Because of her anatomy, a woman has more opportunity to puzzle about what is going on inside her. Women with fertility problems may become obsessed with images of what is "wrong" inside them in a way that few men can really comprehend.

Fertility problems can spoil women's sexual imagery, just as it can men's. This subject is discussed both in this chapter and in Chapter 10.

Jackie, who was having inseminations with donor sperm, was enjoying kissing her husband on a relatively deserted beach. They decided that they wanted to make love, so the two of them got up and moved to an even more deserted and enclosed spot. But the mood was broken, and she found her mind occupied with thoughts of the "cold speculum and strange men coming in and out of the room." She was very upset at the extent to which her sexuality was being affected and asked, "Is a baby really worth all this?"

With one's body constantly under scrutiny, and being the unwilling hostess of so many needles, drugs, dyes, sound waves, and X rays, it would be surprising if infertile women did not find their body images distorted. Many horrifying images spring up in infertile women's minds and then become lodged there, amplifying the pain. Women's associations with their bodies are hateful: "You're ugly"; "You're defective"; "You're useless." A woman with a scar from a myomectomy feels herself "completely deformed." Another woman, who has had several miscarriages, says that she is disgusted with herself because she is "unable to do what even a dumb animal can do." Another woman calls herself a "defective incubator." According to Fisher (1989), girls have an early image of themselves as a "potential creative container" for a fetus, whereas men lack such a vivid sense of their body's potential creativity. This difference may account for infertile women's seeming more vulnerable than men to hateful body imagery.

Sometimes thoughtless comments from medical staff contribute to the horrifying pictures that patients unconsciously harbor of their bodies. One woman was undergoing surgery for endometriosis. Afterward, her surgeon reported to her that it had really been a "mess down there. It looked as if someone had got loose with a bottle of glue and glued everything together." From that point on, as she tried to get pregnant, each time her period came at the end of the month, she thought of the "bloody mess" of her internal organs, pathetically attempting some version of reproduction and failing. Although it may still be possible to get pregnant while thinking such thoughts, it certainly is harmful to one's self-esteem to think of one's body as disgusting, pathetic, or deformed.

When one gets right down to it, some medical terminology evokes vivid negative imagery; *hostile cervical mucus* and *incompetent cervix* are two good examples. Providers would make important progress in preventive mental health care by simply devising less painful terms to use in their discussion with patients. Some of my colleagues at the Tufts New England Medical Center Reproductive Endocrinology Unit have been coming up with some new terms, such as *premature dilation* for "incompetent cervix"; *reduced ovarian reserve* for "premature ovarian failure"; and *empty sac* for "blighted ovum."

Further, there is almost no reference that medical personnel can make to a woman's age that is not experienced as quite hurtful, except possibly the statement that she is still quite young and has plenty of time. And even this flattering statement upsets younger patients, who feel that their sense of urgency is not being well responded to. A twenty-three-year-old patient wrote in a letter:

> There seems to be this belief that panic doesn't touch the younger woman. A person's age has nothing to do with how much a loss upsets them. Whether I'm twenty-five or thirty-five, I still feel the same sense of upheaval. I get just as frustrated and angry and depressed. I can't see how having almost twenty years left of a chance for conception makes us lucky. Think of all of the emotions associated with infertility. Think about how you put your life on hold for medical appointments. Would you really want to suffer through this for twenty more years? I don't think so.

However, the body imagery of younger and older patients is slightly different. Those in their thirties and forties have reported many imaginative variations in body imagery arising from their concern with being "over the hill," such as "My eggs are deformed" and "I see my eggs as all shriveled and dried up."

Basics in Using Imagery for Interventions

All of these instances of negative imagery are amenable to intervention. When using imagery for stress control, as the therapist notices and helps to confront, challenge, stop, or transform the patient's negative imagery, the patient is taught to do the same. One simple technique for stopping images is to have the patient create a competing image of a voice yelling, "Stop! Stop! Stop!" when she notices the offending image. Patients can also be encouraged to increase their consciousness of their negative imagery by sharing their images with partners or friends.

Patients who work well in the imagery mode can be encouraged to concentrate, reprocess, and transform their negative imagery into more positive imagery. However, the self-hatred that patients feel during fertility difficulties means that they intuitively move toward burn-and-destroy imagery when trying to change ugly imagery about cysts, adhesions, infections, and antibodies. The therapist should encourage them to use, instead, cleansing imagery, which is kinder. For instance, a patient who had begun to see her endometriosis as "my insides are all stuck together" was encouraged to imagine a tiny little cleaning person inside her, wielding a bucket of magic scrubbing potion, washing away all the endometriosis until each organ was clean and separate. A man whose stomach was "tied up in knots" about the poor results of his sperm count was asked to imagine untieing the knot (Zoldbrod, 1990).

Images can be more powerful than thoughts. Teach patients that negative spontaneous imagery is normal, not some kind of "voice from beyond" with predictive power. Patients are amazed and relieved when they are given examples of other people's horrible images. They need to know that others, who eventually had good outcomes, had similar negative imagery. The images are not magical or predictive, they are just part of the unconscious processing of this enormous potential or real loss.

Imagery and Technology

The assisted reproductive technologies have made patients' images more concrete, for better or worse: images on the screens during the ubiquitous ultrasound procedures involved in treatment, for instance. Reports of "good eggs" verified visually by ultrasound are very commanding, concrete, positive images. They remain positive images over time, however, only if that particular ultrasound report marked the start of a viable pregnancy.

In a similar vein, an ultrasound image that shows no heartbeat or an empty sac in a precious pregnancy is a concrete negative image that is now encoded as a loss both aurally (as the physician saying, "I'm afraid that this is an empty sac") and visually in the mind of the couple. In this case, technology has created a literal picture of failure or loss. The first picture showed the bleeping point of light: a heartbeat! The second picture showed what is in the couples' hearts: blackness and emptiness. One patient to whom this happened was haunted for a year by the memory of happily walking into the ultrasound office to check on the progress of her pregnancy, having the ultrasound procedure, and then seeing the gray, stressed look on the technician's face and the blank screen. Language or procedures that produce imagery about the embryo encourage the attachment (Fletcher & Evans, 1983; Milne and Rich, 1981).

We're in a new age, when an embryologist can tell a patient, "This is the best embryo we have seen in the clinic in our history. It has eighteen cells!" Having pictured the embryo flourishing, the patient who received this communication was devastated when her magnificent embryo failed to implant and grieved for two years afterward.

According to psychologist Kathryn Faughey of New York City, some in vitro fertilization (IVF) programs give the couple a photograph of the embryo, before it is transferred. She reported (newsletter of RESOLVE of New York City, March 1991) that "most women are deeply grateful for this photograph, . . . find themselves showing this photo off to others, talking to it, encouraging it, expressing love to it. She may keep the photo constantly within her sight for the next two weeks. If the cycle fails, grieving probably is made easier by such a photo. If the embryo grows to be a baby, it may becomes the couple's most treasured photograph."

The kind of imagery "exercise" that the infertile woman is most apt to discover and use repeatedly on her own is picturing in detail the growth and birth of her own biological child. Some caregivers even tell the woman to imagine these images. This kind of encouragement can backfire. In one reported instance (newsletter of RESOLVE of Fort Lauderdale, Summer 1991), an IVF patient from Florida was given a petri dish in the recovery room after her IVF procedure. The IVF nurse said to her, "Here is your baby's first crib." This was a very endearing use of an image. This particular patient, luckily, got pregnant during that cycle; but what happens to the patient when this "baby" doesn't implant and grow and dies instead (a much greater possibility, statistically)? This kind of imagery about successful pregnancy in a particular cycle is common:

> A nurse told Rose, who was undergoing IVF and had just had the embryo transferred, "Now, just imagine this little embryo growing in your uterus." The nurse had never made any reference to imagery before. Rose resented this piece of advice because it was made in a casual (but well-meaning) way, was not in a context of an integrated, therapeutic use of imagery, and did not represent any real attempt to connect with her emotionally.

Was Rose supposed to consciously do something to make the embryo implant? She may have felt that the embryo did not implant because she did something wrong.

Although it is true that, under some circumstances, with repetition and deep relaxation, imagery and hypnosis can cause physical changes, such a use of imagery is not being recommended here. There is a downside to specifically instructing the patient to "imagine this embryo growing" or "imagine yourself pregnant this month." Such images potentially lead to a sense of disappointment and failure, *not mastery*, if conception doesn't occur. They increase feelings and ideas that the future is unlivable unless pregnancy and birth occur.

In fact, the biggest caution that medical psychologists offer about using imagery is that manipulations designed to improve feelings of psychological control can instead produce feelings of responsibility or blame (Taylor, 1990). Other kinds of imagery increase overall coping skills and expand the patient's sense of mastery over infertility no matter what the outcome.

Coping Imagery

Various kinds of imagery exercises that the therapist can suggest will help the patient cope. They work in different ways: Some guided images work through cognitive restructuring; some achieve a sense of mastery through the simulation of events; some heal by regulating physiological states through relaxation; some are confrontational and work by helping the patient to face upsetting events; some clarify issues and choices; and some work by allowing the patient to distract herself, as do some of the imagery techniques for avoiding pain (Burish & Lyles, 1979; Taylor, 1990). Some of the techniques and exercises in this chapter have been pioneered by other psychologists (Meichenbaum, 1977;

Shorr, 1978) or have been inspired by them. Some are original (Zoldbrod, 1990).

The Crystal Ball

The crystal ball (Zoldbrod, 1990) may be the single most useful imagery exercise. (Directions are on page 57–58.) Uniformly, patients come into treatment anxious, depressed, and full of dreadful images of the future. They can picture themselves in the future only as being as unhappy as they are now. The crystal-ball exercise serves a number of functions: It can work to accomplish what Arnold Lazarus calls "anti future shock" by making the patient confront what may come to pass. It can encourage hope. Under the best of circumstances, the crystal ball turns into an exercise in mastery when it results in the patient's picturing a satisfying future:

> Sam and Sue had been trying to get pregnant, without success, for several years. Sue's self-image was worn out from the medical regimen, and she saw herself as "worn and gray," but she couldn't quite stop treatment. For the last year and a half, suspecting that she wouldn't get pregnant, and furious at her ovaries for not cooperating, Sue had been living with anticipatory grief about the loss of their biological child. But as is typical, she had also been plagued by distressful imagery about the sorrows of childlessness. Sam and Sue did the crystal ball together in a joint session.
> Sue paused after performing the exercise.
> "Well, I guess we'd just adopt, wouldn't we, honey?" she asked.
> "Yeah, we would," said Sam.
> They were both smiling now, although they had been quite somber earlier in the session.
> "You know," she said, "it's funny. We used to talk about adopting even before we got married. We talked about having one and adopting one."
> "I always felt good about adoption," said Sam. "We really could do it, Sue."
> At that point, they began to discuss adopting internationally, probably from Colombia. Sue's "old and gray" self seemed transfigured as she and Sam began to share fantasies about their life with an adopted child, as well as Sue's hope to try breastfeeding.

Patients who do the crystal-ball exercise and turn out to have some adoption-positive feelings (see Chapter 3) should be taught to set their sights on the future further down the road of life, not on the immediate outcome of medical treatment, so that, whatever they imagine comes to pass, the outcome will be positive: they will get to love a child. One workshop participant called this "investing for the long term."

Once a patient realizes that she is adoption-positive, she is attuned to this fact and can begin to gather more adoption-positive imagery to use during times of distress:

> Karin produced some adoption-positive imagery during the crystal-ball exercise. She was relieved to see that, in her heart of hearts, she knew that she could love an adopted child. The following week, she came in and reported that she now had another adoption-positive image. She said that she worked with a "wonderful, artistic" Vietnamese woman, Sally. Sally had been orphaned at age nine and had been adopted by a Connecticut family.
>
> Karin commented, "Sally is so fantastic. I kind of forgot what her life story is. And Sally loves her parents and talks about them so adoringly. If I get a picture of Sally sitting at work, talking about how much she loves her parents, it just warms my heart."

Some patients do not produce adoption-positive imagery, but they are able to produce agreeable pictures of a life without children:

> Valerie wasn't sure that adoption was a good idea for her, and her husband was set against it. Valerie did the crystal-ball exercise and pictured her husband and herself surrounded with lots of animals in a scene that was so pleasant it made her smile.
>
> She said, "The animals will give us someone to love. Of course, a relationship with an animal isn't the same as one with a child, but we'd enjoy it. We're both real animal freaks. We could spend some more time with our nieces and nephews, get a nicer house, maybe a nicer car. Yeah, it would be fun with animals."

At the moment when a pleasant image emerges, the therapist should encourage the patient to enrich the picture with as much detail as possible by asking a few questions about the sights, sounds, textures, and smells of the scene. The patient should be instructed to recall that pleasant image when she has irrational and upsetting images about the future during the coming week.

Finally, the therapist should note the specifics of the image in the patient's record, in case the patient forgets. If and when the patient comes to another session quite depressed, fearing that infertility will ruin her life forever, the therapist can recount her explicit good imagery of the future.

I do not mean to suggest that patients should not work through the real losses that will occur if they cannot get pregnant. But patients also need to learn techniques for managing and getting relief from the steady stream of irrational bad images of the future in which they immerse themselves.

The crystal-ball exercise offers the therapist a quick, relatively accurate early assessment of how difficult it will be to help the patient cope. As we will see in Chapter 5, some patients who are characterologically envious do this exercise and can come up with no imagery about the future that does not make them feel "gypped." Some feel that the infertility has permanently damaged their lives and their sense of self, and that they never will recover emotionally from this blow. Unless a patient like this really has a biological child, it may be difficult for the therapist to help her with anything other than long-term reconstructive therapy.

Occasionally, patients who have functioned well in life in the past, who do not feel gypped, and who can imagine themselves succeeding in life in general cannot come up with any good future imagery after doing the crystal-ball exercise. These patients are in deep despair and should be most carefully evaluated. That said, they need a wealth of active help, including bibliotherapy, attending RESOLVE support groups with other people who are trying to find solutions, and going to adoption conferences, as well as an active therapy using imagery exercises designed to explore and examine their feelings about other alternatives to biological parenting. (Such exercises are spelled out further on in this chapter.)

Students sometimes voice concern that the crystal-ball exercise may elicit specific unfavorable imagery about the future "too soon" and so may be harmful to the relatively healthy patient. But imagery comes from the deepest unconscious. We do not ever create bad imagery that was not there before. At the worst, we are just uncovering it. It makes therapeutic sense to uncover the images or beliefs that are upsetting the patient or the couple as soon as possible. They have to be explored eventually.

Of course, the therapist has the discretion not to pursue something she has uncovered that is obviously overwhelming to the patient. But she has gained some important understanding of the dynamics of the case. Whether the members of the couple are adoption-positive, adoption-neutral, or adoption-negative, for instance, will help to determine the course of the therapy.

Bad imagery is fertile ground to plow, often leading to dynamic interventions in cognitions or images. At the worst, one or both members of the couple may have had negative personal or familial experiences with one particular alternative that are so potent that that alternative may be forever unacceptable. The therapist may fail in her attempt to assist the patient in amending such a negative image:

Dolly did the crystal ball and came upon a dead end. During discussion, she revealed that her images of adoption had been spoiled by her sister's experience. Her sister was infertile and had had two "gray market" adoptions. Both children wound up with learning and emotional problems.

Dolly said, "I've seen what adoption did to my sister's life. She loves her kids, but she has had constant trouble with each of them since she got them. I'd be too scared. I just couldn't do it."

Dolly never was able to get past her negative imagery. But no harm was done to her in eliciting these images early in her therapy. They were so vivid that they existed consciously anyway.

At other times, an exploration of negative adoption imagery produces positive adoption imagery:

> Sharon told me that she couldn't imagine adopting internationally. When I asked her why, she said, "I think people will look at us and think we failed."
>
> I asked her to close her eyes and get a picture of herself walking down the street and seeing a family where the kids were from a different ethnic background than the parents. When she did that, I asked her what she thought when she saw such a family. "Oh," she said, surprised. "I just think it is neat." (Zoldbrod, 1990, p. 21)

Thoughts that the parents had failed had never entered Sharon's mind. As a result, she felt more positive about adopting internationally.

Promoting Mastery: The Boulder-in-the-Road Exercise

One technique that promotes feelings of mastery is to have the patient imagine successfully facing something symbolic of a dangerous force or solving a problem. Psychologist Joseph Shorr (1978) called this "task imagery."

This exercise, which I now use routinely, came to me while I was talking with a patient. I saw her walking down the road of life, quite happily, when all of a sudden the road was blocked by a huge boulder. How was she going to be able to continue on her way? Out of my mental picture grew the following guided image:

> Imagine that you are driving, traveling down a beautiful, tree-lined road in the country, going toward a favorite destination. It is a fair, clear day. The air is fresh and clean, the temperature is perfect. The sun warms the back of your neck, your arms. Birds are singing. You are feeling good about yourself and close to your spouse, and you are enjoying the trip. You are looking forward to having a wonderful time.
>
> Suddenly, out of nowhere, an enormous, dense gray boulder appears in the middle of the road. It takes up all of the room. You can't get around it. You have come to a dead stop. What can you do?
>
> In your mind's eye, find a way to continue your trip and to reach your ultimate destination. (Zoldbrod, 1990, p. 17)

Patients enjoy working with the image of getting around the boulder in the road. The use of this exercise with a patient named Ann is described in Chapter 8. Be aware of your own images and associations when working with patients, for they are relevant and can assist in the treatment. Behavioral rehearsal discussed in Chapter 3 is another imagery technique that promotes mastery.

Interventions to Alleviate Guilt and Promote Better Sex

Patients assume that their infertility is a punishment for wrongdoing partly because infertility is a hidden problem. We know that not everyone has lovely looks, for example, because we can look around and see that some people are not especially good-looking. We know that not everyone is able-bodied because we see people who walk slowly or who need help to ambulate. However, we can't watch a person and know that he or she is infertile (Zoldbrod, 1990).

Because patients have grown up believing that *everyone* is fertile, and that *any couple* (or any "dumb animal") can have babies at will, they can only assume that they alone are being punished by God, because they did a bad thing. This belief can be difficult for the therapist to dislodge. Here is an imagery-based exercise that is unusually successful in challenging the irrational belief that infertility is a punishment for sin. Very guilty patients should repeat it several times in different sessions:

> Imagine that you are a young child. When you ask your parents about having babies, they don't automatically tell you that when you grow up, you'll be a parent. In fact, they tell you that some people want children but cannot have them. This has been true for so many years that it is talked about a lot in the Bible, they say. Your parents present this matter of factly and talk to you about how people feel when they find out that they are infertile. They tell you about options people with fertility problems have—childfree living, adoption, donor insemination, et cetera. You ask questions about fertility problems, and they are all answered forthrightly, throughout your childhood.
>
> When you become an adolescent, the dangers of unwanted pregnancies are discussed, but the idea of fertility problems is reintroduced (although you never forgot it from childhood) and discussed. As you grow into adulthood, you meet people born through in-vitro fertilization and third party pregnancy. You notice the numbers of people who have adopted and the other sizable group of people who have chosen not to have children.
>
> Now, imagine that you have married and are having difficulties conceiving. How would your feelings about your problem differ from your current feelings? (Zoldbrod, 1990, p. 12)

Problems with sexual imagery are treated in great depth in Chapters 10 and 11 and sometimes necessitate intensive treatment. However, for couples who had a very powerful sexual attraction before marriage and an active and satisfying sexual relationship before the infertility, one imagery exercise can be a source of pleasure and relief. Once they are relaxed, instruct the couple:

> Recall, in great detail, a wonderful sexual experience you have had with your mate. Where were you? What were the physical sensations involved? What was the most magical thing about it? (Pause). Take several deep, cleansing breaths.

Know that you and your mate will be able to have a wonderful sexual connection like this at some time in the not-too-distant future. (Zoldbrod, 1990, p. 18)

After they open their eyes, you can invite the couple to share their images with each other, if they feel comfortable doing so, or to write down their images to share together in private.

Imagery and Pain

Infertility frequently entails physical pain. The condition of endometriosis, when severe, may cause pain in and of itself. More commonly, invasive medical procedures used for evaluation or treatment cause misery. Pain control is one area in which psychotherapists can be of tangible help to their patients.

As psychiatrist Errol Korn noted, going through pain is a complex phenomenon. Not only do people vary in their pain tolerance, but the same person may have dissimilar responses to equivalent amounts of pain in two different situations.

No one feels "pure pain." Instead, the actual physical sensation of pain is experienced in the context of what the pain means. The more upsetting the meaning of the pain to the patient, the more the patient will suffer. Korn diagrammed the pain experience as a multilayered phenomenon (see Figure 4).

The example becomes more understandable if one considers the example of two hypothetical women who have had three years of infertility. Each has a

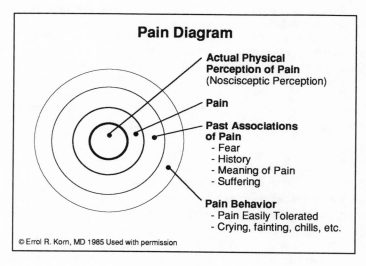

Figure 4

comparable operation, by the same surgeon, with the same medical and nursing management. Each has a six-day stay in the same hospital.

Patient 1, who has had upsetting reactions to both a hysterosalpingogram and an endometrial biopsy in the past, has a myomectomy to remove some fibroids that are suspected of being the cause of her problem. Patient 2, who tolerated a past hysterosalpingogram and endometrial biopsy without much distress, has an elective cesarean because she has finally achieved pregnancy and the baby is nine pounds and in a breech presentation.

Not surprisingly, we find that, even though their bodies have been traumatized in a similar way, they react to the pain completely differently. The patient who has a baby to show for the surgery does not experience much pain after the first day postsurgically, and she does not suffer at all. Although she is very tired when she comes home with her new baby, her attention is focused on learning how to be a mother, and she is more aware of the pain as a slight annoyance than as anything else.

In contrast, the patient who had the myomectomy suffers mightily. She has much more intense pain that lasts eight weeks or longer. She registers more pain during the entire hospital stay, although she finds the nursing care and attention comforting, and she is touched by her husband's consideration. At home, alone during the day, she suffers intense postsurgical pain and sadness about her infertility for several months. She reports more pain at the site of the scar than does Patient 1, and she is more upset by the sight of the scar itself.

Two things account for the difference between these women's pain experiences. One factor is the difference in their prior histories of fear and trauma during medical interventions. More important is the enormous difference in the meaning of the pain to the two women. For one woman, the pain means success. For the other, it means failure again.

Patients find the above explanation of the pain phenomenon helpful, and it is included in *Getting around the Boulder in the Road* (Zoldbrod, 1990). At one workshop on imagery, a participant stood up and said that the diagram in Figure 4 made perfect sense to her. From adolescence on, she had been plagued with severe pain from endometriosis during her menstrual period. For over ten years, she had been able to keep the pain to a manageable level with deep breathing. However, she said, now that she was trying to get pregnant and was having difficulty, she experienced the same pain during her periods as unbearable, and she could no longer control or manage it.

Research has documented the coping benefits of being told in advance what sensations to expect and why, of being alerted to the particular procedures that will occur, and of being given cognitive or behavioral coping strategies to use during the noxious procedure (Taylor & Clark, 1986; Taylor, 1990).

Patients feel anxiety about pain, particularly the first time they are having a particular procedure. Most do better if they are prepared with a plan. In fact, the more a particular client likes to cope by feeling in control, the more specific and detailed the questions she should ask her physician before the procedure. (On the other hand, patients who cope by massive denial will want to know as little as possible beforehand.)

Few patients are sophisticated enough to know what questions to ask ahead of time. Behavioral rehearsal or role playing can be helpful, with the patient playing the physician and the therapist playing the patient.

Asking specific questions may require some persistence on the patient's part, but if it is asked for nicely, many physicians will cooperate with the request for information. Here is an example of the process working beautifully:

An infertile patient was about to have an endometrial biopsy.

"How much will this hurt?" she asked the physician.

"Not much," he said.

"How long will it hurt?" she asked.

"Not long," he said. He smiled at her very kindly, trying to reassure her that it really was a minor procedure.

"Could you be as specific as possible? Tell me exactly what I'll feel and for how long?" she said. She was still anxious.

Her physician, who was a very caring man, paused and thought for over a minute. Finally, he said, "You'll feel the needle going in, a pulling sensation, and you'll have a sharp pain for about ten seconds. Then, you'll feel some stinging for about a minute. Then it will be all over."

Once she heard his detailed description of the brief procedure, she felt more relaxed already. When he put the needle in, she imagined a screen with countdown numbers on it: 10-9-8-7-6-5-4-3-2-1. The acute pain was over. She counted once again after that, and before she got to forty-five, she was pain-free.

As a metacommunication, this process serves nicely as a message that some aspects of going through infertility are controllable. No pain, great gain!

The therapist can help a very frightened patient to increase her control over current or future pain by working through negative associations from the past. People who have already had medical experiences during which their pain and panic were ignored or dismissed by medical staff or family tend to have intense imagery about future agony and abandonment. One technique that is beneficial is to have the patient replay the past scene in her head but, this time, to imagine family and medical staff appropriately comforting her and offering her pain relief through distraction, relaxation, massage, and/or medication.

Behavioral rehearsal is useful here. Have the patient "run a movie in her head" of her worst fantasy of having her pain ignored (again) this time. Help her to keep replaying the scene until she is able to assert herself enough to get appropriate help from medical staff and family.

For more lengthy procedures in which anesthesia will be used but pain will be experienced postoperatively, the therapist can help the patient create a soothing script to use for the hours when the effects of the anesthesia have worn off. The therapist should phrase suggestions positively, in terms of how peaceful or comfortable the patient will feel, rather than how uncomfortable she won't feel.

Eimer (1988) suggested using imagery to change the context within which the pain is experienced. For instance, during an invasive procedure, the patient can imagine herself as an athlete or heroine who can endure or ignore pain in the process of attempting a grand goal. Pachuta (in Sheikh and Pachuta) has developed several useful guided images for pain control, including a magical anesthesia exercise and a healing liquid exercise. Directions for all three guided images are included in *Getting around the Boulder in the Road* (Zoldbrod, 1990).

Exercises for Body Hate and Distress and Pain during Treatment

When patients are in pain, the therapist can help them monitor their associations with the discomfort. They need to get an image of what is wrong and then to transform it:

> Sandra was feeling ill from Pergonal. She visualized the medication as "a red liquid that is making me feel hot." She got some relief from imagining it as a cool, blue liquid when she had her injections.

Here is another example where this technique was used to manage a patient's headaches from Pergonal:

> Clarissa, too, was getting awful, pounding headaches from the Pergonal she was taking. Her physician was notified, but he didn't think the dosage should be modified. She wanted to finish the IVF cycle, so she needed to be helped with the pain.
>
> Clarissa was asked to imagine what the medication "looked like" in her blood. She saw it as a "little ugly dwarf with big flat feet and a beard, running around in my bloodstream." Her association was so awful that she had to laugh. But she realized that her inner picture indicated that she felt the medication was toxic to her whole body. She commanded the ugly dwarf to get out.
>
> After she was reminded of all of the good things that the medication was doing to her eggs, she transformed her image of the Pergonal to "a beautiful, white swan, sailing along on my bloodstream, but not *in* it." She no longer imagined being invaded and poisoned, and her headaches abated. (Zoldbrod, 1990, p. 15).

It isn't unusual for patients to be complaining about pain several days after a relatively minor procedure. When the therapist is working in an outpatient setting, any remarkable pain must be checked out with medical personnel before any psychological intervention is attempted.

However, pain is sometimes more a communication of a feeling state than an actual physical perception of pain. Once the therapist gets the go-ahead medically, these two imagery techniques can be of use in exploring the meaning of pain and distress.

The Talking Chairs Exercise

The talking-chairs technique, given by Shorr (1978), is probably adapted from an old Gestalt psychology exercise. Instruct the patient:

Therapist: Picture two similar comfortable chairs in the same room. Imagine that you are sitting in the first chair. Imagine that the part(s) of your body that are "giving you trouble" are sitting in the second chair. Envision a conversation between you and them. Keep talking until all of you understand and forgive one another.

> Betsy's ovaries hurt after doing GIFT (gamete intra-fallopian transfer). After an ultrasound to make certain that all was well medically, which it was, she had a conversation between herself and her ovaries.
>
> She apologized for the heavy dose of stimulation to which her ovaries had been subjected and asked her ovaries to please be kind to her. She cried when she realized what her ovaries had been through in the last few days. Then she breathed some healing, deep breaths into her ovaries. In about an hour, her pain stopped. (Zoldbrod, 1990, p. 16)

> Another patient, Candy, was feeling miserable during the week before her IVF cycle. She had headaches and blurry vision, and she felt weak. Candy came into the session and said, "Please, don't do anything that will make me feel even worse, I just can't stand another thing." She said, in fact, that her body was "uninhabitable." She was asked to put herself in one chair and her reproductive organs in another chair..
>
> In the conversation that ensued, her ovaries talked about how they were all "pumped up" from Pergonal and were raring to produce "zillions" of eggs. Candy, who is Catholic, sat in the other chair begging and pleading with her ovaries to produce only one or two eggs. Ethically, she didn't feel good about having fertilized eggs that might need to be "thrown out." It became clear that Candy's body felt "uninhabitable" because she felt so conflicted. Candy and her ovaries talked until they reached a truce, agreeing on producing three good eggs. Afterward, she felt much less upset emotionally and better physically. She went on to become pregnant by IVF and delivered a daughter.

Wilma was having trouble adjusting to the scar from her myomectomy. Although she had wanted to have the fibroids removed to try to increase her chance of becoming pregnant, she was resentful that the surgeon "had not prepared me properly."

She felt "weak, scarred, ruined forever. Before, I felt defective, but this makes my sense of being scarred by the infertility more visible." She also complained of fearing that her uterus would "split open" if she got pregnant and tried to carry the child.

Once Wilma was relaxed, she imagined talking to her body: "You're a miserable, ugly failure. Now you even look disgusting. Your stomach is all puffy and mushy, with a big, ugly gash."

Next, she imagined being an imaginary baby-to-be, surveying the scene from the inside of her body and talking to her uterus and the scar. The little baby was happy to see the clean, open-looking uterus, and it talked about how much better and roomier it would be in there. The baby thanked her for "going the distance" to try and have her.

Afterward, Wilma commented that she had a new image of her uterus, that it was "clean and good inside," and that when she saw the scar, she would work on changing her associations to "clean and good" inside and "strong" outside.

Joseph Shorr (1978) created the body-trip exercise. The instructions for your patient are:

Therapist: Imagine becoming very small. Enter your body and take a trip around. What do you see? Talk into a tape recorder or take notes. What you "report" on your trip will give you some insight into how you really feel about your body.

Ceremonies, Ritual, and Imagery in Moving to Resolution

Exercises that help the patient to conquer fears about pain or actual pain or to dispel self-hate are powerful tools that allow her to tolerate staying in medical treatment for longer periods of time if she wants to. But for some patients, medical treatment does not appear to be succeeding, and the task eventually becomes one of searching for ways to resolve feelings about never having a biological child. Imagery is a valuable tool here, as well.

Couples who cannot create a child who is related to both of them must decide whether to remain child-free, adopt, or try to create a child through third-party pregnancy by using donor eggs, donor sperm, embryo adoption, or surrogacy. Whatever the transition or decision point, using imagery and creating ceremonies and rituals with the patient may be fruitful. The techniques suggested here for one alternative can be adapted to each patient's different choice.

Rituals are symbolic acts specific to certain situations and are often repeated from year to year. They mark transitions in life, define relationships, and help people heal if the transition has been a loss. They also work to create an awareness of change and give people a vehicle for expressing their feelings (Melina, 1990).

Serious observances marking important events are becoming rarer in American society today. Significant rites of older days have been transformed into nothing more than an excuse for a gigantic party. Specifically, there is a scarcity of established rituals to mark the loss of biological parenthood (Melina, 1990; Menning, 1977). In recent years, a few groups and individuals have created powerful healing services for miscarriage and infertility (see Appendix 5). More often, patients who need a ceremony to mark an important transition in their reproductive lives must develop it on their own.

When patients must give up on their hope of creating a child related to both of them, the therapist can create a rite such as an "imaginary funeral" (Zoldbrod, 1990) for the child who did not come to be. What would each of the grandparents say about the loss of this child? Who else would be there and what would they say? Have the couple talk about the child they hoped to create. What would she have looked like? What traits did they hope to pass on to her? What talents do they imagine she would have had? Imagine in detail where and when the service would occur, who all of the participants would be, and what would be said and done.

Actual memorial services are soothing, particularly if they are attended by friends and family, giving a sense of "legitimacy" to the grief. One patient organized a commemoration service for her miscarried child at the family's summer home. Parents, siblings, and spouses all participated. The baby's name was engraved on a piece of iron. The grandfather read a poem about the baby's death and cried. Finally, the metal plate with the baby's name was buried in the family's favorite spot near the summer home, overlooking the ocean.

Ceremonies need not always be consoling, however. One patient who had been in treatment for many years imagined collecting all her medical records from each specialist, operation, and clinic and burning them in a big bonfire, while she marched around the edges of the fire screaming about how glad she was to stop the treatments and go on with her life.

Child-Free Living

Having children is seen as normal and normative in society. Positive, varied role models of childless couples are rare because childless people are disparaged as being "pathetic" and "selfish." Barbara Kastner Roundy, past president of

RESOLVE of Puget Sound, made the interesting point that people who choose to make a life without children are making a risky choice; they are sometimes rejected by the other infertile people who have been their lifeline and support over years of medical treatment!

Being married without children is such an unusual choice that patients can frequently use a therapist's help in envisioning different ways in which a child-free life might be lived:

> Sandy was drained by six years of infertility treatment. She had always wanted to be a mother, but it was becoming clear that biological parenthood was unlikely. She did not want to take fertility drugs, which limited the options of her medical treatment. Adoption was unacceptable to her husband, period.
>
> She couldn't imagine clearly how a life without children could possibly be pleasant, but she needed to explore that alternative. Sandy realized that she wanted to find a way to have an ongoing relationship with a child throughout the rest of her life, not "some hit-and-run relationship, like a Big Sister Program."
>
> She first couldn't figure out how to accomplish this long-term relationship. I began to explore "aunt" imagery with her. Her aunt imagery was nil because her mother was not close to her siblings and her father was an only child.
>
> However, I had had three unusually close, lifelong relationships with loving aunts, so my "aunt imagery" is potent. I described the sights, the sounds, and the feel of the development of a niece–aunt relationship and explained how it was possible to have a lifelong relationship with a relative, even one who lived in another city.
>
> We discussed Sandy's good feelings toward her husband's sister and a niece who lived about two hundred miles away. As she talked more, Sandy realized the depth of her feeling toward this child and saw that she had already formed a powerful relationship with her, that she loved her. She began to picture how she could become more involved with her niece. In the following months, she followed up on her images and spent more time and energy with her niece, which was fun and very affirming of her sense of herself as a good mother and a good person. With the inclusion of an important, ongoing relationship with a child, the vision of herself as married with no children of her own seemed to hold more promise.

As therapists, we, too, are molded by the values of the culture at large. Some of us have been subtly taught in our professional training that people who do not have children are immature. But as professionals, we must take the responsibility to examine our own values and to expand our concepts of the possibilities of a life without children.

There are couples who should not adopt. They may have few or no other places other than therapy where they can get the support to carefully examine the possibilities of a childless life. We must be able to give them hope, to provide positive images of life without children. Otherwise, they will absorb our conscious or unconscious bias toward parenthood and may feel pushed to pursue adoption by general societal pressure, and by us.

It is shocking how lacking we are, as a society, of vital images of women who are not mothers. In trying to help women patients explore life without parenthood, I looked high and low for photographs of, and writings by or about, happy, productive childless women. What images do exist, such as the powerful photographs of Georgia O'Keefe, seem to portray women who are so famous, unusual, or powerful that they are of little use to "ordinary" women. This is another area where the therapist may be able to "lend" the patient positive imagery. If you personally have in-depth knowledge and imagery of a happy couple who have no children, you are an invaluable resource for your patients:

Cynthia, a warm, athletic, dynamic thirty-seven-year-old, had had five miscarriages and did not want to keep trying. She was trying carefully to consider a child-free lifestyle, but when she looked into a childless future, she felt panic. All she could think of was her mother's older sister and her husband, Aunt Matilde and Uncle Tom. They seemed such sad figures, with all their money and their eccentric ways.

Uncle Tom seemed to lecture to them as kids, not just to talk to them. Matilde came to visit dressed to the hilt, with glittering jewelry; elegant clothing made of luxurious fabrics; long, bright, perfect nails; and wonderful perfume. Her looks and smell attracted Cynthia as a child, but Auntie Mat never wanted Cynthia or her brother too close, because they were active kids who tended to be sweaty and messy. So, over time, Cynthia had learned to avoid any close contact.

And her mother had always talked disparagingly about Aunt Mat, who spent all of her considerable free time obsessively making mountains out of molehills. If there was something to get upset about, Auntie Matilde would find it. Cynthia's mother, who clearly felt competitive with Mat, used to say that if Aunt Mat had had children, she wouldn't have had *time* to get so self-absorbed. Cynthia's negative imagery about living a life without children was highly developed.

Luckily, as the therapist, I have a competing image of a married couple without children in my longtime friends Carolyn and her husband, Steve. I have been a friend of Carolyn's since 1970, and of Steve's since 1975. They have been married since 1981. Carolyn works as a planner in the state government. Steve is a free-lance writer and consultant.

In 1984, Carolyn miscarried, and she was never able to get pregnant after that. Carolyn and Steve grieved for quite a long time and finally decided to be a family of two. They live in a huge, old farmhouse filled with art and computers.

Carolyn is active in many environmental groups, such as the Four Rivers Watershed Association, often taking a leadership position. She does mountain climbing, takes a very brisk mountain walk daily, knits, and paints. She began studying with a native American medicine woman and experimenting with native American ceremonies. Steve is interested in many of the same activities, especially naturalistic activities and mystical studies, and he travels for his consulting and writing jobs. Both of them come from large families, and they are aunts and uncles to children many times over. They maintain ties with their nieces and nephews.

Besides their professional work, they are very busy with various projects. Steve and Carolyn garden passionately, extending the gardening season for much of the year with various contraptions. They grow every vegetable and flower imaginable and have a commercial-sized raspberry plot that they inherited with the property. They save flower seeds from one year to the next and replant them, and they freeze and can as much as they can every fall. Steve and Carolyn take tremendous pride in being self-sufficient as a household.

They are fulfilled and have created a very appealing and fruitful life together. When I visit them, their garden is so lush and the two of them look so healthy and attractive that I am reminded of the Garden of Eden. Someone else had the same vision, for Carolyn showed me a gorgeous picture someone had taken of her, beaming, her hair down to her waist, clothed in a flowing dress, sitting in her verdant garden completely surrounded by overflowing baskets of home-grown tomatoes, cucumbers, beans, eggplants, broccoli, and flowers.

This particular beautiful image of Carolyn, fertile in many, many ways, is engraved on my mind. I shared it with Cynthia, as an antidote to her picture of Aunt Matilde. It inspired her to expand her own ideas about what a child-free life might hold.

The diagrams of mourning (Figures 1 and 2 in Chapter 3) are another aid in the discussion of a childless life. Patients need to understand that by devoting so much of their energy to the baby quest, they have forgotten how to invest in other activities. After listening to what Carolyn and Steve's life was like without children, Wilma began to consider her life while looking at Figure 2.

She commented that she was giving the baby quest 80 percent of her energy and "getting back very little except an occasional positive pregnancy test." She imagined putting up a sign saying, "This space reserved" for all of her energy. She then imagined other ways to dole out the energy and pictured the next sign, which said, "Coming soon" with smaller signs underneath saying, "Spirituality," "New job," and "Opera."

Here are several guided-imagery exercises for patients considering being a family of two (Zoldbrod, 1990). Relax the patient first.

Exercise #1. Now that you are relaxed, recall the day-to-day details of the life you led with your spouse before you decided to begin having a family. What did you do in the evenings? Can you pick a particularly nice evening and recall the tastes, smells, and sensation of it? What did you do during the weekends? Again, using all your senses, recall a wonderful weekend.

What were the best and worst parts of that life? Could you imagine having a life like that again?

Exercise #2. Think of a couple you know (or imagine one) who have a stimulating and full life without children. Which parts of their lifestyle have the most appeal? Now, given the interests that you and your spouse have, picture what your life could hold if you had the money, energy, and time to focus on the things that excite you. Together, recall some of the peak moments, the most exciting, romantic, or relaxed times you have had together. Now, call up the three most interesting times you have had in your adult life, with or without your partner.

Next, think of the ways in which you have participated in society that have been the most meaningful to you. Have you enjoyed being involved in any organized group projects to help others? Have you done any volunteering? Finally, have there been any times when you have had important spiritual or religious experiences? Might these bring another level of meaning into your life? What about creating a life like this?

Adoption

Each patient, and each professional, responds to the idea of adoption with ideas and images from the present and the past. As with the other alternatives to biological parenthood, professionals need to do their own exploration of these same issues and feelings before they are prepared to help patients.

Patients may have strong feelings for or against adoption because of unconscious pictures they have about birth parents, adoptive parents, adopted people, or the adoption process. As patients are just beginning to considering adoption, it is useful to begin by exploring these images, in individual therapy or in a group:

Good and bad images of the birth mother

Good and bad images of the adopted child

Good and bad images of the adoption process

Good and bad images of the way the community sees adoptive families

Good and bad images of yourself as the parent of an adopted child

Couples becoming comfortable with the idea of adoption as a possibility must begin serious preparation. They must investigate how they feel about the special tasks entailed in assisting their child to deal with her adoption throughout her whole life.

Even parents who are enthusiastic about adoption do not really understand the nature of adoptive parenthood. Adoption is not a decision made once, explained to the child once, and then forgotten about. Parents need help understanding how the lifelong tasks of adoptive parenthood will affect them.

Judith Schaeffer, an adoption specialist, noted that most children are often told about adoption very early in life (before age five), before they can really understand the differences between being adopted and being born into a family. However, when children enter grade school, they do understand the differences, and they get upset. They don't accept the easy answer that they were specially chosen; they see that someone gave them up. Fantasies that they were given up because something is wrong with them or they did something bad abound. They need to be able to discuss adoption throughout their growing-up years.

One nine-year-old child in a slide show Schaeffer presented at the 1991 Open Door Conference in Millis, Massachusetts, commented, "I think about being adopted on my birthday and when I'm angry at my mom." Adult adoptees frequently comment that, as they got older, they hesitated to bring up any questions they had about their adoption because such questions so saddened their adoptive parents, whom they loved. They suggest that adoptive parents not focus on the adoption all of the time, but that, perhaps once or twice a year (maybe on the child's birthday), parents say to the child, "Any questions about adoption come up for you in the last couple of months?" This question gives the child a clear message that the parents can stand to talk about the subject.

The Lifelong Adoption Tasks Diagram

As the diagram in Figure 5 indicates, parents must go over and over the same questions on a deeper level as the child matures: Who am I? Why do I look the way I do? Why was I given up? Do you love me even though I didn't come from your body? Using this diagram, the therapist should have couples imagine conversations with their adopted child at crucial points in his life, say, at ages three, five, eight, eleven, thirteen, fifteen, and eighteen; during the first falling in love; before the child's marriage, when/if the child has his own children; and when the child is thirty-five.

This exercise affects people deeply, as they see that they cannot "forget" about their own infertility once they have adopted. This exercise can easily take an hour and may have to be repeated several times.

Working through the Losses

Each couple's sense of the most salient deprivation(s) is unique. Sharon felt sad that her genetic line was lost and was afraid that if she and her husband adopted a child who didn't look like them, "People will think we failed." Recall Pat

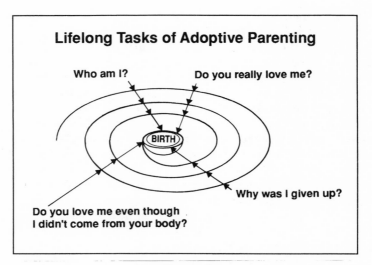

Figure 5

Johnston's point that no solution except biological parenthood addresses all of the losses entailed in infertility. Imagery can help to focus attention on the losses that still remain:

> Helen and Joel, aged thirty-one and thirty-two, respectively, came in for a consultation because they felt that they were almost ready to adopt, but something was holding Helen back. They wanted to figure out what the problem was and work it through, so that they could complete a home study and begin to build their family. They were a marvelous combination of rational and emotional. When they talked about their infertility, Helen got weepy, and Joel hugged her.
>
> They were an unusually optimistic and high-functioning couple. Both Helen and Joel worked as stockbrokers, and together they earned a very good living. A few years before, when they had discovered Helen's fertility difficulties, they had begun saving money in earnest in the event that they should adopt.
>
> They seemed to have discovered that they were both adoption-positive at an early point in their "infertility career," probably because each had an adopted cousin who had, in their words, "turned out OK." At this point, they had twenty thousand dollars earmarked in a special account ready to pursue a private adoption. They had gone to several Open Door Society meetings and had a group of friends who had adopted, and their relatives were supportive of adoption. They were remarkable. If anyone was prepared, they were. And yet something was holding Helen back. What? In

individual work with Helen, using imagery, the problem took only two more weeks to solve.

Helen was the oldest of three children, two girls and a boy. She reported loving and admiring both parents and having a "very upbeat childhood." From her comments, it seemed that Helen had feelings about not being able to carry on her mother's tradition in some way.

Helen was put in a deep state of relaxation. She was to picture her relationship with her mother. She began to object, saying that her relationship with her mother was not the problem. I replied that I knew that, and that it was something *good* in her relationship with her mother that was holding her back. I told her we were working on getting images of how her mother mothered.

All of a sudden, she was flooded with images of her mother's last pregnancy. Helen's mother was very proud of her ability to create life. During the last pregnancy, Helen was ten. For some reason, before the days of ultrasound and amniocentesis, Helen's mother decided that her third child was a boy. Early in the pregnancy, she named the child Jim. She talked and sang to Jim in utero all day and encouraged the two sisters to do the same. She told Jim how much he would love life and how much the family wanted him. She told him how lucky he was to be born in the spring. The sisters sang to Jim and sent him cards throughout the pregnancy. On his birthday, Helen's mother proved to be right, and a little boy was born.

As Helen talked, the tears poured out. Her mother's experience was amazing. It was part of being a woman, and she wouldn't ever have it. As a result of her experiences, she believed that "the pregnancy is the most important time in the child's whole life, and I'll miss it!"

The brief therapy centered on supporting Helen's grieving process, and at the same time challenging some of her specific beliefs (particularly that the mother–child bonding in utero was the most important time in the child's whole life). She was puzzled to hear that her mother's and the family's constant prebirth interaction with the baby was quite unusual.

She was sent home to reminisce with her mother about the period of time when Jim was growing inside her and to grieve together the fact that Helen wouldn't be able to be pregnant. Helen's mother participated in this exercise with great love and talked about the importance of the mother's role once the child is born. As Helen began to realize the importance of the mother–child bond after the baby is born, she felt herself ready to adopt, finally. And that is what Helen and Joel did.

Sharing Positive Adoption Imagery

Adoption-positive people have proadoption imagery to draw on and expand to help them resolve their childlessness. Some couples contain one person who is adoption-positive and one person who is adoption-neutral. In these cases, it is helpful for both members of the couple to relax and listen while the adoption-positive partner shares her imagery about adoption (Zoldbrod, 1990).

In the case of Ann and Joseph, discussed in Chapter 8, Joseph came into the marriage with very vivid and good images about adoption. In discussing adoption, he volunteered that adoption seemed "natural and fine." Jimmy, his favorite first cousin, had been adopted. Jimmy and Joe lived close to each other and saw each other frequently.

They were a mischievous and dynamic duo throughout their childhood and remain close today. When he saw how useful his imagery was to Ann, Joseph intentionally steeped himself in his past memories. He was then able to relate many heartwarming images of adoption to Ann. Joseph's forceful adoption-positive imagery bolstered Ann's own good feelings about adoption as an alternative.

The Imaginary Adopted Child

The therapist can instruct patients to think about their imaginary adopted child:

> It is a funny thing: parents who have biological children quickly and easily have all kinds of fantasies about what their children will be like. But they don't have the time to stop and think about how they will feel when their fantasies don't come true (which they often don't!). When you adopt, you are forced to face the true reality about children: that each child is a unique individual.
>
> Adoption is not for everyone. The child you adopt is not going to be the child you fantasized about having. He is a separate and special person.
>
> Imagine your adopted child at a young age. Imagine that he is attractive, but he doesn't look much like you. Imagine that he is much more/less outgoing than you are. Imagine that he is much more/less stubborn than you are. Imagine that he is much more/less affectionate than you are. Imagine that he is much more/less physical, active, or agile than you are. Thinking of all the kids you have seen and known in your life, imagine a child who is nothing like the biological child you dreamed of, but one who is a cute and lovable child in other ways.
>
> Can you picture playing with that child? Feeding him? Going to school conferences? Taking him to family outings? Can you see all of you being a family? If your images are rich and happy ones, continue building onto them (Zoldbrod, 1990, p. 4).

Imagining Rituals to Help the Child

Lois Melina (1990) commented that there are no rituals for families created in nontraditional ways. In my workshops, couples who become committed to adoption as a way of building their families can enjoy imagining rituals for their family. Some of exercises to use with groups of preadoptive parents are

Can you make a "hello" ritual for the child?

Can you imagine your child's face the first time you see him or her?

Can you imagine being your own adopted child?

What kind of a ritual would make you feel grounded in your home and family?

Can you make a ritual story memorializing how that child came to you?

Professionals' Attitudes

Some professionals are extremely negative about adoption. A study by Kopitzke, (1991) found that infertility patients regarded the decision to begin adoption proceedings as significantly less stressful than did their nurses and physicians (p. 1142). Mental health personnel believe that adopted children are at increased risk of psychological maladjustment and blame this increased risk on the adoptive parents' damaged sense of self (Levy-Shiff, Bar, & Har-Even, 1990).

In *An Open Adoption*, Caplan (1990) quoted a well-known psychiatrist as saying, "No one ever fully resolves his or her grief about infertility. Resolution involves a process of working, and reworking through the anguish and loss of not being able to conceive and give birth to a child. Adoption is no panacea. It is initially a safety net for people who have lost hope; it can become a door through which couples pass to gain some control over circumstances that have made them feel powerless and joyless" (p. 18).

Adoption experiences vary, certainly. Unsuccessful adoptions exist. So do successful ones. Many professionals seem to doubt the possibility of a parent's deeply loving another person (a child) to whom they are not biologically related—and this despite recognizing that married partners are able to do so. When adoption works well, the day-to-day experience is not one of primarily reworking one's grief.

One colleague of mine, an adoptive parent of two children from another country, commented that he knew he had reached a new level of love for his children when he realized that if he could magically turn back the clock and trade his kids in for two biological ones, he would not do it. He commented that the therapist's own model of coping with loss is salient. If the therapist doesn't believe it is ever possible to get over the narcissistic injury of adoption, the patient won't either.

Imagery in Third-Party Pregnancy

Imagery exercises can help couples decide how they feel about having a child through some type of third-party pregnancy. For example, imagery can be an important part of preparing patients for inseminations, whether with husband or donor sperm. Exploratory research has indicated that some women find inseminations in a medical setting more disturbing than they had expected (Zoldbrod, 1988). Patients are surprised that what they anticipated to be a simple process is "cold," "humiliating," or even physically painful. Spontaneous negative imagery is common, for instance, seeing donor sperm as "alien invaders."

Patients will be better prepared if they understand that they may have such feelings and if they can picture, hear, and sense the process accurately: left alone for some minutes, seminaked, in a sterile examining room, perhaps full of a stranger's sperm. Patients can be encouraged to think about what would make the situation more comfortable; for example, their husband's presence (often the best choice), his photograph, a tape recorder with favorite music, or a favorite coverlet.

Because most insemination by donor sperm (DI) is still kept secret, little research has been done on the long-term psychological effects of making this choice. Even though 82 percent of DI couples in one study (Klock & Maier, 1991) felt that they should have had prior counseling, only 9 percent had actually had counseling beforehand.

During interviews with fifteen couples between 1990–1991 to evaluate whether DI was a good option, I found that only three couples had already done reading or had given consideration in other ways to the longer term practical and ethical issues involved. Most had already decided they would keep the child's origins a secret from the child, without even considering the issue from the child's point of view (Klock and Maier had similar findings). Common comments were that no one should know because their extended families and society in general would be disapproving, and that it was pointless to tell the child, anyway, because the donor was anonymous and could not be found later in the child's life. Husbands found it hard to believe that the child would love them if the truth were known.

Once couples are provided with adequate counseling, most are quite responsive, thoughtful, and grateful. A written sheet comparing the pros and cons of using DI compared with another alternative such as adoption is useful in beginning a several-session discussion of important issues, such as secrecy and the parents' unequal genetic contribution to the child.

When assessing couples, it is important to explore the security of the marriage and whether or not the husband is agreeing to DI under duress or out of guilt. How does the wife see the husband? Does her love and respect come through?

Examining the husband's father–child imagery provides important clues to the husband's motivation and unconscious feelings about fatherhood. (Men who are closer to their own fathers feel more loss when they are not able to continue the biological and psychological chain, but they may have a more genuine, internalized motivation for fathering any child.)

Guided imagery about the future consequences of having children by DI provides other important data that need to be included in the decision-making process. Many men feel that the birth of a DI son poses more threat than the birth of a DI daughter. Here are some possible exercises: Can the husband imagine how he will feel when the wife gives birth to a boy who does not look like him? Can he picture how he'll feel when his DI son grows up into a strapping, rebellious adolescent with raging hormones?

One of the major issues in considering DI is the secrecy issue, especially whether or not to tell the child how he was conceived. Although most couples assume when they begin counseling that they will keep this secret from the child, a thorough discussion makes couples begin to think about the possibility of telling the child the truth. Couples desperately want to know the "right" thing to tell the child, and at what ages.

Because the trend toward openness is just beginning, we have no research on which to base firm answers. Figure 5 is appropriate here, as parents can imagine telling the child the why and how of his special conception at different developmental stages.

There is an important difference between privacy and secrecy. Even when couples intend to tell the child, who else do they want to tell, how, and when? How would they talk to the child about how much to tell others about his conception? Behavioral rehearsal is helpful here.

Most couples in counseling at this time will probably continue to choose secrecy, although they will have made a more considered decision than couples who have received no counseling at all. Patients can use imagery to prepare themselves for situations in which the secrecy issue will come up. A couple who thought that they felt perfectly fine about keeping the DI hidden were asked to imagine how they would feel when they had to help their imagined DI child construct her family tree for school or Sunday school. They were startled to find that they did not feel good about keeping the secret.

The issues to be explored concerning other alternatives are similar. Recipients of donor eggs may be counseled with some of the same imagery techniques as those used for recipients of donor sperm (e.g., can the social mother imagine how she will feel when her adolescent daughter, who doesn't look anything like her, idolizes the father and rejects her or gets pregnant out of wedlock?)

Very often, women intend to be completely open about their use of anonymously donated eggs. Such openness eliminates the tremendous problem having a family secret. However, it is a mistake to assume that, if there is openness and a known donor in any third-party pregnancy, there will be fewer problems. The situation still poses moral and practical dilemmas.

In certain situations, it seems clear that those involved cannot actually give "informed consent" because they cannot possibly predict all of the situations that may come up. Imagery exercises provide some help in getting in touch with potential feelings in worst-case scenarios. Take the situation of a woman donating eggs for her sister. Imagery can help her picture the future. What if the child looks just like her, not like the social mother. What if her sister raises the child in a way that is objectionable to her, for example, if an intellectual sister won't let the child try out for cheerleading, the genetic mother's old love, or if the child is raised an atheist when the biological mother is quite religious? What if the social mother develops drug or alcohol problems or an illness that seriously compromises her ability to take care of the child? What if one of the egg donor's children dies? Will she want to have back the child she helped her sister have? What if the donor sister dies? Would her husband want to take the child back?

Given the time constraints, physicians are not able to engage in lengthy philosophical discussions about third-party pregnancies as a choice. Most positively suggest this alternative as a good way to build a family. Some simply reassure husbands that DI, in particular, "can always be kept a secret; no one will know." Clinics and physicians offering any third-party pregnancy procedures should offer patients a well-thought-out decision-making process by a professional counselor. And imagery is a technique that will help couples "see" the future consequences of their choice.

Indeed, imagery is a most powerful tool in helping patients cope with the infertility process in its entirety. It allows patients to regulate their disturbing emotions, to feel in control in the midst of an uncontrollable process, to grieve what will be lost, to find hope, and to consider alternatives and prepare for them. In the next chapter, we look at some of the patient's most difficult feelings.

Much of the material in this chapter was first published in *Getting around the Boulder in the Road: Using Imagery to Cope with Fertility Problems,* Aline P. Zoldbrod Ph.D., Lexington, Massachusetts 02173, 1990.

5
Feelings

T he powerful and pervasive depressed, angry, isolated, guilty, and regretful feelings common in infertility have been well documented in the literature (Borg & Lasker, 1987; Malstedt, 1985; Mazor, 1978; Menning, 1977; Woollett, 1985); along with the stages of the resolution process: surprise, denial, rage, depression, grief, and resolution (Menning, 1977). Note has also been made of the female infertility patient's tendency to have feelings that vary dramatically at different stages of the menstrual cycle, from hope to despair, and back to hope again (Mazor, 1978). This chapter does not reexamine what has been covered so well in other literature on involuntary childlessness. We focus instead on some new comments about the infertility patient's feelings and on some selected strategies for treatment.

Two questions on the effects-of-infertility questionnaire are: "What feelings do you have that you wish you didn't?" and "What feelings would you like to experience more?" When we ask infertile women what feelings they have that they wish to eliminate, responses center on feeling "gypped," isolated, depressed, and envious or jealous.

In an older version, one of the sections of Lazarus's Multimodal Life History Inventory contained a list of qualities that the patient could check as applying to herself, such as "unattractive," "incompetent," "stupid" and "undesirable." Infertile women invariably underline the one which says: "Life is empty, a waste; there is nothing to look forward to." As one twenty-nine-year-old woman who suffers from severe endometriosis said, "I don't have too many positive feelings these days." Often, women comment, "I am angry at the world in general."

Women patients are obsessed to an extraordinary extent with getting pregnant (Lieblum, 1988; Liebman-Smith, 1987); and certainly much more than are their partners. There are good reasons for women's obsession. First, all of the activity occurs inside the woman's body, hidden. Second, all of the treatments depend on the ebb and flow of the wife's menses.

In a sense, success depends on obsession: someone taking the wife's basal temperature daily, being conscious of where she is in her menstrual cycle, and scheduling the treatment or test that is needed next. In almost all cases, the wife accepts the responsibility for these activities. Husbands who take over this task, bringing the thermometer, recording the temperature, and scheduling the necessary treatments, are a rarity. Such husbands may cut down considerably on the wife's obsession.

Even if the problem is male infertility, the female is the patient. The invasive treatments occur regularly to her body (Zoldbrod, 1988). The morning thermometer, each pill swallowed, every injection, each ultrasound procedure reminds her that pregnancy will not come easily, if at all. Last, the obsession continues because each month of "trying" represents a new chance.

One extremely bright, thoughtful, and accomplished woman who had had a happy childhood and a successful adulthood except for the infertility noted that she wished she could change her "absence of enthusiasm." She went on to say, "By now, the only thing that excites me is the thought of having children."

Infertile women respond to other projective questions on Lazarus's inventory with answers that differ significantly from those of all other patients. On a question on "your five main fears," other patients typically list dreads of serious illness or the death of themselves or their loved ones and trepidation about financial issues and then list several idiosyncratic responses. Infertile women typically write, "That I won't be able to become pregnant" and then give few or no other responses in the four other spaces provided. Infertility literally has surmounted life and death as the most important issue.

Skilled therapists who haven't experienced infertility personally or worked with infertile women previously may be stunned and frustrated by the intractability of these patients' feelings of anger and depression. One colleague commented, "I have worked with people with life-threatening illnesses, with cancer, with AIDS, and these infertile women are the angriest patients I have ever seen!"

Along with obsessive preoccupation with pregnancy comes the overwhelming sense of loss of self and loss of direction: "If I can't get pregnant, then what?" Women patients' feelings that life is empty and a waste can be best understood if one looks at the socialization of women, the "Mandate of Motherhood" as psychologist Nancy Russo (1976) called it. Little girls have learned that they should want and have children.

To some extent, the drive for children may be innate. Whatever the reasons women want children, for most women throughout the world being unable to have a child is an unthinkable, unmanageable loss. In *Sex and Destiny: The Politics of Human Fertility*, (1984), Germaine Greer painted a powerful picture of the lengths to which women will go to have children throughout the world. Even in societies where other illnesses cause death and disease and medical resources are scarce, women value treatment for infertility over other important medical treatments and inoculations. Greer commented, "The misery of the childless woman in most preindustrial societies can hardly be exaggerated" (p. 61).

In industrialized countries such as the United States, women have many possible roles other than that of mother. Yet, as Gergen (1990) wrote, even feminist therapists have failed to create a thesis of the psychology of women in adulthood that is separate from women's role as a biological creature, a mother. Right now, psychological theories, and thus mental pictures, of adult women's lives as women-without-children, separate individuals, are "restricted, negative, scarce" (p. 47).

How, then, are women to confront the fears of being childless, or to consider the option of not having children, without feeling that they are stepping into the void? Those of us who are concerned with easing the pain of infertility for future couples must work to generate new pictures of women as dynamic, fascinating, creative people with untold possibilities separate from their roles as nurturers and mothers.

But how can we help our patients to consider a possible future without children now? Empathy and timing are crucial. For many women, this option is unthinkable, ever. For others, this is a choice to consider when they have reached the "end of the road," only after years of treatment and of grieving.

When the "right time" comes, bibliotherapy (reading) helps. *Sweet Grapes* (1989) by Jean and Michael Carter is a personal discussion of how couples can resolve their infertility by choosing to create a rich life without children. However, because Jean Carter is a physician, some patients will not feel that her experience applies to them. Other role models do exist, however. The therapist should ask patients if they know any "ordinary" happy couples who have no children and have them talk about what the wives' lives are like.

Some patients do not know anyone who fits this description. In that case, the therapist who has such friends and acquaintances should share his or her knowledge and vision of a woman who has a full life without children.

Besides offering deep empathy and emotional support and working with the patient's imagery about being childless, the therapist can help the patient gain control over her feelings by using the techniques spelled out in Chapters 3 and 4.

Working with Envy

And when Rachel saw that she bore Jacob no children, Rachel envied her sister; and she said unto Jacob: "Give me children, or else I die."
—Genesis 30:1

Envy is natural to man from the beginning.
—Herodotus, *Thalia,* Book III, Chapter 80.

Envy's a coal comes hissing hot from hell.
—Philip James Bailey (1816–1902)

Envy is a difficult feeling in any circumstances. In *The Canterbury Tales,* Chaucer described the seven deadly sins and specified that, of them all, envy was the worst. Ulanov and Ulanov (1983) commented that, whoever is envied and whoever does the envying, envy has a destructive, dehumanizing effect on both. Jane Ciabattari (1989) noted that envy is an aggressive feeling. The envier feels, "I want what you have, and I want you not to have it. I want to take it away from you! If I can't take it away from you, I'll spoil it or ruin your pleasure in it!" (p. 48).

The literature on infertility makes some references to envy (Borg & Lasker, 1987; Mazor, 1980, 1984; Salzer, 1987), but treatment strategies for the problem are not described. Mazor (1980, p. 43; 1984) began the discussion on envy. She described the infertile woman's rivalry with pregnant siblings and was the first to note women's support group members' jealousy of other group members' miscarriages (for at least pregnancy had been attained, even if not completed), and of women with secondary infertility.

Jealousy of others who are able to get pregnant and carry a pregnancy to fruition is common and is probably the most troublesome and shameful feeling surrounding infertility. On the effects-of-infertility questionnaire, on the topic of unwanted feelings, patients write, "I wish I could accept other people's pregnancies"; "I feel so frustrated and depressed when I hear about close friends' pregnancies"; or "I feel anger and frustration in reaction to other people's easy fertility and casual decisions about abortions."

When patients talk about their envy rather than write about it on a questionnaire, the force behind the feeling becomes apparent: "If I see another pregnant woman on the street today, I'll *kill* her!" or "When I found out that my friend Sally was pregnant again, by accident, I was filled with such hatred and rage that I had to go out running for an hour before my body would calm down," or "When I went to Sandy's christening for her new baby, I was so angry I wanted to break every window in the church."

As a state of arousal, envy feels unpleasant inside the patient's body. Berke (1987) called it a "deep, gnawing, tormenting, excruciating awareness of disparity between oneself and someone else" (p. 325). Ciabattari (1989) described it as a perpetual state of anxious, competitive comparison (p. 48). Envy is one of the seven deadly sins and intuitively makes people think they are evil.

Patients run a real risk of rejection by family and friends if they reveal their covetous feelings. In some cases, men are repulsed by their wives' feelings of envy and make the wives feel even more ashamed of themselves. Recall the case of Betsy and Matt described in Chapter 3. Matt was enraged and disgusted by Betsy's envy of their friends' pregnancies, and he punished her by storming out of the house and painting "No fertile people allowed" on their front door. The partner who doesn't allow himself to feel anger is terrified by the rage that can accompany envy, sometimes feeling that his wife is so "out of control" that she should be hospitalized. Helping the couple understand, accept, and handle envious feelings is a sizable challenge.

Ironically, competition is usually a healthy strategy for handling envy. But competition is impossible in this situation, making the envious infertile patient feel even more helpless. The literal meaning of *competition* is "striving together." If someone envies another's job, she can take steps to get a similar job herself. If a friend is a better athlete, a person can develop her own athletic skill. Therapist and author Betsy Cohen (1986) made a very good case for the proposition that admiring, competing with, and emulating another person transform feelings of envy and the wish to harm into a positive force (p. 255). According to Cohen:

> Competition discharges envy, gives it a needed outlet. In telling yourself, "I can have that, too. What do I do to get it?" you are already thinking competitively. In negative envy, you don't realize that you, too, may have the quality you wish for in the other person. In competition, you try to connect with the quality in yourself that, until now, you have only attributed to the person you envy. . . . In competition, one is provided with the opportunity to become competent. (p. 218)

The awful experience in infertility is that there is no way to emulate the woman who is pregnant or who has children, no way to be as "good" as she is. One cannot will herself to be fertile. Thus one wishes to take away others' fertility.

On no other issue surrounding infertility is the therapist's continual empathy, understanding, and tolerance of hateful affect more important. The more the therapist permits the feelings of venom and destruction to emerge and be accepted, understood, and discussed, the more likely the patient is to get free of the envy.

Once the patient reveals her envy, the therapist should reassure her that envy is perfectly normal. Few others in her life will recognize envy as an ordinary feeling, so the therapist's permission to explore it is crucial. The woman should be encouraged to read accounts of other women's envious feelings. The national and state chapter RESOLVE newsletters contain many articles and poems on envy, sibling rivalry, and the problems of going to other people's baby showers and christenings. Liebmann-Smith's chapter (1987) on "Family, Friends, and the Fertile World" has a vivid story of sibling rivalry, envy, and rejection by parents. Kathleen Weaver's brief writing, "Covenant of Tears" (Glazer & Cooper, 1988) speaks the unspeakable, confessing to "stabbing jealousy" and "hatred" toward other women's pregnancies.

Next, some specific interventions can be used. It is crucial to ask the patient whether she was "an envious person in general" before the infertility. Characterologically envious patients, discussed later on, are much more difficult to treat. In many of our patients, envy is not a pervasive character *trait* in the way described by Melanie Klein (1957); it is a situational *state*.

State-Envy or Trait-Envy?

Envy as a state (let's call it *state-envy*) is likely to disappear when the patient gets pregnant, or when the situation is well resolved by some kind of semiadoption (i.e., surrogacy or egg donation), by adoption, or by a decision to live child-free. Yet the normal definitions of *envy* denote envy as a trait, as a continual, characterological meanspiritedness, if not downright evil.

Berke (1987) wrote:

> The envious *person* is not concerned with possessing, just with preventing others from possessing. . . . Envious anger is different from that aroused by frustration, revenge, rivalry or indignation. The latter presupposes actual hurt, deprivation or injury and is assuaged when the cause of the hostility is overcome or removed. Envy lingers on even after a frustration has been overcome, a specific hurt repaid, a rival removed, or an injustice made right. (p. 323; italics not in the original)

Imagery for Envy

The therapist can ask the patient with state-envy, "Do you think of yourself as being an envious person in general? Do you imagine that this feeling of envy will go on forever?" The patient should imagine that she knows, for certain, that she will be pregnant in two years. While imagining that, she should simultaneously picture seeing a pregnant woman. Does she still feel as envious? When patients who are in state-envy do this exercise, they realize that their envy is transitory. They are not envious people. This realization makes them feel better about themselves.

The essence of envy is feeling inferior. Berke (1987) elaborated on this theme, and his insights may give us insight into why infertile women often find themselves wishing death and destruction on pregnant women and innocent babies:

> Envious tension is a deep, gnawing, tormenting, excruciating awareness of disparity between oneself and something else, inevitably something desirable, beyond one's reach. An immediate wish for discharge follows the tension. The envier aims to eliminate the torment in himself by forceful, attacking, annihilatory behavior. So envy has to be seen as both the tension and the hostile reaction to the tension in the envier. The latter, the discharge, is what most people recognize as envy. (pp. 325–326)

Felice, whom we met in Chapter 3, talked about her envy in a group focused on stress control:

> I feel envious of particular children. When I am outside and I see a cute child with my coloring who is around a year or a year and a half, I feel as

though they have *my* baby. That baby was supposed to be mine! If I had had a baby when I was supposed to, that's the baby I would have had!

Patients like Felice need us to help them grapple with and understand their hateful and destructive feelings toward pregnant women and children. Part of what is being envied is actually the intact nature of the other woman's reproductive capacities. The patient compares herself and is tortured by feelings of pervasive inferiority. These feelings are too painful to remain in consciousness, however: "The infertile woman, regardless of the cause of her infertility, is concerned about her bodily integrity and intactness. She experiences a profound depression over the loss of her reproductive function, and feels herself to be damaged or defective" (Mazor, 1978, p. 148).

Because none of us have X-ray vision, infertile women cannot see inside another women's perfect body to envy it. But when another's body visibly swells, the evidence of one's own defect is in the comparison. Once another woman gives birth, both the woman and her child(ren) are envied. In Berke's theory (1987), the feelings of self-disgust with one's defectiveness are too horrible to stand, and the patient seeks to annihilate the person(s) who made her feel so bad.

If a patient expresses shame about her destructive feelings toward pregnant women, mothers, and children, the therapist should accept them and say something like, "Your feelings are understandable and normal. You feel so depressed, and powerless, and so awful about yourself because you can't have children. You just want her to suffer the way you are suffering."

When the feelings are reframed this way, they are experienced as more reasonable and less shameful. This is the most crucial ingredient in treating envy. Also, consider Berke's cogent comment on the physical tension inherent in the feeling. Patients who experience the emotion physically may try to dissipate it by using intense physical exercise.

One of the hallmarks of infertility is an extreme sensitivity to slights from others, which creates a sense of isolation. In some instances, the patient is deeply wounded by actions or comments by family or friends that seem benign or, indeed, intended to console. The patient's feeling is so exaggerated that something must be amiss in her cognitive appraisal of the situation. The therapist is put in an interesting position. To criticize the patient's interpretation of events is to risk damaging the therapeutic alliance, especially in the beginning of psychotherapy. The psychotherapist must accept the patient's life and reality. Here is an example of an envious woman's extreme and irrational reaction to the ministrations of a friend:

Sally was a thirty-year-old teacher who had moved to Boston from out of town. She came to the office with her husband, Jeff. She had been referred by her gynecologist because she had miscarried, was now pregnant, and was acutely anxious about having another miscarriage. Sally was calling the physician's office at least once a day with some kind of request for medical intervention, such as having a blood test to show that she was still safely pregnant. The office staff were not tolerant of her need for reassurance and became increasingly irritated.

Jeff was a supportive husband, and their marriage was excellent. Jeff stated that he was concerned about Sally's "fragile" emotional state. Sally loved children and was devoted to them. She loved her job. But she was utterly miserable. She was so obsessed by the possibility that she might miscarry that she could hardly concentrate on anything else, and except for Jeff, she felt totally alone in the world.

She was not yet through grieving for the child she had lost a little more than a year before. She was very angry at her doctor's office for not being more sensitive to her anxiety, she was disappointed in the nurse she was seeing there, and she felt at odds with almost everyone. When I commented on her disappointment in other people, she told me a story about how her best friend, who lived out of town, had totally let her down.

Sally and Betty had grown up together, had stayed close through thick and thin, and had been very committed to keeping in touch through letters and phone calls when they weren't in the same city. For the past few years, they had both lived in Detroit. Both had married while living in Detroit and were the maid and matron of honor at each other's weddings. In a few years, lo and behold! one July, both got pregnant. They were delighted and enjoyed fantasizing about how their kids would grow up and be best friends, too. They were disappointed to find out that Sally had to move to Boston because Jeff was being transferred. So Sally moved at the end of the summer.

Unfortunately, at about two and a half months, Sally miscarried. Betty was very sensitive, and Sally felt that Betty had "come through for her." Sally's grieving over the miscarriage was intense, and Betty's contact was consistent. Betty talked it through with her on the phone regularly. One day, at the end of fall, Betty sent Sally a care package with several dozen huge tulip bulbs to plant at her new house. The bulbs would bloom just about when Sally's baby would have been born, as a memorial to the lost baby. Sally was quite moved by Betty's sensitivity.

However, things changed in Sally's mind in April, when Betty's baby, Geoffrey, was born. Around Sally's due date, when Betty's baby was just a newborn, Betty knew that it would be tough for Sally, so she sent Jeff and Sally a condolence card. But Betty had done the unforgivable. She had signed the card, "Love, Betty, Steve, and Geoffrey."

Sally told me that she could never forgive Betty for her insensitivity. Everyone knows that a little baby cannot send condolences! Betty was a terrible friend for being so unfeeling! Sally no longer could bear to be friends with Betty.

This vignette is extreme, but during infertility, many female friendships have floundered on the shoals of hypersensitivity and envy of others' pregnancies. Sally did miscarry again, much to her despair. However, in subsequent sessions, she was helped to explore her past and present life. As she was able to accept and forgive herself some of her past failings and inadequacies, she stopped feeling that she "deserved to miscarry." As she felt more adequate, she began to see that Betty had been a very good friend.

Besides acceptance and empathy, concrete behavioral interventions may be appropriate. Women need help in coping with family occasions, showers, christenings, and other social occasions that include infants and children. the behavioral-rehearsal and stimulus-control techniques spelled out in Chapter 3 are beneficial.

Working with Patients with Trait Envy

There is a group of infertile patients in whom envy has been a constant trait (*trait-envy*). Not surprisingly, their covetousness of others' pregnancies and infants is difficult to unseat. They desperately need to be soothed, but they may well need to be treated within a long-term psychodynamically oriented framework. Some, but not all, of these patients have character disorders. They can be identified by being asked about their lifelong history of envy, as they are aware of it and do not deny it. Their sense of being "gypped" has plagued them throughout life; their current infertility is just the last straw.

Some patients who present this way may be victims of past emotional neglect or abuse, or of physical and sexual abuse. Such patients may be healed by a psychotherapy that addresses the abuse and neglect. We are not talking about this group. Other characterologically envious patients have had what appears to be adequate parenting. The therapist needs to recognize them as a separate set of patients, in individual therapy, and particularly in groups.

Here is a case vignette that illustrates how chronically envious patients respond to exercises suggested by the therapist. None of the cognitive-behavioral exercises seemed to be very effective:

Bonnie and her husband were teachers. She was a lot of fun to have in the group, verbal, bright, and friendly.

When the group leader asked the question about envy, Bonnie revealed that she had been envious all her life. Asked to give examples of early envy, she described being a little girl of seven and envying the fact that the neighboring little girl's parents had taken her on a better, more expensive vacation than Bonnie's family could afford. At an early age, she envied still another neighbor's horse, as well as a different friend's clothes.

When we did the crystal-ball exercise, where the patient's task is to get in touch with what she will do if she finds out for certain that she will never have a biological child, Bonnie had some good adoption imagery. Considering that Bonnie was fearful of pregnancy, this might have been seen as a good thing.

However, Bonnie commented that, even though she "knew" that she could adopt, her husband felt good about adoption, and she believed that she could love an adopted child quite easily, she felt that "Adoption would kill me."

She described how the "unfairness" of the situation would be intolerable: It wasn't fair that she couldn't get pregnant when other people could. It wasn't fair that she and her husband would have to sell a piece of property they owned in order to get the money to adopt. It wasn't fair that life was such a struggle for them in general; they were both bright and should have more money. It wasn't fair that they had to go through a home study. In fact, her life was such an unfair mess that she was certain if she went through all of the time and trouble and money to do a home study, she would "flunk" it. Bonnie said that she could "see how this exercise might help other people, but unfortunately, it can't help me."

An exercise that often works with women with state-envy is to have them do the onion exercise (described in Chapter 3) twice. First, they draw a picture of themselves *before* the infertility, diagramming all of their qualities from the most central to the most marginal. Next, they draw a picture of themselves *now*. The diagrams often look something like Figure 6.

Women with state-envy realize that they actually envy people who are the way they used to be. On exploration, they believe that, when the infertility is resolved somehow, they will again look like their old selves from the "Before Infertility" part of the figure. They often comment that they want to get back to their old "before" selves now, even while going through the infertility. They may find ways to change their lives now in order to feel more attractive, more competent, and better about themselves, so that they can stop envying others as much.

However, women with trait-envy have a different reaction to drawing the two onions. First of all, they may have difficulty getting in touch with what they were like before the infertility. They need to be spurred on with questions like "Who did your husband fall in love with? What was that person like?"

More important, they do not believe that they can ever get back to the person they were before infertility. They sense that no matter what happens, as one woman put it, "My life has already been ruined, and I honestly believe that my disappointment has been so deep that I will never again be the person I was before." They have no prior models of growing through crisis or of adjusting to loss and moving on.

Characterologically envious patients do not profit much from cognitive-behavioral interventions, although the exercises create a structure within which to discuss the deeper issues. Very-long-term psychotherapy with a devoted

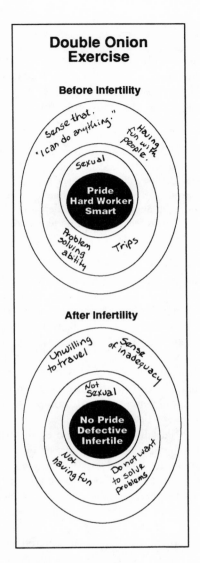

Figure 6

therapist can sometimes heal them. Trait-envious patients who go on to adopt (or do another semiadoption alternative that doesn't use the parent's genetic material or body) may need ongoing professional help in allowing their child to ask questions throughout life about the circumstances of her birth (see Figure 5) because answering such questions will heighten the parent's feeling of being defective.

Shame

Whereas feelings of guilt are often discussed in the literature on infertility, not much is said about shame. Feelings of shame occur frequently in infertile people, often as a result of their pervasive envy.

Perceived inadequacy may also release feelings of shame. According to Berke (1987):

> Shame is a tormenting sense of inferiority and sinfulness. It signals a loss of face and a state of disgrace. It reveals social inadequacy and moral degeneracy. It revels in worthlessness whether in light of oneself, or of others. Shame appears when goodness disappears. . . . Shame is not a mild emotion. It denotes a state of self-damnation brought about by the sudden annihilation of personal integrity. To be ashamed is to feel devoid of goodness, full of sin, and utterly reprehensible. (pp. 319–320)

We see shame in infertility patients when they see themselves as having sinned. Most commonly, patients feel ashamed either because they are envious of others' pregnancies or children or because they think that their infertility is a result of a sin such as masturbation, abortion, premarital sex, or adultery. As noted in Chapter 3, religious patients who feel overcome by guilt and shame because of past sins may find relief in discussing or confessing sins to a supportive pastor or priest.

Shame, like envy, has to do with comparisons. A person may be shamed by another, or she may shame herself. In the case of the infertile patient, shame is often an internal process, the patient drawing comparisons between how she is or was and how she ought to be.

Psychologist Susan Mikesell (1990) warned us that the therapist needs to watch for shame in the therapeutic encounter, as evidenced by the patient's downcast eyes, and should acknowledge the presence of the shame by saying something like, "It is difficult to reveal something you feel ashamed about." In the further interaction, the therapist should make it clear that the client is understood and still respected, not seen as worthless, inadequate, or degenerate.

Besides being empathetic, therapists have some concrete ways to help the patient with her feelings. One important task is teaching the patient to pay attention to her "tracking order," and to trace what thoughts, sensations, or images cause her sad, depressed, empty feelings. Some women can gain a sense of mastery over their feelings by looking at the sociocultural pressures on them to have children. Last, the therapist can use some specific techniques to help the patient cope with envy and shame. The therapist should be careful to determine whether the patient has envy that is a characterological trait or envy that is a temporary state. Patients with trait-envy may not respond to cognitive-behavioral interventions and need a therapy focused on the underlying issues.

6

Social Support and Interpersonal Relationships

The disastrous effect of infertility on interpersonal relationships has been extremely well discussed elsewhere, as have some excellent coping techniques (Liebmann-Smith, 1987; Menning, 1977; Salzer, 1986; Woollett, 1985). Problems with intimates and coworkers may be so troublesome that RESOLVE, the national support organization for infertility, has put out a fact sheet on the topic of "Dealing with Friends and Family." Patients will be well served by reading such material, which documents how inevitable and pervasive these interpersonal difficulties are during infertility. This chapter adds a few new thoughts about how infertility affects relationships.

A person's social world affects her or his physical and mental health (Lieberman, 1982). Adequate social support has been shown to help recovery from surgery, to protect against clinical depression in the face of adverse events, to reduce psychological distress and physiological symptomatology following job loss, to mitigate the effects of bereavement, and to reduce the number of complications of pregnancy for women under high life stress (Hamburg & Killilea, 1979).

Throughout life, the majority of people perceive their social network to be a major source of help (Lieberman, 1982; Litwak & Szelenyi, 1969; Wellman, 1976a,b), and evidence suggests that these perceptions are veracious (Croog, Lipson, & Levine, 1972). In fact, social networks are such a powerful source of support that several studies have shown that, during crises, people turn to professional agencies only when assistance is not given by their interpersonal network (Kasl, Gore, & Cobb, 1975; Quarentelli, 1960).

It is very sad, then, that one of the major losses during infertility is the sense of alienation from friends and family (Woollett, 1985). In the infertility literature, friends are occasionally noted as a source of support. Borg and Lasker (1987) noted that friends were very supportive of infertile couples' attempts at high-tech pregnancy. But more often, the infertility experts agree that, in many cases, the reaction of family, in-laws, and friends to infertility leaves much to be desired (Liebmann-Smith, 1987; Mazor, 1978; Menning, 1977; Rosenfeld &

123

Mitchell, 1979; Salzer, 1986; Woollett, 1985). Competition with siblings is frequently devastating. In large families with many daughters of childbearing age, the feelings may seem too intense to manage.

Here is a good example of infertility's complicating sibling relationships:

Maria and Mike, both in their late twenties, were very excited about Maria's pregnancy after several long years of trying to conceive. Unfortunately, Maria miscarried at four and a half weeks and was desolated. Meanwhile, Kristin, Maria's sister, got pregnant.

Maria was still upset about her miscarriage eight months into Kristin's pregnancy, and Kristin probably was disappointed that Maria couldn't share her joy. She commented to a friend, within Maria's hearing, "I can't understand why Maria is still so upset over the miscarriage. After all, it wasn't a full-fledged baby like mine."

Maria was really hurt. So was Mike. Mike commented, "Of course, Maria was offended. What did Kristin mean 'it wasn't a full-fledged baby'? It wasn't going to become a squirrel or a chicken! It was a little person. Just like Kristin's baby, it had a soul!"

In another case, a mother who had miscarried repeatedly had finally used diethylstilbestrol (DES) and had given birth, eventually, to three daughters. The mother sought support now because the three daughters, all in their late twenties to thirties, had married and were each trying to conceive and experiencing infertility. This sad situation did not draw the siblings closer. Instead, the young women were fiercely competitive with each other, each sister wishing that the other sisters would not succeed in having children until she herself had had a live birth. The mother, feeling guilty, of course, about taking DES, could not stand to see the ugliness of the way her "girls" were treating each other.

Although competition is primary with siblings, there are often different problems with parents. Sometimes parents are intrusive, poking and pressuring the couple for news at every turn. Other patients are disturbed because their parents do not seem to understand how overwhelming the problem is and do not ask questions, seeming not to care. The couple must decide whether to reveal the true extent of the problem to families and friends or to be private. Each choice has its drawbacks. Each time the couple opens up to others and gets an unempathetic or insensitive response, there is a tendency to try to reevaluate whether being open is a good policy.

When the people in the social network fail to understand or support the infertile couple adequately, the husband and wife are thrown back onto each other for support. This strengthens the relationship of some couples. For other couples, the differences between male and female socialization, as discussed in Chapter 2, make for rough going.

The effects-of-infertility questionnaire asks, "In your dealings with other people, what gets in the way of close, personal, loving, and mutually satisfying interactions?" Patients answered:

"People do not understand the pain of infertility."

"I am very sensitive to verbal and nonverbal clues. I easily feel rejected by my husband."

"I feel sad, as though I have nothing to offer. I feel too self-consumed."

"With my husband, I am not open enough with my feelings."

"I don't like it when others offer me unsolicited advice."

"If I talk about it to others, I feel as if I am talking about it too much, am boring, and so on."

"I am not able to trust my feelings, and I am very cautious in expressing my feelings to anyone other than my husband, including my mother or my sisters."

"It hurts me so much when people are insensitive and talk about how much they are excited by their pregnancy or their children."

"I feel isolated from other people."

"When I see people with children, I feel I have trouble relating to them because we no longer share many mutual experiences."

"I talk about it so much, I worry about using my friends up."

"I'm afraid to talk about it with friends. I don't want them to pity me."

Why is it that the victims of infertility feel so misunderstood by others, when victims in other situations do not? In this situation, why doesn't the social network provide the necessary support?

First, people do not respond empathetically because they do not understand. Infertility has been a hidden problem. We see pictures on television of a family's house being washed away in a flood, and we get in touch with how awful they must feel. If we hear about a plane crash, we imagine how horrible it would be for us if a loved one were killed. But we cannot see pictures of an "infertility crisis" on television. People who are unaffected have not stopped to think about how they would feel if they were infertile. They haven't paused for a moment and imagined themselves walking a mile in the infertile person's shoes, so they are unempathetic.

Second, others are puzzled by the unpredictability of the hope–despair–hope pattern common in infertility. This unpredictability significantly undermines coping abilities as well. Other crises are linear, or more nearly linear. To understand, one must imagine that an event, such as an illness or a flood happens. There is an acute crisis, a special stage in which a friend or loved one can offer help. Then there is an adjustment to the situation and maybe a recovery. In other words, there is a predictable pattern. The victim is initially upset, gets help, and gets better as time progresses.

Even when the final result of an illness or an accident is unknown, the likely parameters of the outcome may be known in a relatively short time. For instance, Jim has an accident. Initially, it is not clear whether Jim will ever walk again. As his recovery progresses and he makes progress in physical therapy, it becomes clear that he will walk again, but probably with a limp. Jim adjusts to the aftermath, and so does everyone around him. The progress has been in one direction.

Even in the case of an unpredictable disease process, the victim and her friends usually have some sense of the likely outcome. Let us say that Jane has liver cancer. In January, when they find it, the physicians are not very optimistic, and they present Jane and her family with the depressing survival statistics. Jane does well on chemotherapy until the spring, and she feels relief. Everyone thinks that maybe Jane has beaten the cancer. But when she gets worse in June, she does not have the sense that maybe, in July, she'll be better than ever and have an amazing recovery. Nor do her friends and relatives think that she will have a miraculous cure.

Compare these situations to the course of infertility. A patient who has been telling her family that she is losing hope may switch to a new physician or a new treatment program, and the story of the struggle with infertility begins anew with new tests, new treatments, a new prognosis, new uncertainty, and new hope. Patients get very sophisticated medically, understanding the nuances of the options in a way that takes many hours of study. It is difficult for family and friends to understand or even keep up with a constantly changing situation.

Infertility patients do not appear to cope as well as people facing other kinds of crises. They do not get more adjusted to the situation with time; instead, they may get more upset. A fascinating article by Taylor, et al. (1983) reviews the scientific literature on coping with tragedy. Studies have shown that most people who suffer from tragedy overcome the victimizing aspects of their experience and often find something positive about it. The authors quote a person whose home was devastated by a flood who says that the disaster enabled him to get to know his neighbors, a polio victim who found that her disability had sensitized her to other people, and many examples of breast cancer patients who found solace in the fact that "It could have been worse if . . ."

Why do most people make the best of tragic situations? Taylor et al. believe that the condition of "victimhood" is aversive because victimization represents a loss of status, value, or resources, a loss of self control, and a loss of self esteem. Victimization may also be aversive because it forces people to group themselves with other "stigmatized" individuals.

Victims of other kinds of tragedies use a number of cognitive techniques such as "selectively evaluating" themselves to make themselves feel that they are not victims after all. They may, for example, compare themselves with people less fortunate, create hypothetical worse worlds, or see themselves as having benefited from the victimizing event. Taylor et al. commented that "the scientific literature on coping with tragedy . . . suggests that relatively few people feel like victims for very long." (p. 20). Without realizing it, we expect this behavior from people who suffer tragedy: adjusting, not complaining, and making light of their situation a short time after the crisis has passed. Medical personnel, in particular, are accustomed to find patients with more serious and life-threatening events than infertility behaving like brave little soldiers, being cheerful, cooperative, and happy to be alive.

In contrast, infertility patients stay upset. They don't see anything good about their infertility. They don't compare themselves with others and find that they have a better situation than people who have less than they. Instead, they feel that everyone else in the universe is luckier. They don't "adjust," because they don't know what the end will be. They feel angry, depressed, and gypped, and they stay feeling that way for a long, long time. They may seem to be unhelped by emotional support. This attitude has a negative effect on some of their relationships. Because the lay public does not understand that the cyclical nature of the crisis negatively affects attempts to cope with it, they make negative attributions to infertility patients, believing, for example, that they are not coping well because they are "spoiled" or "selfish," and people pull away.

The phenomenon of victims' receiving ambivalent or rejecting reactions in social situations was called "blaming the victim" by Ryan (1971). The same concept was commented on by Lerner (1970) in his conception of the "just world." Lerner believes that the notion that innocent people are victims is threatening; that is, if bad things can happen to good people, then we ourselves are not safe. People thus try to derogate the victims' behavior or character in order to show themselves that the victims deserved to be victimized. Perhaps the long periods of distress and agony suffered by the victims of infertility are just too much for some other people to bear.

One patient, aged thirty-six, said:

> This damned infertility has ruined my relationships. My birthday was last week. I didn't get a single card, not a single one. And I have five good friends who have sent me cards every other year. How could they all forget? How could they all abandon me now, when I need them?
>
> They know I am going through IVF [in vitro fertilization]. Why don't they call to see how I'm doing? I know sometimes I act as if I don't want to talk about it, but wouldn't you think they would know to ask me something? God, what has happened?

The pain of feeling one's beloved family and social networks being destroyed is indescribable. There seem to be few other life crises in which social relationships are equally dismantled. Patients need to understand why this is happening, or at least that their experience is universal in the world of infertility. It doesn't represent a personal failing. And this, too, is a temporary situation. When the infertility crisis is resolved, old friendships will reappear.

Close friendships and empathetic relationships appear to be more salient to women's sense of self-esteem and well-being than they are to men's (Rubin, 1985). Some of our patients are encouraged and soothed by accounts of others who are struggling with their interpersonal relationships. Liebmann-Smith's examples (1987) of the infertility patient's acute sensitivity to slights, descriptions of sibling rivalry, and stories of friends' insensitivity are particularly graphic and helpful (also see Glazer & Cooper, 1988; Menning, 1977).

Men such as Matt, who painted the "No fertile people allowed" on his front door because he could not understand his wife's feelings of envy, need to understand that their wives' envious reactions are so common that they ought to be considered entirely normal, not selfish or pathological. But men can feel socially isolated and envious, too, and they need to be given the opportunity to air these feelings.

There are techniques that patients can learn and use to help control the stress during interpersonal relationships. Menning (1977), for example, suggested that patients set limits on intrusive families. A woman with a mother who calls her weekly to ask what's new can be told, "Don't call us. We'll call you."

The techniques described in Chapter 3, such as stimulus control and behavioral rehearsal, can ameliorate the trials in certain social situations. However, there are times when the patient is really right in complaining, "These sound good in theory, but things are much more complicated in real life."

Here is a case where a letter to their kin made it easier for a couple to get through their first IVF cycle. Tom and Cathy Richardson published this letter in the RESOLVE of the Ocean State, Rhode Island, chapter newsletter (Summer 1991). They sent it to members of both families. Family members responded very positively to the letter, with phone calls, letters, and flowers. Cathy and Tom found that the support from relatives was very helpful during the IVF process. The letter is reprinted here with permission. Perhaps patients who have supportive families can use such a letter with similar good results:

Dear Family,

Hope this letter finds everyone well. I know this may seem a little formal in writing this to everyone instead of a telephone call, but sometimes it is very hard to find the words. The fact is that we need your help. We are about to undergo the most complicated but exciting journey ever. We have been fighting the battle of infertility for 4½ years. On March 22nd, we will begin the process of in vitro fertilization. For 6 weeks, Tom will be giving me shots of medicine and hormones—first for 4 weeks, once a day, and then for 2 weeks, 3 times a day.

(Hopefully, for my sake, he is having a good day, ha ha.) He has to become the cheerleader, and I the patient. Egg retrieval will be done the first or second week in May. The eggs will be fertilized and in 48 hours put back inside my uterus. Two weeks from that day we will know if the pregnancy has taken. If yes, then all our prayers would have been answered. If no, well then we have to decide if we would do this again or live with the fact that we will not be able to have any children of our own. In any event, it will mean the end to a very long and sometimes quite painful emotional and physical ordeal. Thank god our relationship is strong enough to endure all that has happened and is about to happen. Many couples do not make it through.

I hope you all can understand just how alone and alienated we can feel sometimes in the midst of this big, beautiful family full of wonderful children, whom we love so very much. This is where your help is needed. We've come to realize that we cannot go through this alone. We need to know that we have your understanding and support and prayers. The doctors have this procedure down very scientifically, so really there is nothing more we can do but keep a positive attitude and pray that we will be successful. Of course, all of this could not be happening at a worse time with Tom being out of work and having a bad back. But there will always be circumstances out of our control, right?

We honestly feel that with everyone's support and prayers it would certainly help us through. That's what families are for, and we certainly are blessed with a beautiful family.

Well, the words came much easier on paper. Hope you all understand. Thank you. We love you all so very much.

Tom and Cathy

The following is a case in which all the therapeutic advice in the world didn't create a good outcome:

Donna, who was very attached to her mother and to her sister, wanted to get pregnant for the second time. Her first child, a boy, was ten. Her secondary infertility had lasted for eight years, but she wouldn't give up. Talking to her sister, Serita, who knew how pained she was by the secondary infertility, Donna mentioned that she wanted to name her hoped-for child Vanessa Louise after their mother.

Serita, who was almost seven years younger than Donna, got pregnant several months later. She told Donna that if the child was a girl, she planned to name it Vanessa Louise because she wanted to name her child after their mother, too. Naturally, Donna was very upset. Donna spoke with her therapist, who encouraged her to tell Serita how much turmoil this name would cause her. Donna did reveal her feelings, but Serita countered by saying that Donna might never be able to get pregnant again, whereas she, Serita, was already pregnant. Serita felt that she had every right to use that name. Seven months later, little Vanessa Louise was born to Serita. Donna was so wounded that she couldn't speak to Serita for months. It is hard to avoid a sister, so they were speaking again, but they were most certainly not close. Donna was still not pregnant. What was the right and the wrong in this situation?

In another case, a patient's attempt to ask for what she needed and to use the stimulus control technique to handle her envy and sadness at her sister's babies' christening did not work out satisfactorily:

Cindy and George had been trying to have a child for six years. Cindy had severe endometriosis, and surgical and drug treatments had not been effective. She was trying in vitro fertilization.

Cindy was the eldest girl in a large, close, traditional Catholic family. All the siblings had gone to the same Catholic schools, and all had similar interests. The sisters were especially close. They ranged in age from the early twenties to the mid-thirties, and all were married and planned families.

In the winter, Cindy's younger sister Kathy got pregnant, with twins. At exactly the same time, Cindy was undergoing IVF, for the third time. She had a successful egg retrieval, and in a few days, the embryologist contacted Cindy and George to let them know that there were two eggs that had fertilized so beautifully that they had divided into eighteen cells each. The embryologist had never seen anything like this and was very inspired. They scheduled the transfer immediately.

Meanwhile, Cindy was so excited that she called Kathy. The two of them talked about getting together and jointly taking walks, each of them with a twin stroller. These phone dialogues went on for several days because Cindy was confined to her house so as to allow the embryos the best chance to implant. Unfortunately, the embryos did not develop. Because she was Catholic and because she knew that embryos were so very alive, Cindy was devastated and experienced the loss as a miscarriage.

Cindy went into a full-blown grief reaction for about a month, during which time the members of the extended family were supportive. She seemed to be feeling a little less depressed for a while. But as the weeks progressed, Kathy got larger and larger with her twins, and her physician was afraid that, if she didn't get full bed rest, she would deliver them very prematurely. The whole extended family network of women began to rally around Kathy. Kathy's twins were the center of most of the conversation and activity.

As one might imagine, all the talk of Kathy's twins reminded Cindy over and over of the twins she and George had lost. She began to get more depressed again. She wanted her mother to come over and be with her, but her mother was tied up with driving Kathy to her doctor and with ultrasound appointments, with cooking for Kathy, with cleaning for Kathy, and on and on. She had to make sure that Kathy's twins, who were very much alive, had the best chance.

Cindy then wanted to get some support from her other sisters, but they didn't understand her loss. She talked to her mother and told her that she was thinking of giving her siblings some pamphlets and booklets on supporting people emotionally through infertility.

"No," commented her mother, "they'll just think that is silly." Cindy would just have to accept that Kathy needed to be the center of attention right now. Cindy, the eldest, shouldn't expect understanding from her younger siblings.

The months were excruciating for Cindy. Kathy was doing very well on bed rest, and her babies were getting to be a considerable size. Soon, Kathy's babies were born, by cesarean section. They were quite healthy, and the family was elated. But because of the C-section, Kathy continued to need the mother's help, particularly during the day, when Kathy's husband was at work.

Cindy tried to get some time with her mother at night at the family home. She was depressed and envious about the twins. Her mother was getting fed up with Cindy's neediness and depression and complained to her that she "brought a black cloud into the house with her when she came." The mother was basking in the joy of having two new, healthy twin granddaughters, and Cindy was raining on her parade.

The time came for Kathy's babies' christening. Kathy wanted Cindy to be the godmother, which Cindy agreed to, remarkably enough. Cindy was sufficiently mature and giving to know that someday she would feel better about her loss, and she did not want to alienate Kathy, who was probably her favorite sister. However, Cindy asked that someone else stand in for her that day at church. She did not feel she could remain composed while standing in the limelight with her sister, the priest, and the two thriving babies. She offered to prepare the food for the celebration afterward and to show up at the family party at the house.

This is what did transpire. However, Cindy knew that she had no one's blessing in protecting herself. She had dampened their ability to enjoy the christening themselves. Basically, her sisters and her mother made it crystal clear that they thought that this decision was very selfish of her. Cindy felt isolated and censured for weeks afterward.

In situations like Cindy's and Donna's, the therapist becomes a special part of what may be a very small support system of people who do understand and accept the feelings of infertility. Hopefully, these cases provide the reader with a good understanding of why joining a support group can be so valuable to infertile people.

Encouraging Patients to Join RESOLVE

The one group of people who truly understand the stresses of infertility are people who are experiencing it. There are many accounts in the lay literature of the benefits of joining RESOLVE, the national support group for infertility (Borg & Lasker, 1987; Liebmann-Smith, 1987; Menning, 1977; Salzer, 1986). Furthermore, research studies by Simons (1988) and Cooper (1979) have shown that participation in RESOLVE support groups lessens anxiety and depression and increases a sense of being in control of life. Although not all patients are willing to identify themselves as being infertile by joining this self-help organization, therapists who practice in areas where RESOLVE groups are available should encourage membership.

Summary

There are many reasons why patients are disappointed in the help and understanding they get from the fertile world. The patient's loss of a valued social network is a threat to her emotional well-being and self-esteem.

The therapist must be instrumental in helping the patient to cope with difficulties in existing relationships by sharing concrete techniques and suggestions. Such approaches are not guaranteed, however, and the question of how to relate to one's family, particularly, often remains a challenge throughout the course of infertility. Therefore the therapist should encourage the patient to form new bonds with others who comprehend the experience of infertility. Participation in a RESOLVE support group is invaluable, if there is one nearby.

7

The Realm of the Physical

Two of Lazarus's modes (1981) speak of the world of the physical body, the mode of drugs/biology, which has to do with how well a person treats her body, and the mode of sensation.

The first mode typically needs little intervention by the therapist. Both partners in infertile couples tend to have good health habits. They don't usually drink, don't use drugs (except fertility medicines), often eat well, and sometimes exercise. The men are trying to develop healthy sperm, which are negatively affected by drugs. The women are trying to prepare their bodies to create and nurture a baby, so in their conscious health habits, they pay scrupulous attention to their physical practices.

The second mode, sensation, is a major arena for therapeutic work. In the initial evaluation, the therapist should give the patient Lazarus's extremely detailed checklist of physical sensations (1991) to fill out. (See Appendix 1) Even though patients consciously take very good care of their bodies, one is struck nevertheless by the tremendous physical toll of infertility. The stress of trying to cope and the side effects of the fertility medications together create many discomforts and unpleasant physical sensations.

Compared with women who come into care for other reasons, women with infertility tend to have many more somatic complaints. Because they are inclined to tolerate significant bodily anguish in order to bear a child, frequently they do not disclose their physical discomfort if the therapist does not inquire.

The therapist must query frequently, and very specifically, about tension, inability to relax, trouble sleeping, stomach trouble, fatigue, back pain, other aches and pains, tremors, chest pains, rapid heartbeats—the entire panoply of possible physical symptoms. No one else in the patient's world will probe in detail into how well she is faring physically. The patient doesn't share this with friends; if she talks about it at all, it is only to say that she feels "rotten and depressed." When her physician inquires, at each meeting, about how she feels, she will reply, "Just fine," meaning that she is still alive and will willingly tolerate the next round of medical interventions.

Common answers to queries about patients' physical sensations are myriad complaints about "fatigue and exhaustion," "awful insomnia after my last failure at in vitro fertilization (IVF)," "heart pains," "a total inability to relax," "anxiety and twitches," "heartburn," "restlessness," "eternal vigilance and tension," "obsession with every sensation," "racing heart and headaches" (from medications), "feeling bloated," "vicious headaches and eye problems" (also from medications), and "no energy, total apathy."

Answers about physical sensations from week to week are often the best gauge of a patient's stress level. When a patient reveals negative physical sensations indicating that the infertility is taxing her beyond her limits, an important part of the treatment plan is teaching relaxation skills. Patients can learn not to create as much tension in the first place by paying attention to their *tracking order* (see Chapter 3). Aside from the side effects of fertility medications, many physiological reactions are a response to the patient's upsetting thoughts or images:

> Karen had felt better after a few weeks of psychotherapy. She wasn't feeling as "fragile and tense" physically, and she wasn't angry at her husband anymore. But at the fourth session, she came in complaining of a bad headache. With detailed questioning, we were able to track the origins of the headache. It had appeared after she saw her fertility specialist. In the course of her appointment with him, he had mentioned that the scarring in her fallopian tubes may have been a result of pelvic inflammatory disease (PID). He said that she could have had PID and not even known about it.
>
> Apparently, this observation set off a whole chain of thoughts and beliefs in Karen's mind. She thought that the infection may have been the result of a rather unhealthy love affair she had had with an unsavory fellow two years before she had met her husband. She felt guilty and ashamed about this affair. As one thought led to another, she blamed herself for her own infertility. The headaches soon followed.

As patients learn to identify and control distressing relationships, upsetting beliefs, and painful imagery, they gain some mastery over their physiology.

Along with helping the patient to use imagery to relax (see Chapter 4), the therapist should offer her several other stress-control techniques. Stroebel (1982) created the "quieting reflex" (QR), which patients can learn in a few minutes. The QR helps stop the physiological feelings of arousal. Part of the sequence involves movements of the head, neck, and chest that reduce physical tension in these areas. It also includes breathing and imagery. The sequence is so rapid that it can be used, in public, as often as needed. For instance, patients sitting in a physician's waiting room and getting progressively more tense can do the QR while waiting without attracting attention to themselves.

Reid Wilson's cue-controlled deep-muscle relaxation exercise, in the book *Don't Panic* (1986), takes about forty minutes and is the best deep relaxation exercise for patients who haven't mastered any particular relaxation technique. It is useful to make a tape of the instructions and to send the patient home to practice with it. Wilson claimed that research has shown that people who experience predominantly physical symptoms of anxiety can diminish these tensions best through physically active techniques such as cue-controlled deep-muscle relaxation, rather than meditation. Both Wilson and Shoebel's exercises should be detailed for the patient.

Of course, a regular physical exercise program can help control anxiety, but patients frequently complain that they are too depressed to maintain regular exercise schedules, even if they did so before infertility. I am more likely to recommend to women patients that they occasionally "treat themselves" to the kind of nonaerobic stretch-and-tone class that works the muscles in the pelvis, giving the exerciser pleasant, relaxed sensual and sexual feelings.

Happily, professionals are beginning to tout the necessity of stress control techniques. Domar et al. (1990) described the success of a ten-week stress-management program for infertile women that includes learning about the physiology of stress, relaxation training, training in meditation and breathing, and cognitive restructuring.

Making a Recuperation Plan

Occasionally, patients become severely depleted physically, and no one acknowledges this depletion or addresses it, not even the patient herself. Some women who go through intra-uterine insemination (IUI) with Pergonal or in vitro fertilization and fail to get pregnant experience total physical exhaustion afterward, along with regret and depression.

However, after the cycle is over, their ties with the medical clinic loosen until it is time for the next intervention. The therapist needs to acknowledge the patient's physical weariness and help her to make a plan to address it, not just to offer emotional support. Here is the plan created for a woman named Jill:

Jill was a very astute and articulate woman of thirty-three. She was a totally lovable person, warm and nurturing. She came from a large, happy family. All she ever wanted was to be a mother. She had married Sal, her warm and funny husband, when she was very young. The union was solid, passionate, and committed. They had had one child, Sal, Jr., who was eight and a handful. Jill prided herself on being an excellent mother.

Jill and Big Sal had wanted several children, but Jill developed tubal problems. She had been in infertility treatment for six years at the same clinic. Tubal surgery hadn't worked. She was on her third attempt at IVF.

During the weeks when she was medicated to prepare for the IVF attempt, everyone in Jill's life tried to support her. Jill needed a lot of shots, around the clock. Sal gave her the shots, much as he hated it, because she couldn't stand to do it to herself. She had a terrible reaction to the fertility medications each time; her whole body raced and she had chronic headaches, so her husband had learned to take over the care of Sal, Jr., during these weeks. The hospital staff had treated her for years, and her physician and nurse were quite attached to her. They kept in close touch with her to make sure that her ovaries didn't hyperstimulate. Her siblings and her mother checked in periodically to see how she was doing.

Unfortunately, the third in vitro attempt failed. The next scheduled session after the failure, a few days later, Jill felt too exhausted to come to her psychotherapy appointment. She wanted to sleep while Sal, Jr., was in school and come to her session the next week.

When I saw Jill again, nine days after the failed IVF attempt, she was in shambles. Her skin was pale, she was listless, and she complained of muscular aches and pains at the sites of the injections and exhaustion due to insomnia. What had happened?

During the prior weeks, her body had gone through the wringer. The timing of the medication is crucial during IVF. Jill had been afraid to go to sleep before 10 P.M. each night because she was afraid she would not wake up in time to remind Sal to give her her injection. Once she had the shot, the medication would make her "speedy" so that she couldn't fall asleep until much later. When she finally fell asleep, she wouldn't sleep for long. Sometimes she wanted to be up to say good-bye to Sal, Jr. More recently, she had had to get up at 5:30 A.M. to get to the hospital for the morning ultrasound procedure. In two weeks, she had become quite sleep-deprived. And now, after the failure of IVF, she was very upset and had been having insomnia.

Meanwhile, it was assumed that she no longer "needed" Big Sal because the in vitro attempt was over and she wasn't on medication. So Sal wasn't helping out with Sal, Jr. Big Sal was awfully beat anyway, after taking such good care of Jill, and doing his regular job plus all of Jill's household and motherly duties. (Well, he did what he could. The house was a wreck.) Jill felt too grateful to Sal for his past help to ask for any more now. Anyway, Jill felt guilty about having spent so little time with Sal, Jr., during the IVF attempt and wanted to spend a lot of "quality" time with him now to make up for it. She also wanted to get the house back in order.

Now that the attempt had failed, some of the other sources of support had dried up. The hospital no longer called her daily. Her siblings knew how disappointed she was, but it was hard for them to tolerate her feelings, so they weren't in such close contact. No one really knew the sad physical state she was in.

Jill and I created the following plan to deal with her exhaustion:

• I spoke with her internist and got her some light sleeping medication for five nights, to get her back on schedule.

- Even though she felt she should spend every available minute with Sal, Jr., Jill agreed to take a one-hour break when Sal, Jr., was home and let him play a computer game while she rested (i.e., to let up on "quality time").

- She was to massage her black-and-blue marks from the injection and praise herself for surviving the ordeal.

- She would get a notebook and list her negative thoughts during the day and refute them. She would stop negative thoughts at other times, especially at bedtime.

- She would listen to a relaxation tape every day. She was not to catch up on housework until she felt better.

- She was to tell Sal that she wanted to go out to dinner as a family several times during the next two weeks so that she wouldn't have to cook and clean up.

The plan worked. In one week, she was feeling much better. The very-short-term sleeping pills were a significant help, as they allowed Jill to get several straight nights of good rest. That rest, in turn, helped her to control some of her most depressing thoughts, so she focused less on aches and pains and felt better.

The psychotherapist needs to be attuned to the infertility patient's physical state. Often, the therapist is the only person who will give the patient permission to "baby herself" in order to recuperate.

Helping the Patient to Find Pleasure in Her Body

In this society, men are taught that they have to be strong and powerful and to be good providers, and women are taught that they must be pretty to attract a powerful and wealthy man to take care of them. When a woman feels that her body is defective, she may feel that she no longer has any value as a person. Often, women who don't feel good about their bodies do not feel that their bodies deserve sensual (or sexual) pleasure. Thus whether or not an woman can get any pleasure from her body during infertility hinges on her body image (Fisher, 1989).

In answer to a question about what sensations she would like to have more often, one woman was in touch with the connection and wrote, "Ugh. I can't get into this. I see myself now as fat and ugly, and I weight only 112 pounds."

The feelings of depression and depletion engendered by infertility are so overpowering that without help from a therapist, many patients cannot rationally answer questions about their sensual selves. After traveling down the road of life with infertility problems for a while, people just plain stop loving their bodies. I am not talking only about the sensual pleasures connected with sexuality. People struggling with infertility are not attuned to their *senses* anymore and no longer realize that what they see, smell, touch, and hear can be soothing, exciting, or nurturing. (However, many people, probably most, do remember taste as a source of pleasure. I hear frequent complaints about overeating to dull the pain.)

Patients need assistance in realizing that they have disowned their own bodies. The imagery in this parable may help:

Therapist: Let's say that you buy a brand new car. You love it madly. It takes you to great places, gives you no trouble. You depend on your car, and it looks so shiny and bright. It works so well that it contributes to your good feelings about yourself, and to your security. Your car is your friend for several years.

Given the laws of the universe of cars, the situation changes. One day you take your car on a long, supposedly relaxing trip to the mountains, or the ocean, or the big city. And when you are far, far from home, the car dies. And there is a big problem. And a long, expensive towing job. And a large repair bill.

But you forgive your car, for the time being. You go to some more nice places in it, and it behaves OK. But you don't feel quite so great about that car of yours.

So you go about your business, driving the car. But life goes on, and time and time again, the car continues to let you down. It makes you late to work and needs to be in the shop for long stretches of time. By this point, your entire feeling about the car has changed. You no longer like your car, let alone love it. You feel hostile toward your car. It doesn't add to your secure feelings in life; it makes life feel more precarious. It no longer contributes to your good feelings about yourself. When you get into your car, you are seized with what does not seem to be an unreasonable feeling of dread: What is this damned car going to do next?

Assuming that you have the money, you begin to make plans to dump the car. And you do so. You get rid of this damned unpredictable and unpleasant car, and you feel more in control of your life again.

The problem with infertility, of course, is that bodies aren't cars. We go through this same feeling of rejection toward our bodies, but we can't really get rid of them. And enjoying anything about our bodies during infertility seems to hold about the same amount of joy that we might have in the prospect of taking that damned old car out, again, for a long "pleasure ride" deep in the boondocks some dark, chilly December night: "Gee, do I have to?"

Another technique to help the patient regain some positive association with her body is to have her focus on pleasant sensations that are not tied to thoughts of sex and reproduction. Have the patient brainstorm: What are things that I will still enjoy, even in the midst of infertility? What are sensual things my partner and I enjoy together? Watching a beautiful scene, like . . . ? Going to a museum and looking at . . . ? Listening to . . . music? Listening to the ocean and smelling the salt air? Smelling . . . ? Stretching? Lying in the sun? Riding a horse? Sailing? Exercise? Sitting by the fire and feeling the heat and seeing the flames? Lying by the fire and hugging? Petting the cat? Feeling . . .?

Appendix 3 contains a patient worksheet exploring sensuality.

The therapist is the only person in the patient's life who will pay close attention to the realm of the physical and of sensation. The therapist should therefore ask specifically about discomforts, teach relaxation skills, and make a recuperation plan if necessary. During times that are not acute crises, ask the patient what pleasurable experiences she and her husband have given themselves.

The patient won't thank the therapist for doing this, of course. When meeting up with the inevitable resistance to doing these things, the therapist must explore the patient's irrational thoughts that she does not deserve pleasure because she is infertile.

8

Using a Multimodal Approach to Work with an Infertility Patient: The Case Of Ann

I n the preceding chapters, we explored in some depth how infertility affects the patient's behavior, feelings, sensations, imagery, cognition, interpersonal relationships, and physical self. This chapter uses the case study method to illustrate how a psychotherapist, taking a multimodal approach, treated Ann (not her real name), a woman who entered psychotherapy because of overwhelming distress about her inability to conceive. While going through the case, the reader should bear in mind that multimodal therapy (MMT) is created to match each patient's particular constellation of symptoms. This was Ann's treatment. Different techniques and approaches would be used with other patients.

Ann's Presenting Problem

Ann was a tall, quiet, intelligent, thirty-seven-year-old Catholic woman who worked as a lawyer in downtown Boston. She had been married for several years to Joseph, also a lawyer. Referred by RESOLVE, a nonprofit, national organization that helps infertile couples, Ann sought help for severe depression after three years of unsuccessful attempts to conceive. Ann felt her marriage was deteriorating because of the stress of childlessness.

She had seen another therapist who understood the emotional aspects of infertility, but Ann felt that this woman was not comfortable with Ann's anger. Ann said to her new therapist, "I just hope that you can help me deal with my anger, frustration, and disappointment!"

Indeed, Ann was full of fury. At the beginning of her medical treatment, Ann's original physician had missed diagnosing her endometriosis. When she switched to a very highly respected specialist and he did exploratory surgery, she found out that she had "wasted two years trying." She could not have conceived

140

because she had needed surgery to take care of some scarring in her fallopian tubes. She was very angry at the first physician.

Over the past year, she had been undergoing an aggressive series of infertility treatments with this top specialist and had had several surgeries. She finally became pregnant, much to her and her husband's joy. Unfortunately, she had an ectopic pregnancy (where the embryo begins to grow in the fallopian tube instead of the uterus). As a result of the ectopic pregnancy, in order to save her life, she had still another surgery to remove the damaged fallopian tube. This procedure further diminished her chances of conceiving.

At this point, she was taking several powerful, commonly prescribed infertility drugs, which she tolerated quite poorly. Ann did not feel well physically. She had severe stomach trouble and suspected that a lot of her fatigue was also a result of the medication. She was "just waiting to see if she would get pregnant again." If she did not get pregnant spontaneously on the medications, the next step would be in vitro fertilization (IVF). This would mean frequent treatments with even more powerful fertility drugs and certain invasive surgical procedures each cycle. Ann was not at all sure that she could bear the medications, the ultrasound procedures, the invasive procedures, and the loss of control over her own body during the IVF process.

Ann complained of feeling anxious and obsessed about getting pregnant. She also reported feeling depressed, angry, withdrawn, and in "despair."

Ann's History

Joseph, Ann's husband, was a bright, serious, attractive and ambitious man. Ann felt her six-year marriage had been on the whole, a good one. Joseph seemed to be "on her team" in most areas.

As a couple, they were basically in agreement in their values and beliefs, and each of them interacted well with the other's extended family. Before the stress of the infertility, they had enjoyed their leisure time together doing "fun things" and had spent pleasant times with mutual friends.

However, Ann found one aspect of Joseph's personality very trying. Joseph was not warm or especially open emotionally, physically, or sexually. He had difficulty expressing his feelings verbally and didn't talk much. Ann complained that he was not affectionate enough. And his level of sexual desire was not as high as hers. Ann blamed this side of Joseph's behavior on his "cold and distant" family.

Ann's early life had been quite happy. She came from a large, affectionate, religious family. She recalled wonderful memories of having her siblings as her closest friends and playmates and of many joyful family gatherings at holidays throughout her life.

She felt close to her siblings and to both of her parents. She described her father as "loving and caring" and her mother in the same way, and as "always willing to listen and help me as best she can" and as "strong emotionally." Ann felt loved, respected and understood by her parents.

The Evaluation

At the end of the first interview, Ann was given the MMT life history questionnaire (see Appendix 1) to complete and mail back to the therapist. This tool is used by multimodal therapists to pinpoint problem areas across all of the seven modalities (behavior, feelings, physical sensations, imagery, thoughts, interpersonal relationships, and biological factors).

A bright and highly motivated woman, Ann filled the questionnaire out thoroughly. She pinpointed several problem behaviors: withdrawal when she was among other people, sleep disturbances, crying, and outbursts of temper, especially with her spouse. She reported that she wished she could read, garden, and work on her handicrafts more often.

Ann revealed that she was plagued by a number of unpleasant feelings often: anger, annoyance, sadness, anxiety, fearfulness, envy, conflict, hopelessness, unhappiness, tenseness, loneliness, and low self-esteem. She had a negative body image because of her surgery. She naturally wished to experience more happiness, relaxation, and optimism.

Stomach trouble, fatigue, and tension were unpleasant sensations that Ann suffered often. When asked to list pleasant sensations, she replied with being held, massages, and eating favorite foods.

Ann was a person who used imagery a lot. She was full of helpless images, and images of being hurt, losing control, and not coping. When asked what was her most unpleasant image, she cited an image of herself in the hospital, intravenous needles in her arm, weak, sick, and in pain after surgery for her ectopic pregnancy. She was frequently upset by spontaneous imagery of pregnant women or women playing with babies and young children. When queried about a safe place, she offered: "tucked deep under the covers of my bed."

Even though she had quite a good self-concept, seeing herself as intelligent, sensitive, loyal, trustworthy, considerate, honest, and hard-working, Ann was bothered by some very negative thoughts. Mainly, these centered on ideas such as "Life is empty, a waste; there is nothing to look forward to." She worried that she might never be happy again. She recognized that her "bad attitude" was a problem in and of itself.

Her interpersonal relationships usually were good, but they had suffered because of the infertility. She had two close friends and was very close to her mother and her sisters. However, she was not sharing her feelings about her infertility with family or friends. She commented that she was "very cautious about expressing my feelings to other people."

Ann had difficulty with some of her feelings. She felt envy when friends or relatives were pregnant. Also, it appeared that she had a difficult time being assertive about her needs and waited until she exploded with anger.

In the physiological area, Ann was living a very healthy life. She engaged in aerobic exercise regularly. She took no drugs at all except for the prescribed fertility drugs (Serophene, Parlodel, and progesterone. She never ingested alcohol or caffeine. She ate three well-balanced, healthy meals a day.

The Treatment

First Session

The first session, Ann looked gray and grim. As she told her story, she alternated between anger, bitterness, and great grief, and she did not seem to have a happy cell in her body. She felt all alone in life.

She had little good to say about her marital relationship. She said that she and Joseph were no longer close, and that they never had any fun anymore. She was furious at her husband for not "being more sympathetic" and warmer to her, and she stated that if she were not so "damaged" by her infertility, scars from the surgeries, and loss of one fallopian tube, she would consider leaving him. However, she said, she no longer felt attractive to herself, let alone to other men.

She was being eaten up by envy of an unwed cousin's accidental pregnancy. She felt disappointed that her husband did not understand her feelings of resentment of this cousin. In general, she portrayed her feelings toward her husband in such negative terms that the therapist wondered if permanent damage had been done to the marriage.

Although Ann was usually very close to her mother, she had felt alienated since the mother had commented that the infertility was perhaps "God's will." Ann had not revealed her problems to her mother-in-law, who was pressuring Ann and Joseph for grandchildren. Ann felt that the infertility was too personal to discuss with her friends. When the therapist commented that Ann might benefit from joining a RESOLVE support group or sharing more with some other people, she replied that all she needed was for the therapist to "be there" for her.

The therapist began treatment by acknowledging Ann's real suffering, both because of her grief at not knowing whether she could ever give birth to a biological child, and because of the insult to her body from the surgeries, the loss of part of her reproductive system, the scarring, and the drugs. The therapist assured her that both anger and envy were common among infertility patients. At the same time, the therapist proposed taking some steps to control the anger.

Ann's tendency to isolate herself and not to get support during this life crisis was of concern. It was particularly sad for Ann to feel so estranged from her mother, her lifelong best friend. The therapist explored Ann's beliefs about why people said hurtful things to her about her infertility. Soon Ann acknowledged, "I guess that I tend to see malice where there is just ignorance."

In the same vein, they looked at Ann's rage at her husband. First, Ann talked about her resentment of Joseph for being so "cold and factual." The fact that he was not visibly upset about their inability to have children disturbed her and made her feel like the "crazy one." The therapist explained in detail why it is common for husbands to act less disturbed than wives about infertility, because of the differences in how men and women are socialized. Culturally, motherhood is seen as being the important role for adult women to a greater extent than fatherhood is for adult males.

As she talked, Ann revealed that she actually blamed Joseph for her infertility. She had wanted children a few years before he had felt they could afford them. His wishes prevailed, and they waited. It became clear that, every time she got her menstrual period, and she was filled with grief and longing for a child, she told herself that this horror was his fault. Maybe if they had begun trying sooner, she would have been more fertile. They might even have had a few children already.

The therapist pointed out the irrationality of this belief and explained the concept of the tracking order. Ann's conviction that Joseph had caused the infertility by postponing having children fueled the fires of Ann's anger toward him. Did Ann think that Joseph would have made them delay childbearing if he had thought that this would be the outcome?

Ann stopped short. She had not noticed how frequently she had angry thoughts and feelings about Joseph. She immediately realized that there was no way that Joseph would have intentionally made them go through all of this travail. His makeup was simply to be cautious, and assuming that they would be fertile, he had thought it best to wait until they had more cash. Ann was a bit startled to realize the degree to which she had blamed Joseph, the irrationality of her position, and the relationship of her thought process to her feelings.

But she wasn't done with her anger at her husband yet. She said that she needed a lot more touching in the relationship. She needed him to be affectionate and hold her, but she could not bring herself to ask him. The therapist wondered out loud whether, given Ann's anger, Joseph would think that she wanted physical affection.

As it turned out, Ann's "outbursts of temper" occurred when she needed to be comforted and Joe did not soothe her. She then provoked a fight, which made the two of them feel more distant. The therapist asked Ann to keep track, in a notebook, of the times she picked a fight with Joseph and what she had been feeling in the minutes before the fight. Ann agreed that she needed to control her irrational anger at her husband and then, when he began to sense that she felt friendly toward him again, be assertive and ask for affection.

Before the session drew to a close, Ann was asked to participate in the crystal ball exercise. The therapist said, "Imagine that I have a crystal ball that tells the future. As I look into the crystal ball, I see that no matter what you do—no matter how much you suffer, no matter what medical treatments you undergo—you will never have a biological child. Now, what would you do?"

Ann paused and thought, and then said that she and Joseph could adopt. Joseph felt fine about adoption. She went on to say that, when she had been small, she had once thought of having a big family and adopting several children. She spontaneously offered that she thought that she would have no trouble loving a child who was not related to her genetically. And remarkably, she added that she figured that an adopted child would want to search for her biological roots. Once the child reached adulthood, Ann would help her in the search.

The therapist commented on Ann's openness to the idea of adoption. As you will remember, Ann had a great deal of spontaneous imagery about childlessness. The therapist instructed Ann to consciously picture the pleasures of life with adopted children when she was feeling despondent about the idea of never having any children to love.

Adoption seemed like a very real emotional and financial possibility for Ann and her husband, even though Ann was still in the middle of the process of grieving the loss of her fertility. The therapist suggested that Ann monitor her thoughts over the coming week. When she found herself thinking that "Life is empty, a waste—with nothing to look forward to," she was to counter this thought with the thought that "Although we may never have a child who is biologically related to us, if we adopt we will still have a child to love."

Between the first and second sessions, Ann mailed her completed questionnaire to the therapist. The scoring of the results showed that Ann was a person who scored very high in imagery. Also, despite what she had said about her husband in the first session, she gave her marriage relatively high marks when she answered the marital satisfaction section of the questionnaire.

An MMT Evaluation of Ann

Behavior	Unable to express her feelings when hurt in social situations.
	Doesn't communicate with husband when angry or disappointed.
	Withdrawal.
	Outbursts of temper.
Affect	Sad.
	Envious.
	Anger often based on irrational thoughts.
	Tremendous guilt based on ideas.

Sensations	Fertility medications cause physical distress.
	Stomach trouble.
	Fatigue.
	Tension.
	Negative body image.
Imagery	Imagery about childless future causes depression.
	However, images of adoption are positive.
	Maximize positive adoption imagery.
Cognitions	Has perfectionistic standards.
	Beliefs about husband's causing infertility are a problem.
	Beliefs that God would let her have a biological child if He loved her are a problem.
Interpersonal	General deficiency in assertiveness skills.
	Isolation is increased by her difficulty in telling others when her feelings are hurt.
Physical	Takes good care of her body.
	Fertility medications cause extreme physical distress.

Second Session

Ann entered the second appointment looking like a different person, much less angry and tense. She reported on a rather unsatisfactory consultation with a new infertility specialist, but she said that she felt somewhat less trapped by her infertility, now that she was considering adoption as a possibility. She asked the therapist for some books to read on adoption and took one home with her.

She had had a better week with her husband and was seeing the marriage in more positive terms. She had done the homework diligently. Having to document her critical thoughts about Joseph had caused her behavior to change. When her husband disappointed her slightly, she monitored her reactions and was able to avoid seeing his actions as malicious.

Furthermore, she had been more assertive, too. She had taken the initiative to discuss infertility with her mother again, this time telling her that the comment about "God's will" had upset her deeply. Her mother understood her and apologized. Ann felt much more safe in two important relationships, and considerably less isolated in the world.

Still, she was desperately hoping for a biological child. And she was very upset and angered by her cousin's illegitimate pregnancy. Ann thought that this cousin knew of the fertility problems that she and Joseph were having and that she was purposely flaunting her pregnancy in front of Ann by constantly talking about how she looked and felt and touching her stomach. Ann was going to have to attend a picnic with this pregnant cousin, and she wanted some help with managing her anxiety, her hate, and her envy.

The therapist reassured Ann that jealousy of other people's pregnancies was extremely common among infertile women. They discussed what an upsetting and unpleasant experience it was for Ann, a religious person with a strong sense of right and wrong, to feel so envious. However, the therapist also commented on Ann's persistent sense that people were trying to hurt her, when in fact they simply may have been insensitive to her infertility. Ann's belief that her cousin's behavior was intentionally hurtful made her feel even worse—feeling really angry and hateful toward her cousin, as well as sad about her own lack of fertility and jealous of her cousin's obvious success.

Together, Ann and the therapist constructed a plan to help Ann handle seeing her cousin at the picnic. Ann was asked to monitor her thoughts during the next week and to use the technique of thought stopping when she told herself that her cousin was intentionally being cruel about Ann's infertility. The therapist also invited Ann to think of a constructive way of telling her cousin how painful the experience of infertility was.

Next, the therapist used the technique of behavioral rehearsal. She helped Ann to "walk through" the dreaded scene in her own mind. Ann was to imagine each and every unpleasant situation that she anticipated would happen at the gathering. She was to project it in her mind, frame by frame, as if it were a movie. In her imagination, she was to try out different responses to the interactions until she came upon one that worked well. Once she came upon a good way of handling a given situation, she would practice it.

Ann closed her eyes and began to run through the scene in her mind. The first time she did this, Ann imagined kicking her cousin right in her pregnant stomach! She was a little uneasy at revealing the depth of her hostility to another human being and laughed nervously. Although she noted that she could never do such a thing, and that it was no solution to the problem, she felt some relief in bringing the ugly feelings into the light.

Because this image didn't work as a real solution, Ann kept running through the scene in her head. She finally came up with a good script: She could bring her cousin a lovely baby gift and give it to her soon after they arrived at the gathering. That would give Ann a simple way to acknowledge the pregnancy. After that, Ann felt that, if she needed to, she could avoid her cousin for the rest of the evening.

Next, she thought of talking to her husband ahead of time about how difficult it would be for her to be in the same room with her pregnant cousin. Even though Ann knew that her husband would probably never share or even understand these feelings, Ann felt that Joe's just knowing what she was going through at the time would help.

In addition, the therapist taught Ann a quick relaxation exercise (the quieting reflex), that she could use, unobtrusively, right at the picnic if she felt her body begin to tense up. (Stroebel, 1982).

After Ann came up with her plan, she felt more relaxed about getting together with her family. The session was drawing to a close. The therapist reminded Ann about her homework for the coming week.

Third Session

Some important breakthroughs came during the third session. Ann was pleased by how well she had handled the picnic with her cousin. She had used all of the strategies that she and the therapist had rehearsed. She had kept her anxiety to a minimum during the days preceding the picnic by monitoring her thoughts. She had used "rational self-talk" to dispute the idea that her cousin was purposely flaunting her happiness with her pregnancy whenever this idea arose. She had told her mother and Joseph before the event that she would be feeling vulnerable and could use an extra knowing glance or hug. And she was pleased with herself because she had been able to give the cousin her baby gift and act appropriately by wishing her good luck. After her "performance," she had allowed herself to unobtrusively avoid much contact with her cousin for the rest of the day.

But Ann felt the problem was far from solved. Although she had acted rationally, she said that she felt as angry as ever about the cousin's pregnancy. She began by talking about how hypocritical she felt her whole family was being. Because they were such good Catholics, how could they be so enthusiastic about this illegitimate pregnancy and celebrate it? As she talked about this, she began to cry.

She was trying to figure out, if God is just, why God would let this particularly unwholesome and promiscuous cousin become pregnant, when Ann, who had been good, was barren. In the course of her moral accounting of lives, she had dug up a whole list of major and minor sins that she herself had committed. She wondered if she was being punished for being mean to a younger sister when she was baby-sitting, or whether she was being punished for living with a boyfriend. Or perhaps it was punishment for having used birth control before she was married. She didn't see how God could love her if he didn't let her get pregnant.

As was described in Chapter 3, Ann finally saw the trap that she had set for herself with her belief system. She could not stop trying these highly stressful medical treatments of the last few years because it would be possible for her to see herself as forgiven by God only if He allowed her to have a biological child.

As she sat with the therapist and pondered this revelation, Ann began to consider a few alternative ways of thinking about God and her infertility. It made some sense to her that God knew something about her that she didn't, for instance, that her back, which was weak from a congenital abnormality, may in fact not have been able to support a pregnancy. She also thought that perhaps God's plan for her was that she would adopt a special child who would flourish under the care of her and her husband.

Finally, she began to be able to imagine a God who didn't direct every tiny event that happened to each person on earth at each moment. She started to be able to let go of the thought that the infertility was her punishment for wrongdoing.

The session was almost over. A great deal had been accomplished. The therapist commented that it was as if God had put a gigantic boulder down in the middle of the life path that Ann had planned to take, but that Ann could find a way around the boulder and continue walking down the path.

Fourth Session

Ann walked into the fourth session smiling. She said she had been imagining adopting quite frequently, and that she and Joseph were excited by the possibility. Ann told the therapist that the image of walking around the boulder in the middle of the road had come up in her mind several times over the past week, and that it had made her feel good to picture herself walking around the enormous obstacle and getting back on track.

Ann was a hard worker and a resourceful person. Having liberated some energy from the task of getting pregnant, she had already begun to collect the official information on various adoption agencies. In addition, she had contacted local RESOLVE members and had got the "scoop" on several agencies from couples who had successfully adopted from them.

Because of her recent reading about adoption, she knew the costs could be steep. With some trepidation, she had spoken to her mother about the possibility of help. Her mother, who had previously voiced doubts about adoption as an option, had agreed to give them substantial financial aid. So Ann was feeling connected again, to her husband, to her mother, and to the future.

Further Sessions

As is natural, in the next few weeks, particularly when she saw babies, Ann felt occasional twinges of still wanting to pursue becoming pregnant. However, Joseph came right out and told her that he did not want her to pursue any more medical treatment now. He finally had the old, happy Ann back, and he did not want to lose her.

Ann's rational self agreed with Joseph. She let her feelings about wanting her own pregnancy come and go, and she continued to put her energy into exploring adoption. When she felt bothered by sadness about not being pregnant, she soothed herself by promising herself that, after their adopted child was two years old, if she wanted to pursue pregnancy again she could. She purposely called up images of romping with their adopted child in the near future. She and Joseph discussed the merits and drawbacks of the different adoption agencies they could use.

Ann no longer felt anxious, depressed, or angry. She felt more comfortable in social situations and was relaxed and outgoing, even in situations where others had small children. Her unpleasant sensations—stomach trouble, fatigue, and tension—had disappeared. Instead, she felt hopeful and optimistic. Her self-esteem was back to its normal high level, and she felt certain that she and Joseph would be good parents.

She was a much happier person, and she felt enthusiastic about her husband again. As her anxiety about and obsession with becoming pregnant dimmed, she had more energy and love for Joseph. Their relationship became more affectionate.

Joseph and Ann adopted successfully. Joseph agreed to try to work on their sexual relationship together and, if there was no progress, to go into sex therapy.

Discussion

This example is in some respects a typical case of working with an infertile woman. Here is illustrated many of the facets of infertility that are documented in the literature: Ann's initial sense of a life devoid of meaning; the way her interpersonal relationships were interrupted by envy and hurt feelings; the enormous stress on the marital relationship; her loss of self-esteem; and her damaged sense of body image.

Ann's case was unusual, though, in her immediate ability to accept adoption as a positive resolution during the crystal-ball exercise. After three years of very draining treatment, including surgeries, many women are deeply depleted and discouraged. Unbeknownst to her, however, Ann had preexisting and unusually positive adoption imagery. Tapping into this imagery early in the treatment allowed her to make a rapid change in her outlook.

For many women, much time must be spent looking at feelings, beliefs, and imagery surrounding the loss of their genetic line, as well as their unconscious sense that, if they don't produce a child in their bodies, they are not truly adult women like their mothers. Many may need the therapist's help in mourning their loss of the ability to experience pregnancy and to breastfeed.

Ann deserves credit for being a highly motivated patient, too. She took every shred of help, every technique, every insight and used it.

A number of issues in this case are typical aspects of taking a multimodal perspective on working with infertile women:

1. The seeming appearance of serious character or marital problems in highly distressed women; then, the rapid transformation of the patient's personality and marital relationship when the patient "does her homework." The patient uses specific techniques that allow her to appraise the situation accurately and to regain a sense of control.

2. The advantages of assessing how *each* mode of the patient's personality is affected by the problem of infertility. In Ann's case, her imagery, a

modality not explored by many therapists, held the key to helping her feel better.

3. The way in which intense exploration of cognitive processes, including the patient's tracking order and various beliefs about the cause(s) of her infertility, can alleviate the symptomatology.

4. For patients who are driven and ambitious, the powerful benefit of giving back a sense of control by teaching ways to intervene and manipulate their own imagery, tension, beliefs, and behavior. After all, homework can be successfully mastered when becoming pregnant cannot.

Selected Comments on Ann's Treatment

Infertility can make even relatively healthy women appear to be deeply disturbed. Ann's initial presentation of general rage at life and seething, irrational hostility toward her husband is worth noting because it gave her the appearance of having a character disorder.

Ann's rage was remarkable even for an infertility patient, and as a therapist having a first contact, I was not sure how healthy she was. By offering her concrete coping techniques initially, I was doing what I would do in any case. However, her determination and strength became clear when she made such good use of them, and her cooperation and her quick relief during a few sessions of psychotherapy were, in themselves, diagnostic. Ann was a healthy woman who had been stretched beyond her limits by her grief.

As was discussed in Chapter 3, infertile patients rarely create adaptive, self-protective distortions or illusions about their situation, even though most other victims of tragedy do so (Taylor & Brown, 1988; Taylor, Lichtman, & Wood, 1984). Professionals and paraprofessionals without a background in infertility are stunned by the anger and hostility that infertility patients display. People with life-threatening illnesses, such as cancer patients, are more likely to act optimistic and pleasant than are infertility patients. Patients get angry at delays or at "mistakes" in treatment and may develop negative institutional transference to all the staff in a particular hospital or clinic.

I have heard such patients labeled as having very unpleasant personal attributions ("spoiled," "entitled," "demanding," or "impossible") or diagnoses indicating character disorders (e.g., "narcissistic" or "borderline") by office staff in physicians' offices. At times, the situation almost feels like class warfare. The young nonprofessional staff feel insulted by the often older, more educated patients' free-floating anger, making comments such as, "Well, all along, she has had everything she wanted: the right job, a fat salary, the perfect house, the right husband. She thought she could control everything and have a baby exactly when she wanted one. But, hah! she has finally run up against something she couldn't control!" The patients, in turn, are so wounded by the staff's lack of empathy that they may begin to feel and act hostile to them. Some staff training on how to work with patients' anger would be a welcome addition in most clinics.

Therapists should cherish and nurture any positive thoughts or explanations that patients have about the meaning of their problem. While exploring her views about God and her infertility, Ann arrived at some beliefs that made her feel better about her infertility: She decided that God knew something about her that led him to believe that she could not physically tolerate a pregnancy; or that she had been put on earth to adopt a very special child and make him happy. Therapists shouldn't question such beliefs or label them as denial.

The financial factor figured prominently in this case. Ann was saved not only by her positive adoption imagery, but by the fact that she had a supportive mother who was willing to help Ann and Joseph pay for an adoption. Once Ann came to her rapid realization that adoption would be a wonderful way to be a parent, her mother's positive response to her assertive request for financial help allowed her to see the road ahead as being totally unblocked. If Ann had again been frustrated, by seeing that adoption was emotionally viable but financially impossible, it is very likely that her feelings of rage would have emerged again.

Last, literature on infertility does not take enough cognizance of the common undesirable side effects of the fertility medication (Greenfield et al.'s 1984 article is a notable exception). Some patients are not very bothered by side effects, but Ann was. For three years, determined to get pregnant, she had taken the medicines. She had been ingesting fertility drugs for so long that she had forgotten that feeling nauseous and tired was not her normal state. If we think of the concept of her "tracking order," her physical discomfort certainly contributed to her difficulty in feeling that life was worth living because it led to the thought, "I feel rotten." Why did Ann feel so much better after only a few weeks of treatment? One simple factor that should not be overlooked is that, once she had decided that she would adopt, she stopped taking the fertility drugs. When she began to say that she felt much better, her reaction was partly a reflection of her renewed sense of comfort in her body.

Using a multimodal framework, we more clearly see all the possible avenues for intervention. As time goes by, therapists hopefully will discover more and more concrete techniques that help patients like Ann cope with their infertility. In the chapter that follows, we look at the application of behavioral techniques to miscarriage and to anxiety during subsequent pregnancy.

9

Treatment of Anxiety during Pregnancy in Patients with a History of Recurrent Miscarriage

Women who habitually miscarry can do so for many medical reasons, including genetic error, abnormal hormone levels, structural problems in the uterus, infection, and immunological causes. The American Fertility Society (1991) now feels that it is reasonable for physicians to begin extensive testing to attempt to find the cause after two consecutive losses. However, in approximately 40 percent of couples, no cause for the miscarriages can be detected (and treated), so the "treatment" for many women with a history of recurrent miscarriage is to keep trying to get pregnant. Even after several miscarriages, the American Fertility Society reassures women that they have better than a 50 percent chance of achieving a healthy pregnancy.

Couples who experience repeated pregnancy loss may begin to doubt that they will ever have a child to take home and love. After the first miscarriage, each subsequent pregnancy is filled with anxiety. Although the supportive counseling strategies used to help the couple deal with their grief after a pregnancy loss have been well described in the clinical literature, no one has set forth a therapeutic strategy to help the woman cope with feelings of stress and anxiety *once she succeeds in becoming pregnant again*. Because of the intensity of the patient's anxiety, a therapeutic style of being supportive and simply listening to feelings is not adequate to contain potentially damaging amounts of anxiety. A behavioral-educational therapy that helps the patient contain her anxiety while pregnant after recurrent miscarriage is described in this chapter. Such a treatment plan should be used in the context of a generally supportive and empathetic therapeutic relationship.

One in every six pregnancies ends in miscarriage. Clinicians and researchers now recognize the extent to which miscarriage is a traumatic event for the patient, her husband, and her family (Borg & Lasker, 1981; Friedman & Gradstein, 1982; Peppers & Knapp, 1980a,b; Woods & Esposito, 1987). The professional and lay literature on how to help families grieve their loss after

153

miscarriage is now excellent. Nothing in this chapter should be construed as denying the need of the woman and her family to grieve after miscarriage and the importance of supportive and exploratory psychotherapy in supporting that process.

However, some women have a pattern of repeated miscarriages, miscarrying in the first trimester two or three or more times consecutively. Once pregnant again, these women have different needs from women who are in the stage of grieving a past miscarriage.

Medical sources disagree somewhat, but estimates are that women who have had three consecutive miscarriages still have between a 50 percent and a 70 percent chance of having a live birth (American Fertility Society, 1991, "better than 50%"; Friedman & Gradstein, 1982, p. 112, between 20 percent and 80 percent, Plouffe & McDonough, 1982, 70 percent). After a careful evaluation of the possible causes of the miscarriages, many of these women are urged to persevere and become pregnant once again.

The problem is that, for a woman who has once lost a pregnancy, it no longer feels safe to be pregnant. The pregnancy has a "cloud over it" (Berezin, 1982), and the first few months of the pregnancy (and sometimes much longer, if the pregnancy holds) may be filled with unremitting anxiety (Berezin, 1982; Kirksey, 1987; Limbo & Wheeler, 1986).

It is difficult to describe adequately the agony of patients who are pregnant again after two or more previous miscarriages. One of my patients who had miscarried twice said, "I was in a much more intense state of anxiety when I was pregnant. It was much worse than after I miscarried. Then, I was in grief; it was different, not anxious, not as bad. From the time I found out I was pregnant to the time I finally started bleeding, I was so full of anxiety, it was horrible!"

The first miscarriage is a terrible shock and an awful loss. It is a discrete, direful episode in the life of the couple. Grieving may take a long time (Reinharz, 1988). The second loss also comes as an alarming jolt because the woman has been hoping that the first miscarriage was a "fluke." The mother mourns specifically for the second baby, too. But many women with subsequent early losses, when the babies are so tiny and the pregnancies are so tentative, find that everything blends into a tapestry of hope and loss, and it becomes difficult to grieve for specific losses. After two miscarriages, it seems as if the anxiety that women experience when they are pregnant may be much worse than the grief that they feel when the feared event—a miscarriage—actually occurs.

These patients' excruciating anxiety during pregnancy expresses itself in many symptoms. Berezin (1982) mentioned terror, insomnia, obsession with eating the right food, and magical thinking and these are the symptoms in a patient who has lost only one prior pregnancy.

> Unconsciously, the expectant mother has made a connection between the optimistic mood of her prior pregnancy and its tragic outcome. As a consequence, she now tries to gain a measure of control over things by

proceeding with the utmost caution—not sharing the news with friends or relatives, perhaps postponing the appointment with the gynecologist—in the hope that by ignoring the pregnancy, she can magically influence its outcome. (Berezin, 1982, p. 122)

The magical back-and-forth nature of the thoughts about the past loss(es) torture the woman, making it impossible for her to feel secure or happy about the pregnancy. During an interview, a patient named Arnis described this process: "I would just keep thinking, going back and forth, mostly scary thoughts. Sometimes I would think happy thoughts, but when I did, I would be afraid. I would tell myself that I shouldn't, because maybe this wouldn't work out. So I'd go back and forth, back and forth."

Later, Arnis talked about her ambivalence about whether to tell her friends about this pregnancy, and again, the obsessive ruminating back and forth was evident: "Well, sometimes it is a happy feeling, and I think, 'Isn't it wonderful? I'm pregnant and no one knows it yet, but soon they'll all know and they'll all be excited and happy.' I'm just sitting on it for the time being. But then I think, 'But something might happen, and I wouldn't want anybody to know that.'"

The pregnant woman is obsessed with her past loss. Patients' imagery is profoundly affected. Berezin (1982) discussed a patient who sees herself as a "defective incubator." Friedman and Gradstein (1982) quoted a patient who saw herself "as a fragile vessel carrying an even more fragile cargo." My patients have shown profound changes in self-image. One, whose husband wanted to have sex with her, commented, "I can't imagine why my husband would want to put his penis down that dark hole where things keep dying." Another commented that her uterus was like "the dark hole of Calcutta. No one gets out alive." Another was frightened of having sex while she was pregnant and said that she pictured the "fetus attached to my body by only the thinnest of threads." This patient saw her husband's penis as a "giant intruder that will destroy the baby."

Thoughts and memories of the past pregnancies are prevalent. Recollections of past losses include remembering the physical pain (see Reinharz, 1988), so sensory imagery and intense fear of the pain of the next miscarriage are common. For some patients, the memories are frighteningly visual, including spontaneous visions of fetuses being sucked out into metal bowls during a D and C, or memories of involuntarily expelling a fetus into the toilet and having to scoop it up and take it to the physician for genetic analysis, or picturing going for an ultrasound and seeing the gray look on the technician's face when she could no longer find the fetus.

As in infertility, cognitions and beliefs are affected. The patient thinks that the miscarriage is her fault (Berezin, 1982; Seibel & Graves, 1980; Reinharz, 1988), and she feels guilt. The miscarriages are seen as punishment for sins such as past abortions or premarital sex (thoughts that cause still more anxiety). Or they are punishment not for sin but for her own bad judgment, perhaps for having had the nerve to attempt to postpone pregnancy for a few years in order to get on better financial footing.

The patient feels utterly out of control. Arnis said, "By the third time, I realized that this is totally out of my control. If something bad is going to happen, it is already there. I just have to let it play itself out. There is nothing I can do to prevent it, to control it, to affect it. There is nothing I can do. And that was an intense and horrible feeling."

Eternal Vigilance to Internal Sensations

The patient keeps expecting another loss (Kirksey, 1987). Previous miscarriages have been heralded by unpleasant abdominal and pelvic sensations, so she scans all of her internal sensations, watching out for one which will spell *danger*. There is a tremendous amount of involuntary activity going on inside women's midsections all the time, especially during pregnancy, and the pregnant woman who has even once had a miscarriage begins to scan her body and to pick out sensations that she might otherwise miss or dismiss and to be frightened of them.

Friedman and Gradstein (1982) commented that such a patient is "eternally vigilant—every twinge, pain or cramp is noted, amplified, and feared" (p. 159). In fact, at any and every abdominal or pelvic twinge, the patient runs to the bathroom to check her underpants for blood. In addition, the focus on bodily sensations is frequently the beginning of a whole stream of negative thoughts, images, and feelings. One of my patients commented on her own tracking order: "As I remember, I had a lot of gas while I was pregnant the third time, and every feeling I had in my stomach, I would get visions of the last time I was in Dr. T's office, getting the D and C for the last miscarriage. And then, of course, I would remember the sights, and the pain. And then I would get scared and upset." If we were to make a schematic drawing of the tracking order of this event, it would look like Figure 7.

Clearly, most of the patient's strategic attempts to try to gain control in this out-of-control situation, such as the obsessive focus on physical twinges or searching through past history to find the "reason" for past miscarriages, only serve to create a vicious circle in which the patient becomes more and more watchful and more and more anxious.

Any sensitive therapist immediately understands why the pregnant patient in this situation is so worried. Most of the authors of books on miscarriage state that the patient who has miscarried needs special support during the next pregnancy. But to my knowledge, no one has described a systematic treatment strategy for controlling, containing, and hopefully even lessening, the anxiety. Simple support is necessary but not sufficient as a therapeutic technique in such an instance. The patient needs coping strategies that provide her with a sense of control over anxiety, for several reasons.

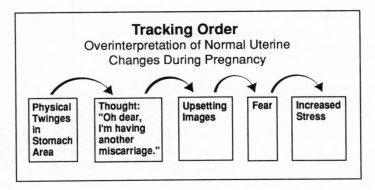

Figure 7

First of all, although we do not know for certain that the patient's anxiety may be a factor in miscarriage, this hypothesis cannot be ruled out. I am not positing that the patient's feelings necessarily caused the original miscarriage, but a high level of anxiety during a subsequent pregnancy cannot benefit the patient physiologically or psychologically.

Infertility and miscarriage both involve a great interdependence of endocrinological and psychological factors (Birnbaum & Eskin, 1973). The limbic system, which is known to be involved in the emotions, also plays a major role in reproduction. In fact, the limbic system receives sensory and emotional input and responds with hormonal secretions. When there is an imbalance in the process, one of the results may be "hormonal or structural defects that can . . . terminate a pregnancy" (Mosley, 1976, p. 412). More recently, Seibel and Taymor (1980) commented on the negative physiological effects of the stress of coping with infertility: "Catecholamines, prolactin, adrenal steroids, endorphins, and serotonin all affect ovulation, and in turn are all affected by stress. Such stress might result from infertility or habitual abortion" (p. 16). Infertility causes stress, and subsequent stress may cause infertility and habitual miscarriage (Seibel & Taymor, 1980). On a physiological level, then, it makes sense to design interventions that will help the patient keep herself as calm as possible.

Second, in order to have the greatest chance of a live birth, the woman needs to be able to have the strength and the courage to become pregnant repeatedly after a miscarriage. Typically, couples experience more difficulties coping with each suceeding loss. Friedman and Gradstein (1982) commented, "How long to keep trying is a highly individual decision. Many couples do finally succeed in having a child after numerous losses" (p. 111).

If each pregnancy is more horrible than the one before it, pregnancy is negatively reinforced psychologically, and the woman will give up earlier in the process than she might wish to. Psychologically, then, we also want to shore up the patient's sense that she has a repertoire of new coping strategies with which to reinforce (or replace) her natural coping mechanisms.

Psychotherapeutic Strategies That Relieve Symptoms of Anxiety

To begin with, the patient must understand the general nature of the stress response and learn one or more techniques (deep breathing, deep-muscle relaxation, self-hypnosis, or meditation) to relax herself physiologically whenever she feels herself becoming tense. Part of the therapy sessions must be spent in practicing different relaxation techniques, and the practice must continue on a daily basis at home. Resources for the patient include Wilson's *Don't Panic* (1986), Borysenko's *Minding the Body, Mending the Mind* (1987), and Kabat-Zinn's *Full Catastrophe Living* (1990).

The patient needs to understand the concept of the tracking order and to realize the many experiences that serve for her as cues for anxiety. The pregnant woman who has had several miscarriages may be reminded of her losses by a myriad of everyday sights, smells, sensations, beliefs, thoughts, feelings, or sounds.

Partial List of Cues That Can Begin an Anxiety Sequence for a Pregnant Woman with a History of Recurrent Miscarriage

- Abdominal and pelvic bodily sensations (cramps, twinges, gas, "I'm not as nauseous. Maybe I already lost it.")
- Breast sensations ("They aren't as swollen today. Maybe I'm not still pregnant.")
- Sights or smells found in hospitals or doctors' offices
- Appointments for blood or ultrasound procedures
- Blood
- Pregnant women
- The word *abortion* or anything about abortions (e.g., abortion clinics)
- Hearing that someone else miscarried
- Ambulances
- Needles
- Toilets in general
- Going to the toilet
- Sex
- Babies and children

- Seeing "baby items" in any kind of store (drugstore, variety store, food store, clothing store)
- Anniversary of a past due date
- Anniversary of a past miscarriage
- Seeing or hearing about a child that was born when her child should have been born
- Eating ("I'm pregnant, so I should eat well. But maybe I won't keep it, so it doesn't matter. I might as well enjoy myself.")
- Friends ("Should I tell them or not?")

The therapist should teach the patient to challenge her response to anxiety cues. However, the therapist in this situation has to walk a very thin line. In order to keep the therapeutic alliance, it is critical that the patient feel the therapist understands that the anxiety has a basis in reality. Certainly, she will deeply resent being told "not to worry" or "just think happy thoughts" when she has had such devastating losses. On the other hand, she needs to be taught how her own rational and irrational beliefs, thoughts, and images and her reactions to her own sensations can create an inner message of *"Danger,"* which in turn sets off a chain of events inside her body that makes her feel even more anxious. She must notice when her stress response is being turned on and learn to interrupt her response and relax her body and her mind.

In the first trimester, the most powerful and common cue for anxiety about another miscarriage is hypervigilance about internal abdominal and pelvic sensations. Psychologist David Barlow's brilliant work on the dynamics of anxiety and panic attacks has an important application here. Barlow discovered that panic attacks are actually set off by a learned fear of internal sensations. Once the patient has a panic attack, with the associated sensations, any hint of these same sensations is feared.

Craske & Barlow (1990) wrote that "unlike fear of an external object, fear of internal sensations . . . generates positive feedback looping effects [see Figure 8]. That is, fearing an internal sensation (e.g. I am having a heart attack) serves to generate increased arousal, which in turn increases the intensity of the cue that is feared, and hence a spiraling effect occurs. . . . Crucial to this model of panic attacks is the role of anxious apprehension of the recurrence of panic" (p. 82).

A similar process happens in the case of a woman who has previously miscarried. Unless she is trained in physiology, the patient does not understand the close placement of the intestines and the uterus (see Figure 9). She also does not know that many of the normal sensations of pregnancy can cause sensations that seem to threaten miscarriage.

The patient needs to understand the biology of pregnancy. During normal early pregnancy, abdominal and pelvic sensations are produced by many different benign processes:

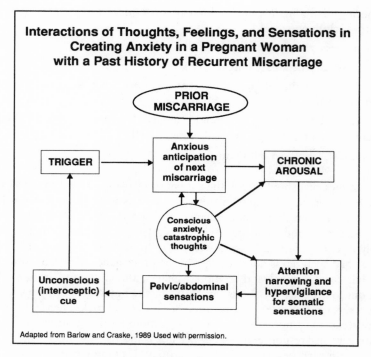

Figure 8

1. Most women will notice a feeling of pelvic pressure and congestion as the uterus is enlarging by the fourth to eighth week of gestation. This feeling is caused by the increased weight of the uterus and the increasing vasculature in the area.

2. As the uterus grows, the surrounding muscles stretch and contract.

3. In addition, the enlarging uterus will exert pressure on the bladder, causing midabdominal discomfort difficult to distinguish from uterine discomfort.

4. Because the uterus is not fixed in place, it shifts internally. Even seemingly small movements may result in pain that is mild to sharp.

5. The digestive process is changed considerably during pregnancy because of mechanical pressure of the uterus on the internal organs as well as hormonal changes that slow down the digestive process. Constipation is frequent in pregnancy, and can cause sharp, annoying gas pains that the patient may not recognize as such.

6. Finally, and much less frequently, there may be an occasional pain that

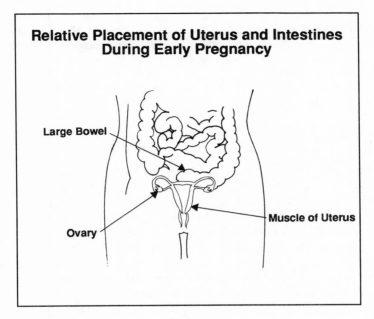

Figure 9

goes along with the enlarging ovary (sometimes cystic) that contains the corpus luteum of pregnancy.

Against a backdrop of increased general arousal because of fear of another miscarriage, a patient's increased attention to and misinterpretation of normal abdominal and pelvic sensations generate still more arousal, which in turn may actually increase the feared sensations, for example, nervous stomach, cramps, or gas. During a full-blown stress reaction, the blood flow to the digestive systems shuts down, as does digestion, so that the body can deliver more blood to the arms and legs. The rerouting of the blood flow in times of stress can be felt as "butterflies in the stomach" (Kabat-Zinn, 1990, p. 251). All of these sensations are misinterpreted as dangerous. As Figure 8 shows, the reaction is a vicious circle.

A pattern of learned fear of certain sensations results in an acute sensitivity to these sensations. Craske and Barlow (1990) noted that the hyperattention to somatic cues occurs at both the conscious and the unconscious (perceptual) levels:

The misinterpretation of symptoms is related to two concepts.
(1) Cognitive misinterpretation occurs at a conscious level. [That is, the

patient does not understand that some internal sensations in the pelvic and abdominal area are normal.]

(2) The second is *interoceptive conditioning,* which refers to a strong, automatic association between certain cues and fear reactions based on past repeated trials. Hence, one is a more consciously elaborated process and one is a more direct perceptually based process. (p. 8-2; italics on the original)

Interoceptive Cues

Barlow and Craske's down-to-earth example (1989) of how one becomes superattentive to interoceptive cues makes the process understandable to patients: In a large crowd, although you are unable to hear all of the conversations, you may hear your name if it is mentioned. This is an example of the process of attentional selectivity to cues that are salient and meaningful to you. The therapist should explain to the pregnant woman that the cues she feels portend a danger of miscarriage (e.g., reminders of the cramping that preceded the previous loss) are most meaningful to her, and so she tends to unconsciously scan through her body, to focus on any pelvic and abdominal sensations, and to misinterpret them. In fact, she should be told, she is so sensitive to danger signals that, without even being aware of it, she is always scanning her body for danger, and that this anxious scanning and feedback loop makes her generally anxious all of the time. In other words, it is like telling herself that the house is on fire or that a bear is chasing her when it isn't.

The pregnant woman should be taught about the healthy and normal causes of abdominal and pelvic sensations, the concept of interoceptive cuing, and how the stress response is turned on. A diagram of the relative placement of the uterus and the intestines in the body, such as the one in Figure 9, is most helpful at this point.

Once the patient is pregnant, the therapist should question her weekly to find out if she is being frightened by her own sensations. With enough explanation and instruction, she will see the importance of tolerating the sensations, reinterpreting them, and not connecting their presence with evidence of physical risk. We cannot make any guarantees, sadly enough, but under any circumstances, it is better to stay as relaxed as possible and "hope for the best." Her life will begin to feel more predictable and more safe, and the result should be a significant lowering of general arousal.

The patient also needs to learn that, during times of high anxiety, people tend to treat their thoughts as if they were fact. Two of the most universal negative thoughts, which should be controlled as much as possible, are "I am going to miscarry" and "I did X and Y bad things, and I am miscarrying as punishment for them."

Richardson (1969) gave a useful example of the self-escalating effects of chronic worrying in his illustration of the horse that notices itself running, assumes it must be fleeing some real danger, runs faster, notices it is running faster, infers that the danger has increased in magnitude or is closer at hand, runs even faster, and so on. The patient must realize that just feeling vulnerable or thinking that she will not carry this baby to term does not mean that her thoughts are the truth (Friedman & Gradstein, 1982; Limbo & Wheeler, 1986). In fact, the therapist should tell her of other women who were equally sure that they would miscarry and who went on to give birth to healthy children.

As described in previous chapters, the patient needs to learn to interrupt upsetting thoughts, feelings, sensations, or images immediately (thought stopping) and to substitute soothing thoughts, phrases, feelings, or images.

Edwina, a forty-one-year-old pregnant woman who had suffered two first-trimester losses, came into psychotherapy for help with her anxiety about having another miscarriage. Edwina was a strong and wonderful woman who was active in trying to help herself. She was seeing a first-rate physician who knew a lot about miscarriage, and she was being treated for a medical problem that might be causing the losses. She had terminated therapy with her old therapist because she felt that she needed help with her current anxiety more than she needed general supportive or exploratory therapy. She sought me out because she learned that I was an expert in treating anxiety in pregnant women, through seeing an advertisement for a continuing-education course I was teaching on behavioral treatments for infertility and miscarriage.

In the same vein, Edwina had been very responsible in working on her own issues in life. She had grown up in a dysfunctional family. Her mother had been rejecting and hostile to her and had been physically abusive to her on occasion. There had been some sexual abuse for several years from an uncle. Edwina had worked for years in psychodynamic psychotherapy because she believed that she had to resolve her feelings about her own childhood before she herself became a mother. When she and her husband decided that they were ready to become parents, they felt wonderful about their decision.

Unfortunately, after two miscarriages, Edwina's old feelings of self-doubt and worthlessness came up again. She began to report "thoughts that I had done it wrong. I had waited too long, not like my younger brother, who got his wife pregnant at thirty-two. I began to think that this was happening to me because I was promiscuous in my twenties, that I didn't deserve to have a baby."

I told her a number of things that she was subsequently able to use as *positive* self-talk when she blamed herself for the miscarriages: (1) that she was being much too hard on herself; (2) that most people who miscarry feel somehow to blame for the miscarriage because of some past sin or mistake in behavior; (3) that, actually, she had postponed childbearing because she was extraordinarily responsible and wanted to be the best mother possible;

(4) that she did deserve a child; and (5) that in fact, she especially deserved a child and would be a good mother, and if things were fair in life, she would never have had a miscarriage; and (6) that it was just bad luck, and that her physician believed that her chances for a child were still excellent, probably at the 70 percent or 80 percent level.

Edwina reported at the time I made these comments that they were soothing and made her feel much better. She was given a sheet on which to keep track of and dispute any other irrational ideas about the causes of her miscarriages. The following week, Edwina reported that the statements continued to have a pacifying effect on her. She had stopped blaming herself for the miscarriages. Luckily, on her third try, Edwina went on to give birth to a healthy baby.

The Mantra

As we have seen, the pregnant woman has great difficulty in controlling her obsessive thoughts about whether she should invest emotionally in this pregnancy. She cannot figure out what the "correct" or "balanced" point of view is about the pregnancy. Swinging back and forth between these two very different poles, from "I'm going to have a baby" to "I'm going to have a miscarriage," is difficult on the woman both psychologically and physiologically. But she does need a point of view about the pregnancy.

I teach my patients to replace their conflicting thoughts with the mantra (or cue) of "So far, so good" or "We'll see" (depending on their degree of optimism and the number of previous miscarriages), said while taking some deep, relaxing breaths. It is important to have some appropriate and specific thought or phrase that can be substituted for the previous back-and-forth thoughts because the old behavior of ruminating may have gained some anxiety-reducing properties through its obsessive-compulsive nature.

"So far, so good" represents a rational and reasonable stance about the pregnancy because it neither promises a perfect outcome nor damns the pregnancy to certain failure. It merely takes a wait-and-see, but faintly hopeful, position. Here is what Arnis said about using the phrase "So far, so good" during her third pregnancy:

> It helped. It really did. It was like a mantra. It was something—when that whole cycle was going on—it was something to stop on. I thought of it as a mantra, and it is also one of those standard little phrases. "So far, so good" being a mantra would make me laugh, so that would stop me, the humor of it. When I get to my humor side, I am in much better shape. The humor sort of takes away the fear, and taking it all too seriously, and the not seeing the bright side of it. And also the wisdom of the statement would stop me, because I

would say, "That's right. Nothing has happened yet. Up to now, it's OK. Everything is OK, so, keep going."

Patients also say and think things like "If I lose this pregnancy, too, I'll go crazy," or other statements that indicate that they feel they have no more inner coping resources left. Unless the patient now seems so fragile that the therapist believes that she is actually in danger, the response to this kind of statement should be an offer of some help with additional coping strategies and more frequent meetings with the patient, in person or by phone.

Women with whom I have worked have created special positive coping statements that helped them when they felt they could no longer stand to persevere. One tactic is to be less invested in each pregnancy at the beginning, in order to be less devastated by the possible loss. Arnis, mentioned above, began to see pregnancy as simply a "biological event" and told herself that she was brave and was *consciously deciding* to risk another loss, that she was not being a victim.

Another patient, who had had a bout of infertility before she began miscarrying, told herself that waiting to see if the pregnancy would hold was not any more difficult than waiting to see if she would get her period, which she felt she had become good at coping with.

Some patients think or say, "I'm afraid of the pain of another miscarriage. If I lose this one, I don't think I have the courage to continue to try once again and potentially have still another miscarriage." Obviously, this situation is tricky. The therapist needs to be quite empathetic and in tune with the patient to deal with such a statement. She has the right of self-determination, of course. On the other hand, this is another form of a negative thought: "Having a miscarriage is so horrible that another one would destroy me. So I'll never have a baby." Patients often voice this feeling after two miscarriages, and yet after two miscarriages, their odds of giving birth to a child are still reasonably good.

The appropriate response, I believe, is equivocal. It both gives permission to stop and holds out hope of "bringing in the reinforcements" to help the patient cope better with the pain if she chooses to go ahead. The therapist might say something like

Therapist: It is natural to be afraid of the pain of miscarriage, and I know that is what you are feeling right now. When to stop trying for a child is your decision, a very personal one. The people who care about you will support you in whatever decision you choose.

But if you ever want us to, I think we can work on helping you to feel less afraid of the physical pain of a future miscarriage, so that you can keep trying if you want to. There are exercises we can teach you to prepare you for the pain [Zoldbrod, 1990]. And as you have already experienced (two) miscarriages, you probably have no more nasty surprises in store. You know what you are up against, physically, and can become better prepared than ever, this time, to handle the pain. I can speak with your physician to make certain that you have more pain medication, if you would like. And I'll be there to help you through the grief process, too, of course.

Suggested Interventions by the Medical Staff and Therapist

What is the role of the physician in treating anxiety in these patients? Seibel and Graves (1980) made the good suggestion that physicians working with women with a history of recurrent miscarriage see them every two weeks during a subsequent pregnancy, in order to answer questions and provide additional support.

It is most appropriate for the physician or nurse to gently introduce the patient to the idea that if she becomes pregnant again, she may well experience some anxiety in the first trimester of pregnancy. The physician can ask the patient to call her, if this happens, for some concrete help in managing the anxiety.

At the point at which the patient calls, the physician or the nurse should at least take the amount of time needed to teach the patient about how to deal with her fear of her bodily sensations and to encourage her to get help in learning to relax in response to feared sensations, thoughts, images, or feelings.

Women who are pregnant after recurrent miscarriages need to have concrete behavioral strategies for containing their anxiety about miscarrying once again. Several such strategies have been outlined here.

Many patients are helped by having a card that they can carry with them with instructions and hints that will help them calm down. Such an instruction sheet might contain the following suggestions:

If you miscarried, you did nothing wrong. It was not your fault.

When you feel anxious, remember:*

1. Breathe deeply, do muscle relaxation, or meditate.
2. Ask yourself, "What is the evidence for the fear?"
3. Remember not to overinterpret physical sensations. Because of past losses, you have become supersensitive to your bodily sensations and are anxiously scanning your body for all abdominal and pelvic twinges. Normal pregnancy is full of such sensations. The sensations you are tuning in to are most probably the perfectly normal sensations of digesting food, the normal stretching and contracting of uterine muscles, pelvic congestion, or constipation and gas pains. If you look at a diagram of a female body, you will see the close proximity of your uterus and your intestines.

4. Stop upsetting thoughts and images. Instead, relax.
5. Use "So far, so good" or "We'll see." Don't concentrate on loss imagery.
6. Remember, after three miscarriages, the chance of a live birth is still better than 50 percent.
7. Tell yourself, "I am learning to handle this situation better and better, so that if I do lose this pregnancy, I will have the physical and emotional strength to get pregnant again if I want to."

In the third part of this book, we take a look at infertility and sexuality.

---

*A "calming card" explaining these principles to patients is available. See Appendix 5 for ordering information.

Part 3
Sexuality

10

Men, Women, and Sexuality

A s a sex therapist, I cannot help but be amazed that some infertile couples are able to enjoy sex occasionally or frequently during their evaluation and treatment. But in many cases, much of the time, infertility spoils the sexual experience until the crisis is resolved. The husband and wife are able to perform the act, but the feeling is gone (Drake & Grunert, 1979; De Brovner, and Shubin-Stein 1975; Menning, 1977). Keye and Deneris (1983) surveyed almost five hundred infertile men and women and found that, at one point or another, most of them experienced some sexual dissatisfaction or dysfunction.

What is it about desperately trying to have a child that is so poisonous to sexuality? According to Keye (1984), patients believe their sexual problems are caused by dyspareunia; medication-induced inhibited sexual desire; goal-oriented "sex on schedule"; "unrealistic sexual demands by partner"; poor body image; depression; guilt; and ambivalence (p. 764). In a different article, Keye (1984) noted that the medical evaluation process itself may be traumatic, a factor that is discussed in the following chapter.

On the most elementary level, conflicts caused by infertility may make the couple feel estranged from one another (Bierkins, 1975). Their sexual relationship presumably had been an expression of love in an intimate relationship. That is, the partners trusted each other, helped each other, and were known to each other. That, of course, was part of the reason they wanted to create a child together to begin with (Douglas & Atwell, 1988).

When couples indicate that there are sexual problems, the therapist should ask specific questions and obtain a sexual history before offering any reassurance or advice. Each couple is unique. Sexuality is affected by many factors, among them socialization, family history, religious history, the kinds of sexual information they have received, permission to act sexual, sexual experience, intimacy issues, defenses, addictions, negative messages, and blocks and resistances. These factors color a couple's sexuality before the infertility occurs and can continue to have an effect. Other sexual strains arise because of the special demands of medical evaluation and treatment.

171

General Issues

Sex therapists rarely, if ever, see couples struggling with infertility because of complaints about the partners' lack of desire, lack of excitement, or female anorgasmia. There may well be, in fact, a tremendous lack of desire, no excitement whatsoever, or female anorgasmia, but that is not the point. All the emphasis is on adequate *performance* by the male if he is fertile. If he's infertile, and the treatment is inseminations, the wife's focus is not on sexual pleasure; it is on the proper timing of inseminations or other treatment.

The stereotypical sex act, mid-cycle, for the woman with a fertile husband is nothing more than a means to an end, "a job you have to do." The big question is: "Can my husband get an erection and ejaculate the sperm in the proper place: my vagina?"

Is there a warm afterglow? Not usually. In fact, in some cases, the wife quickly spins around with her head toward the bottom of the bed, puts her feet up against the wall, tilts her pelvis, and assumes this position for some minutes, doing her part to make the sperms' trip up the vaginal canal an easier one.

The men in one RESOLVE couples support group tell a story that sums up a common sexual scenario beautifully. One wife had a "code sentence" when it was one of the nights when intercourse was important. She would say, "I'm going up to bed, and I'm going to be asleep in *five minutes*." That meant the husband had to drop whatever he was doing immediately, come into the bedroom, get an erection as fast as he could, enter her, and ejaculate forthwith! Given this insane sexual script, the husbands in the group made this into their own joke. Whenever they were discussing sexuality, one of them would hold up one hand, fingers spread apart, and say to the others, "Remember now, *five minutes!*"

According to Walker (1978), the most common complaint by both men and women is low libido. This should come as no surprise, given the prevalence here of sexuality without desire.

Depression causes low libido, and some infertile women are quite depressed (Bell, 1981; Daniluk, Leader, & Taylor, 1985). Depression in fertile women increases when their husbands are diagnosed. Men struggling with the infertility crisis become depressed, too (MacNab, 1984; Wright et al., 1991).

Under other circumstances of great loss—the death of a friend or relative or some other kind of tragedy or disaster—the sex drive is naturally dampened. But in this case, although depressive feelings may predominate, sex during the fertile time of the month is a ritual.

"This is the night," the wife says. Often, what she is thinking is "I'm so depressed I wish I were dead. If I don't get pregnant soon, I don't know what I'll do. Lord, I hope he can get it up." There it is: no desire, no excitement, just a desperate quickie to make sure that the sperm gets a crack at the egg. Probably, he'll cooperate anyway.

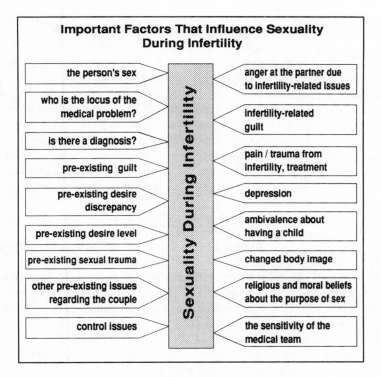

Important Factors That Influence Sexuality During Infertility

Sexuality During Infertility

- the person's sex
- who is the locus of the medical problem?
- is there a diagnosis?
- pre-existing guilt
- pre-existing desire discrepancy
- pre-existing desire level
- pre-existing sexual trauma
- other pre-existing issues regarding the couple
- control issues

- anger at the partner due to infertility-related issues
- infertility-related guilt
- pain / trauma from infertility, treatment
- depression
- ambivalence about having a child
- changed body image
- religious and moral beliefs about the purpose of sex
- the sensitivity of the medical team

Figure 10

This kind of cooperation can come at a price. The therapist should not minimize the tremendous effect of having intercourse with no desire. Sex therapist and psychologist Judith Silverstein of Cambridge, Massachusetts, compares forced sex with forced feeding. Even if you love chocolate, if you continually eat it day after day when you don't want it you will soon find chocolate distasteful. So it is with forced sexuality.

Several of the wives of infertile men commented on their loss of libido and lack of sexual pleasure in an article on women's reaction to artificial insemination (Zoldbrod, 1988) One said:

"Any interest or desire for sex which has been lost by us began well at the beginning of the infertility work-ups. This is due to the general feeling of 'Why bother? It is not going to produce anything anyway.' I guess when you're a Roman Catholic, and so much about when sex is permissible and when it isn't is poured into you, it becomes difficult to tailor the 'rules' to your own situation. You're rather reluctant to give yourself a break and make what you're doing OK in your own conscience." (p. 165)

Another source of low libido exists. Fisher (1989) wrote that "the passionate anti-body, antisex themes dominant in the Christian imagery (and still powerfully present today), are remarkable. They call for a rejection of the body as an object worthy of being equated with the self. They classify the body as lowly and depraved and hardly worthy of representation in one's self awareness" (p. 4).

Because infertility is intimately tied to sexuality, any free-floating sexual guilt can easily become attached to it. Mosher (1966) began studying guilt about body sexuality ("sex guilt") as a personality trait. Sex guilt has been shown to be correlated with repressed sexuality, low sexual drive, and inhibited sexual response (Galbraith, 1969; Janda, O'Grady, Nichelous, Harsher, Denny, & Denner, 1981; Mosher, 1966; Mosher & Cross, 1971). We would expect people with preexisting high levels of sex guilt to have an especially hard time with sexuality during infertility.

Changes in self-concept and self-image are tremendously significant. As Mazor (1980) noted, patients frequently feel defective, like "damaged goods." The sense of defectiveness is not confined to reproductive function. Instead, it spreads to encompass sexual function and sexual desirability.

In a 1983 study of 500 infertile men and women, Keye and Deneris's subjects spontaneously mentioned poor body image as one of the top seven factors leading to their sexual problems. In fact, more subjects mentioned poor body image than mentioned depression.

Body image mediates sexual behavior. Seymour Fisher (1989), a psychologist who has spent his whole academic life studying sexuality, commented that even under normal conditions, "body shame is everywhere" (p. 1).

Any person with preexisting shame about his or her body (e.g., "My penis is too small" or "My breasts are too small") may find it more difficult to allow himself or herself to feel sexual pleasure. There are studies by Eichler (1973) and by Young (1980) that indicate that the more women approve of their own body features, the more sexually active they are.

In addition, people tend to feel guilty when something is wrong with their bodies. In studies, children and adolescents with different kinds of illnesses and deformities all indicated that they believed that the illness or deformity had happened to them because they deserved to be punished. In short, there is normally an "inappropriate readiness to attach blame to one's body" (Fisher, 1989, p. 2).

The examples of changes in body imagery cited thus far have been, in large part, examples of changes in women's images: the womb that is like "the dark hole of Calcutta"; the woman with multiple miscarriages who wanted to know why her husband "would want to put his penis down that dark hole where things keep dying"; and the 110-pound woman who felt fat and ugly. Men, too, have changes in body imagery, but they are much less likely to reveal them. Remember Stan, in Chapter 2, who was so frightened about whether his sperm would "pass" the hampster egg test. Infertility causes men to question their bodies, to feel less masculine than other men, even if the medical evaluation has not found a male factor.

I worked with a highly educated professional couple in their mid-thirties, obviously very much in love. They were having trouble conceiving, although a thorough medical evaluation found nothing physically wrong with either of them.

> The husband, Lew, had wanted a baby before his wife did. At this point, Bonnie was desperate to get pregnant, and they were both depressed and worried. Their physician referred them to me for sex therapy because she suspected something might be wrong with their sexual technique that was causing some of their difficulty.
>
> They were an attractive pair, about the same size and coloring. Each of the spouses seemed a bit shy and younger than their years socially. They did have a lot of problems with sexual technique, because neither of them was comfortable with their sexuality, and neither was able to tell the other what was pleasing. Their erotic relationship, even before the infertility, had been tentative and not a central focus of the relationship.
>
> Lew and Bonnie had married while quite young, and neither of them had received any sexual education in his or her family, so they were totally naive. The bulk of the therapy was teaching them the basics of adult sexuality and helping them to set up a sensual environment that would be inviting to both of them. For example, Bonnie was always physically cold during sex and hurried to get it over with, but it had not occurred to the couple to think ahead and heat up the bedroom.
>
> Lew was medium height, with a slight build. He had no trouble with erections, and his sperm count was good. Nevertheless, his insecurity had been immensely heightened when he and Bonnie were unable to conceive. His frank discussion of his worries gives us a hint of some other men's sexual disquietudes:
>
> "But do you really think I am normal? Maybe something is wrong with me. I am so thin, and I don't have much hair on my body, not like other men."
>
> ". . . and I don't think I ejaculate as much as some other men do. I have no trouble ejaculating, but not much sperm comes out unless I abstain for a day. And, you know, I have trouble getting deeply into Bonnie unless we put a pillow under her rear end. I've watched all kinds of movies. Other men don't use a pillow. Is needing to use a pillow normal?"

When there is already a physical disability, body imagery may become a worse problem during infertility:

> Brian, a twenty-eight-year-old man, had had uncontrollable colitis for years and had had a colostomy after three years of marriage. His wife, Sandy, was

not bothered by Brian's appliance. His illness had been life-threatening, and she was relieved to know that her husband's problem was controlled—no more long and frightening hospitalizations.

But Brian was bothered by the colostomy. He felt ugly and deformed. He thought the bag was disgusting and was certain that Sandy thought he was offensive. He was very worried about having a bowel movement during sex.

Sandy's attitude was that she loved Brian. If he had a bowel movement during sex, she could handle it. She had "bought the whole package." She figured they could problem-solve and find the most optimal time of day to have sex.

At the point at which they discovered that they were infertile, Brian still hadn't become completely comfortable being sexual. The combination of his hatred for his body, his fear of having an accident, and the pressure on him to have erections on command was terrible.

Another important factor is the dynamic of the husband and wife. The relationship can become so tense that the partners hate each other. Hatred has never been an aphrodisiac. Coping with the actual mechanics of the crisis strains the marital system, seemingly to its limits: the physicians' appointments, the intrusive tests and procedures, the early-morning temperature taking, the scheduled sex, the depression. Some couples have their worst fights around mid-cycle.

It is common for one or the other of them to become more sexually demanding of the other, or to try to regain control by refusing to have intercourse (Keye, 1984). At other times, they may collude in avoiding sex, mid-cycle (if they haven't tried, they didn't fail). Salzer (1986) wrote a particularly good chapter for couples to read on common sexual interactions and foibles.

Couples may begin keeping secrets from each other. For instance, a wife who irrationally blames her infertility on her husband's postponement of childbearing may feel too blocked by her resentment to want to have an intense, intimate lovemaking session with him for months and months. A man who feels that his wife is obsessed with pregnancy and emotionally withdrawn from him may not feel much like having sex with her at all, even if a particular night is her fertile time. The husband and wife may be afraid that if they express the conflict or the disappointment in their hearts, the marital system will not be able to withstand the added burden. Without support and a strong therapeutic intervention from outside itself, the couple system will get frozen in a bad adjustment to a taxing situation, and the couple may get stuck in a sexual relationship that "works" physically but is empty emotionally.

Women's Reactions

Sexuality is markedly affected in women patients (Kaufman, 1969; Menning, 1977). De Brovner and Shubin-Stein (1975) reported women's common reactions to be decreased libido and sexual enjoyment, difficulty achieving orgasm, and a change in roles so that the wife begins to initiate sex frequently, even though she has no desire for it. Keye and Deneris (1983) reported the results of a conflicting study that found sexual dysfunction, including desire disorders, to be no higher than average among infertile women. However, my clinical impression is that diminished sexual enjoyment *is* quite common among infertile women who unambivalently want children. (Men's sexual responses are more variable.)

In the Multimodal Life History Inventory (see Appendix 1), women patients were asked, "Is your present sex life satisfactory? If no, please explain." Here are some typical responses:

"Sometimes it is, but lots of time I am either very tired or have so much on my mind that I cannot be in the mood and I really don't enjoy it" (woman aged twenty-seven).

"No, I have lost most all desire to have sex, even though I enjoy it somewhat when I push past that" (woman aged thirty-five).

Often, wives blame their sexual difficulties on their husbands, as if their husbands are enjoying the process:

"I feel that Sid is not being sympathetic enough. He could try to make our intimacy more special without being reminded, 'This is the week' " (woman age thirty-three).

"I feel cheated and scared when he doesn't want to cooperate at ovulation time" (wife of Jarred, a fertile man who hates to perform on command).

"I don't think it is fair when he complains about only having to have sex a couple times a month, compared to me, who has to do all the treatments and consultations" (woman aged thirty-one).

One very significant aspect of low libido for women may be the particular assault on their body image. Fisher (1989) wrote, "One would presume that since the idea of being pregnant is so central to feminine identity, the average girl starts early to come to terms in fantasy with the phantom fetus who is already a part of her body image" (p. 266). Fisher called this a potential "someone else is or will be within me" state.

Hees-Stauthamer, who followed four Dutch women through their pregnancies, learned from extensive interview material that, even before conception occurs, a woman who is thinking of becoming pregnant may explore what this will mean for her body and her relationship with her spouse. One of the women Hees-Stauthamer studied said that the idea of "Having a baby made me feel finally like an adult. My body will finally become a woman's body" (quoted in Fisher, 1989, p. 230). According to Fisher, "One of the major distinctions between male and female is the fact that the female's body becomes the site for the developing fetus. By the time of adolescence and probably earlier the vast majority of girls have constructed images of self as a potential creative container. The concept of being a protective womb is universally linked to womanhood" (p. 263).

Women can engage in a unique body-image fantasy, as Fisher wrote: " 'I will serve as a protective, enclosing envelope for my child' " (p. 236). This "potential for pregnancy gives the average woman a greater sense of meaning and purpose with regard to her body than a man can muster for his own. She can see a creative mission for her body. Men, on the other hand, who have defined the utility of the masculine body primarily in terms of strength and power, find there is less and less regard for muscular output, as such" (p. 264).

The womb of the infertile woman is far from a protective space that will house a new person. Thus negative imagery of wombs that are "defective," "empty," "a black hole," or "that black hole where things keep dying" occurs. Intercourse makes the woman focus attention on her vagina and womb when she feels hatred and rejection toward them.

And orgasms? The women who are the most successful in having orgasms are attentively focused on their own pleasure, on their own genital sensations, on their bodies. But that focus is probably upsetting.

One female participant in a workshop on infertility and sexuality commented:

> You're right. People just don't understand what a blow infertility is to women's sexual self-image. Often, men are told to imagine how they would feel if they lost their job and work identity in order to comprehend their wives' feelings of upset. That's not the right comparison.
>
> I finally got fed up with my husband's lack of understanding. I told him to imagine how he would feel if he couldn't get an erection at all, and every other man in the world was walking around with a huge erection, and people walked up to all those other men and stroked their erections and told them how terrific they were all of the time. My husband was stunned by this comparison and said that he would feel really rotten. This infertility has ruined my sexual identity.

Fisher (1989) commented:

> There is a widespread stereotype that sexual excitement comes from abandoning self to sexual inputs. This notion is often applied to women. Presumably, if a woman is sufficiently femininely receptive to sexual stimulation directed to her body she will build to orgasmic excitement. . . . this is not the case. Multiple studies show that women most likely to be orgasmic are those who

actively set goals and who value being individually effective. They are women willing to put out energy persistently. (p. 278).

In order to have an exciting experience, the woman has to be relaxed and yet actively focused on the enjoyable sensations of the lovemaking. Because her womb imagery has been spoiled, she may find it unpleasant to focus her attention on her body enough to get sexual enjoyment. In addition, mid-cycle, the infertile wife might feel concerned that her own focus on pleasure may distract her husband, so that he will not ejaculate into her vagina. No wonder many infertile women want to get intercourse over with as quickly as possible.

When the medical problem includes severe male-factor infertility, there is a different dynamic. The lovemaking isn't as frantic or as pressured because he can't make her pregnant anyway. He knows that. She knows that. It makes them both sad, and it may be an unspoken, painful truth between them (Keye, 1984; Menning, 1977). Or the husband may find it hard to share his sadness about not being able to father their child. Perhaps he doesn't even recognize this loss, but he finds himself feeling strangely unmasculine.

Although the fertile wife of an infertile man isn't frantic about scheduling sex with him, her sexuality may be spoiled, too, if she is being medically inseminated. She is acutely conscious of when her fertile period is and has organized her life around it, including taking her temperature daily or doing a test on her urine. She knows where she is in her cycle, and she has carefully called up and scheduled the insemination at the correct time, hoping that the fertile days won't fall on a weekend or a holiday when the physician's office won't be open. As described in a 1988 study of women's reactions to insemination (Zoldbrod, 1988), scheduling is handled in many ways, depending on the physician, and it is sometimes complicated. In several cases, the women wrote to their physicians, sending them temperature charts from the preceding month. The physician would then write back, scheduling the appointments for the days she or he thought were correct and at the hour that would accord with the physician's schedule. Scheduling difficulties happened around weekends, holidays, and physician's days off. These led to the wife's obsessive concern with when her next menstrual period might start, an obsession that began shortly after the last menstrual period and continued until the inseminations were completed and the temperature charts showed that the fertile period was over, longer than half of each month.

Because of AIDS, frozen donor sperm is often used now, so that some of the scheduling conflicts abate because the couple no longer have to coordinate with the needs of the donor. But the fertile time still must occur when the office is open. When the husband is subfertile and his sperm must be treated and then used to inseminate the wife, coordinating the timing of the doctor, the wife, the husband, and the lab can get complicated.

Patients' comments included "scheduling of medication and appointment times was a hassle right from the start" and "It's hard to describe how difficult the scheduling problems became" (Zoldbrod, 1988). One AIH (artificial insemination by the husband) patient commented:

> "Because of our jobs, my husband and I could not come in for the standard 9 A.M. appointments. Scheduling of medication and appointment times was a hassle right from the start. Although my doctor was part of a clinic, he wanted to have his staff do the insemination, and that meant working appointments around his day off and Sunday. As we needed to come in one day for the insemination, skip a day, and then come back the next day for the second insemination, we had to be sure that the Clomid was started on the correct day. . . .
>
> It's hard to describe how difficult the scheduling problems became. I was a school teacher at the time and my school was 35 miles from the doctor's office. Of course, I couldn't be gone mornings every month for 9 A.M. artificial insemination appointments. Also my husband was working many miles from the office and never sure exactly what time he could get away. Both bosses had to be told a little of what was going on . . . Neither of us enjoyed always asking permission to leave early. Fortunately, both bosses were very understanding of the situation." (Zoldbrod, 1988, p. 166)

Fatigue

In her book, *Night thoughts: Reflections of a Sex Therapist* (1981), Avodah Offit talks about good sex as taking certain ingredients: enough time, a special environment, and perhaps a substance that acts as an aphrodisiac. Another crucial ingredient is adequate physical energy. To have a really intense orgasm, the body has to have some excess energy to discharge.

Undergoing infertility treatments can be exhausting for the woman, no matter which partner is infertile, because the wife is always the recipient of the treatment. Remember Jill, whom we met in Chapter 7. She was tired from getting up at the right time to get to her ultrasound appointments in the morning, and she didn't sleep well because she was afraid that she would miss the proper time for one of her injections. She also had headaches as a side effect of the medications. Jill had secondary infertility and had responsibility for a child. Luckily, her husband took over. In cases of both primary and secondary infertility, the wife may be physically depleted.

There are many reasons why wives' sexual functioning tends to be more disturbed than husbands' sexuality. On the other hand, helping personnel ought not to make assumptions that the wife's sex drive is diminished and the husband's remains intact:

> Laura, thirty-four, and Todd, thirty-six, had been married for six years. They had attempted pregnancy immediately. They had had two years without conceiving, followed by eight pregnancies in the past four years.

Laura had had five miscarriages and three ectopic pregnancies. She had lost a fallopian tube with the second ectopic pregnancy and the other fallopian tube with the third.

Laura and Todd were feeling very drained. Laura was still trying to come to grips with the loss, and they were having difficulty talking about how they felt. Laura described herself as "very depressed, but I keep my pain very private. Friends think I am terrific and strong." Laura and Todd were considering in vitro fertilization and were on two adoption lists, too.

In the midst of this, Laura commented "Our intimacy has been affected in ways we don't understand." Todd's sex drive was very low. But despite the losses and her depression, Laura's sex drive was strong.

Men's Reactions

The negative effect that fertility problems have on male sexuality has been discussed repeatedly in the literature (Debrovner & Shubin-Stein, 1975, 1976; Elstein, 1975; Sturgis, Taymor, & Morris, 1957; Walker, 1978), particularly performance anxiety and erectile dysfunction (Bullock, 1974; Drake & Grunert, 1979; Keye, 1984), and especially at mid-cycle.

The focus on erectile dysfunction has been so strong that one might be led to think it is quite frequent. Walker (1978) wrote that "impotence and transient ejaculatory disturbances [are] believed to happen in more than half the cases." Keye (1984) wrote that "not a few men" have ejaculatory failure undergoing an infertility evaluation (p. 761). And Abbey et al. (1991) declared that "viewing sex as a homework assignment often produces impotence" (p. 297).

Yet these accounts don't adequately represent the sexual issues we see in the real world of consulting rooms and group therapy rooms. Ongoing performance failure seems to be rare among fertile husbands. None of my sex-therapist colleagues see much of it, and clearly, wives who watched their chance of achieving pregnancy being missed month by month because of erectile dysfunction would drag their husbands into treatment, kicking and screaming.

But men have other common problems with the sexual aspects of medical treatment that are not adequately recognized: sad feelings about the lack of genuine sexual connection with the women they love; insecurity about their masculinity; and hurt feelings about how they are treated by medical personnel. No man feels as good about his sexuality during an infertility crisis as he did before it.

What is true and what is untrue about men's sexuality and the infertility crisis? One truth is that, on the whole, men still do seem to be able to experience more sexual pleasure than women (Abbey et al., 1991; Daniluk, 1988; Lalos et al., 1985b).

Second, men inevitably have a negative reaction to the medical interventions involved in infertility workups and treatments and resent the scheduled intercourse. MacNab's respondents (1984) complained about the "lack of dignity of the sperm tests," and about "invasion of my privacy." Others felt "manipulated by the charts, the timing, the sex on demand" (p. 117). One spoke of "unpassionate, joyless sex on demand" (p. 125).

Third, hurt feelings about being ignored or treated coldly by medical personnel during evaluation or when doing sexually sensitive infertility tasks are commonplace. We cannot assume that everything is fine when men do not complain. Levant (1990) commented that "the male sex role requires that men be independent, strong, self-reliant, competitive, achievement-oriented, powerful, adventurous, and emotionally restrained." This "self-denying and stoicheroic" script takes a tremendous toll on men's physical and mental health (p. 309).

And fourth, it is perilous to assume that we know how *most* men feel or how they function, day to day, during this period. Men, far more than women, vary in how they react sexually to the infertility crisis (DeBrovner & Shubin-Stein, 1975). Men are poor reporters. Their reticence in talking about their reactions has frustrated several researchers. In the gathering of data for a study of critical incidents in medical care (Zoldbrod, 1988), not one man wrote in to talk about how he was affected, emotionally or sexually, by how he was told his diagnosis, by having biopsies, or by taking medications. MacNab (1984) had to contact 400 men in order to get 30 subjects who would participate in his dissertation on men's reactions to infertility, and even his respondents were not particularly open about their sexual feelings.

Menning (1977) noted, and MacNab's research verified, that there is a myth that infertility is a sexual disorder. Men fear talking about their sexual problems because perhaps their listeners will assume that their sexual problems *caused* the infertility.

Men's Secretiveness about Sexuality

Men are secretive about how their sexuality is affected by their infertility experience, in large part because they are secretive about their sexuality in general. According to Zilbergeld (1978) "One of the cornerstones of the masculine stereotype in our society is that a man is one who has no doubts, questions or confusions about sex, and that a real man knows how to have good sex and does so frequently" (p. 3).

The current stereotype of male sexuality is that men are always ready to perform (Zilbergeld, 1978), and both husband and wife may subscribe to this notion. We can be certain that the respondents who wrote down "unrealistic sexual demands by partner" as an answer to Keye and Deneris's survey (1984) of the causes of sexual problems during infertility were men. Some infertile wives are totally lacking in empathy with their husbands' feelings when it is time to "just do it." Recall the "five minutes" story told earlier.

Legends about male sexuality abound. The myth is that women need closeness, communicating, and relating in order to get in the mood for sex, to be aroused, but that men are very simple creatures when it comes to sex. They have no special requirements; they are almost always ready and willing, and their only problem is how to get enough of it.

Zilbergeld (1978) humorously and crudely summarized the myth: "A man's sexual tastes are easy to satisfy. He will take it any way he can get it, but what he really wants to do is stick it in and hump away until he has an orgasm, with as little tenderness, communication and relating as possible" (p. 2).

Ironically, this script comes amazingly close to describing what the mid-cycle sex act is for some couples when the man is fertile. For a husband with no preexisting sexual anxieties or control issues, this regimen will not create any physical problem. If one considers what this sex act entails, all the wife is insisting on is a process similar to masturbating, but at the end, the penis is inserted in the vagina and ejaculation occurs. The husband feels no anxiety about whether or not she is willing, aroused, and lubricated, and he need not pay attention to how she is feeling during the thrusting and ejaculation, or to whether she has an orgasm. The point is simply to deposit the sperm in the right place. And given the folklore, men *should* be able to perform quite well at this task. Not to be able to do so would be "unmanly." But for some men, the obligation to have sex this way is upsetting and demeaning. However, because of the standard views of male sexuality, men who resent the sexual burdens are silent about their sentiments.

In 1991, I appeared on an hour-long radio show about the psychological effects of infertility on men and women. A man called in and talked about the awful pressure to have sex so frequently during mid-cycle. I asked him if he ever talked to his friends about it. He said that, when he tried to talk to his male friends about this problem, they made jokes about the fact that they'd *love* it if they had to have sex all the time. No wonder few men complain to their buddies when they have to perform to try to get their wives pregnant.

In reality, wrote Zilbergeld (1978), men are not all that content with their sexuality. In a survey of fifty-two thousand people by *Psychology Today* that he cited, over half the men said they were dissatisfied with their sex life. Thirty-nine percent reported various problems, such as premature ejaculation and lack of interest in sex. Zilbergeld was very sympathetic to the plight of men who completely break the masculine sexual stereotype, the ones who feel that any kind of sex is a burden or a duty. Such men are far more common in the general population than anyone suspects, he wrote, because they cannot admit their feelings. Of course, men may feel that sex is work, wrote Zilbergeld. They have so much to do to fulfill the mythical masculine sex role. They must (1) initiate the whole event; (2) get their partners turned on; (3) orchestrate the whole event; (4) make sure their partners are satisfied; and (5) find their own satisfaction (p. 6).

Under normal circumstances, Zilbergeld encourages men who don't like sex to say "no" when they don't have the desire. Imagine what happens to these men and to the marital relationship when they must have intercourse at specified times in order to conceive a baby.

One husband, Jarred, expressed his feelings of disgust in this way:

> I hate to perform at certain times of the month, like an animal, at my wife's request. Sometimes it's five to seven times a month. I feel loving two or three times a month, but I feel used the rest of the time. The rest of the month, we may have sex, but I'm very turned off, to the point where I don't want to do it. I love my wife very much. She is what is important to me, not a possible child. If and when we have a child, she will still be the most important person in my life. If we don't have any children, I still plan on leading a full life.

Even some professionals are shocked by this statement because they buy into the Kinsey view of male desire as an incessant and invariant appetite. Some professionals make judgments about how immature this man is, how he probably is threatened by the fear that a child means the loss of his wife's love.

In order to be of support to men, professionals must do some self-examination. Don't men have the right to have their own biologically set levels of desire, which may be less than the desire levels of their wives? Maybe we should act as if this is the case with each man. If we "mistakenly" empathize with a man who has no problem with sex on command, no harm is done. To the man who does feel used, our empathy will come as a tremendous relief and as reassurance that he is, indeed, masculine.

And many men need a safe place to discuss their sadness because their old sexual closeness to their wives has been lost. They're getting regimented sex during mid-cycle with depressed wives who have no interest. The rest of the cycle, it isn't much better. A large part of men's sexual enjoyment comes from pleasuring their partner, despite the male mythology. Derogatis (1977) found that men whose wives had a sexual dysfunction were as anxious and depressed over sexuality as were men who themselves had a sexual dysfunction.

MacNab's respondents (1984) expressed grievances about sex occurring only when the timing was optimal for conception and its being "scientific rather than personal and intimate." One commented that he could still enjoy sex for other purposes than tests, but that his wife could not. He expressed concern that she did not feel affection for him and that she would never enjoy sex with him again. Another member of MacNab's study, who now has a child, commented: "'Sex is still different; I still worry whether or not my wife enjoys it.'" One of my male patients commented, "I can't stand the regimentation of what is supposed to be the happiest and most spontaneous part of our life together."

Each man going through infertility needs our support. Even if he has a normal sex drive, it takes a remarkable man to avoid periodic feelings of resentment at having to perform. Men who are insecure in their marriages, men who need a lot of intimacy before they feel like having sex, and men in marriages in which they are the lower drive partner in a situation of long-standing desire discrepancy have an especially hard time during scientifically prescribed intercourse.

One last assault on men's sexuality deserves attention. Even though they may act stoic, men are deeply affected, positively or negatively, by their interactions with medical personnel. Recall that MacNab's subjects complained about the "invasion of privacy of the diagnostic procedures." Professionals appear to treat wives with much greater consideration than they do husbands.

Stu, my colleague, is a forty-one-year-old psychologist whose wife lost both her tubes. They are pursuing in vitro fertilization (IVF). He complained about the sexism of the medical process, saying that the clinic had treated his wife quite sensitively but had treated him "like a piece of meat."

As an illustration, he imitated how the nurse interacted with him. Playing the nurse, he walked up to me, without smiling or greeting me with words, and thrust a small dixie cup about three inches from my nose, saying "Here! The bathroom is over there." "Fine," he felt like saying to her, "tile and toilets really turn me on." This little drama seems to be in the "man as sexual machine" mode that Zilbergeld articulated. Stu was hurt, but he didn't say anything.

In another case, my colleague Charlie was being examined by a urologist for a varicocele on his scrotum. When he entered the room, the physician was talking to another male physician about a golf date. He nodded a brisk hello to Charlie, then turned back to his friend, in the opposite direction. While facing his friend, he casually said to Charlie, "Just drop your pants," and meanwhile continued the golfing conversation. Charlie felt humiliated and hurt. Again, he said nothing to the doctor.

Relatively, these can be seen as mild interactions. Here is one which was much more painful:

> Jack, at that time a twenty-three year old, went for a sperm count. He was told by the urologist, Dr. Byron, simply this: "Well, you'll never be a father. You'd better adopt." When Jack asked if there was anything further to test, or any treatment, Dr. Byron simply stated, "No, it's hopeless. I'm sorry." Then he got up abruptly, excused himself to see more patients, and left the room.
>
> Jack never forgot this experience. He was so devastated that he became temporarily impotent. He never told anyone (except his therapist) how this experience had hurt him. He and his wife, Sylvia, eventually adopted.
>
> Years later, they wanted a second child. Wondering if medical science had anything new to offer, and consciously taking an emotional risk, Jack went to get a second opinion from a different urologist.
>
> He was moved to tears in talking about how sensitively this urologist, Dr. Madding, handled the situation:
>
> Dr. Madding took the time to ask how the first diagnosis had been presented to Jack. Jack felt relieved because Dr. Madding listened carefully

to his description of how he had felt the day he received the news about his poor sperm test. Dr. Madding directly expressed sympathy for the shock Jack must have felt, and for his hurt.

After hearing the story of how painful the first medical workup had been, Dr. Madding took great care to make a plan for when Jack could call for the results of his sperm count this time. He fixed his own schedule to make certain that Jack would call at a time when he wasn't at work and when Dr. Madding would have quiet time to discuss the results. After this affirming interaction with a male physician, Jack felt better about himself as a man and as a sexual being, even though the results of this sperm count were as dismal as before.

These episodes illustrate how socialization influences providers, as well as patients. Some nurses and physicians are so affected by cultural stereotypes that men should be stoic that they really believe men don't have feelings. Perhaps some male physicians cannot stand their own identification with the infertile man's pain.

Precisely because men do not speak up when their feelings are hurt during medical treatment, there is a vicious cycle, in which professionals—nurses, psychotherapists, and physicians—assume that if men are not talking about distress, they are not aggrieved. Keye (1984), a physician himself, pleads with his colleagues to be very careful in how they report the results of sperm counts. Hopefully, in the future, more physicians will put a hand on a male shoulder or look the man in the eye and say, "I'm so sorry. I'm sure this is very difficult to hear," when discussing poor results from a sperm assay.

Sexual problems are not always insurmountable, of course. One of my couples did a wonderful job of negotiating about forced sex. Sally, the wife, objected to pornography. Bob, the husband, liked it. Before infertility, Sally would not allow any adult movies as part of their sexual relationship. But she loved Bob and was very aware of the pressures she had been putting on him mid-cycle for years. As a gesture of her love and her gratitude for what had really become a distasteful monthly job at her fertile time, she laughingly presented him with an explicitly sexual movie, to "make his job easier." They watched the film together, had playful and pleasant sex, and enjoyed themselves.

Sometimes it helps to address what is happening, not to ignore it. One colleague had sex while saying, "I don't want to do this. I don't want to do this," over and over, and waving to the physician he imagined to be watching over them in the corner of the bedroom.

Suppose that we have a couple who are very close, and who view the infertility crisis as something they are handling as a team. Despite the additional task of coping with the infertility, both of them might want to have wonderful sex. To put it another way, as Levine (1984) wrote, they each have the "desire for desire."

How would they go about this? First of all, the multiplicity of the stresses of the infertility struggle would have to be consciously counteracted. The wonderful sex would not just happen; it would have to be planned for. Avodah Offit's recipe for good sex (1981) would be a useful guide: Leave a lot of time, set up a special environment, and find a way to set this time off from ordinary time.

Given the kind of busy lives young couples have today, they would have to set aside the date ahead of time. If the husband or wife has been physically depleted by lack of sleep, or if the wife is struggling with the unintended negative side effects of fertility medications, she would need to take a nap ahead of time, perhaps a long one. If any injections are to be given, the timing of the sexual experience is important because the couple won't want to be interrupted by a reminder of the infertility. If this couple has secondary infertility, plans need to be made for child care.

Last, certain things must be set up ahead of time—"planned spontaneity," as some sex therapists call it. If the logs are set up in the fire and the CDs or records or tapes are ready to go, and if the massage oil and the incense and the sheepskin rug are out, then *if* something sexual and special happens, there will be more of a sense of an easy flow of things.

Given the primacy of intercourse to "get the job done," to get the sperm to meet the egg, an approach that doesn't rigidly divide the sexual experience into "foreplay" and "doing it" makes much more sense. It is the "doing it" that has been forced, month after month, at times when it was neither convenient nor desired. During infertility, sex has been quickies all too often.

Foreplay is a terrible misnomer, in general, but particularly in this situation. The unhurried, loving touches and the caresses that might have been seen as the "appetizer" might well be the whole meal here. Or perhaps this sexual experience will evolve into intercourse. But if it does, the intercourse will have a much deeper meaning than it usually does during infertility.

The therapist can offer a couple this recipe for good sex *if they specifically ask for suggestions* to make their sexual relationship more pleasurable. In general, though, the therapist shouldn't say anything implying that the sexual problems of infertility are easy to overcome, or that couples should want to work on improving their sexual relationship right now.

When a couple indicate that they have some kind of sexual problem, it's necessary to understand what kind of help they want and need, and what each one feels. The therapist should assess all the variables noted in figure 10, taking a very good sexual history that will make clear the meaning of the infertility to the couple. No assumptions should be made, particularly as to what the man is feeling.

When medical personnel are "prescribing" some kind of sexual activity, they should acknowledge the issue and normalize the couple's reactions ahead of time. They should mention that men may have difficulty performing and occasionally may need to "cancel out" of a test or a managed reproductive cycle because men's reactions vary markedly. Zilbergeld (1978) wrote a marvelous popular book on male sexuality that, when read by the couple, may increase empathy and understanding and alleviate some of the performance anxiety when the husband doesn't enjoy sex.

Salzer's chapter (1986) on couples' dynamics and sexuality is outstanding. Also, patients may take a look at RESOLVE newsletters, which frequently mention what a problem sex may become. Couples' support groups, such as the ones run by RESOLVE, give men a safe arena in which to discuss what they really feel.

Last, therapists should confront their own difficulty in discussing sexual topics, if there is difficulty. They should explore their own unconscious stereotypes of male and female sexuality. Once they feel comfortable, their patients will sense it. The therapist's office should be a secure place where men and women, especially men, can reveal themselves.

11

Medical Treatment as Rape: Sexual Problems in Women as an Aftermath of Treatment for Infertility

As we have seen, infertility may lead to sexual problems (Kaufman, 1969; Lieblum, 1988; Liebmann-Smith, 1987; Menning, 1977). Such problems are usually attributed to the medical workup (Cook, 1987; Keye, 1984), the necessity for taking temperatures daily, the increasing focus on sexual performance; the pressure to have sex during the "right time"; and the changing purpose of sex from pleasure to conception. For women whose quest for fertility involves years and years of treatment, is it possible that the medical treatments themselves—repetitious internal exams, painful procedures, operations that may leave scars on the body, and thoughtless comments by the medical staff—may cause sexual dysfunction? In the two cases reported here, this appears to have been true.

Mazor (1979, 1980) warned about the invasiveness of medical procedures and noted the infertility patient's pervasive sense that she is "defective." In an excellent article on psychosexual responses to infertility, Keye (1984) wrote, "The evaluation of infertility may be emotionally traumatic and a threat to each patient's emotional, physical, and sexual self image" (p. 761). Keye went on to note that the physician's manner and words in reporting the results of tests can be "devastating," and that "positive findings should be used to reinforce positive feelings, but negative results must not be described in terms that may have a negative psychological impact" (p. 761). Yet none of the nearly five hundred infertile men and women he and Deneris studied blamed any of their sexual problems on medical treatment. Instead, they faulted other things, such as their guilt, having to have sex on schedule, or drug-induced inhibition of sexual desire. However, Keye and Deneris's (1983) five hundred respondents did name "poor body image" as one of the causes of their sexual problems. Much of the poor body image comes with the diagnosis, and a portion of the insult to the body image may come from the invasiveness of the medical treatment.

189

Some evidence exists already that the patient's experience of repeated medical procedures may cause sexual problems. Medical interventions may cause changes in sexual imagery (Zoldbrod, 1988, 1990). In addition, as will be described here, medical procedures may cause pain and later anticipatory anxiety, which the woman may link to the penetration of her genital area. Or repeated invasive procedures may amplify her sense of being defective, causing a feeling of disgust and self-hate that, sooner or later, translates into sexual problems.

Imagery about Medical Treatment: Pain, Invasion, and Shame

A striking example of medical treatment's changing sexual imagery came from a woman who was part of my 1988 exploratory study of women receiving donor insemination: "Bill and I were on the beach, necking and petting. I got very turned on, so then we had to move to a place down the road, so we wouldn't be seen. By the time we actually made love a few minutes later, I wasn't turned on. My head was full of images of speculums and metal stirrups. . . . Sometimes I ask myself, is a kid worth this?" (Zoldbrod, 1988, p. 165).

Consider the factor of pain, and the special meaning of genital pain to a woman who is lying down, relatively helpless, during medical evaluation and treatment. In the 1988 study cited above, several women reported pain: "Artificial insemination not only takes all the emotional contact out of a couple and makes it very cold and regimental. It is painful during the procedure and after" (p. 168). Another patient said, "The doctor did explain the physical procedure that would be performed, but did not mention that there would be cramping and other discomfort" (p. 168). A third patient reported, "I guess I must have been really tight, because every time they put the speculum in, it hurt" (p. 168).

The same research (Zoldbrod, 1988) found that women undergoing inseminations felt shamed and embarrassed by having strangers present at the "sex act." One patient said:

> The clinic where I am going for artificial insemination has a large nursing staff, who rotate their duties frequently, so that I have been inseminated, examined, injected, weighed, questioned, and poked at by at least a dozen different people besides my doctor. The nurse is often present when I am undressing or when the doctor is examining me. I feel that my privacy has been violated. There are just so many people involved in my care. As our hopes dwindle, it is hard for me to maintain any equilibrium when I go to the doctor's office, and having to deal with a succession of strangers is difficult for me. (pp. 167–168)

Another patient said, "I am just sick of spreading my legs. . . . When this process began, I just never dreamed that I would have to spread my legs for so many strangers" (p. 168).

A young foreign-born woman who was undergoing inseminations and having a lot of difficulty with her feelings read the article containing the above quotes and commented, "That's exactly how I feel, I feel humiliated! I'm going to translate this article into Japanese so that other people can read it and know that they are not alone in what they are feeling."

Women are horribly *confused* by their feelings of distress about medical treatment, particularly when a given procedure is not one that causes pain. They have sought out and initiated this treatment because they desperately want children. In the past, during their healthy and seemingly fertile days, internal exams were not upsetting. Why are they upset now?

Medical personnel are also unclear about the symbolic meaning of their interventions. In training to become an obstetrician, a gynecologist, or a nurse, they learn to desexualize medical procedures. By their attire, cool manner, and "professional" behavioral cues, they are supposed to take away the possible stigma of the internal exam. "This is not a sexual or embarrassing matter," their behavior seems to say.

On the whole, for routine exams that are performed once or twice a year, this kind of role playing works well. But this approach may not be the correct one to use with women who have been undergoing invasive infertility treatment, particularly for a prolonged period. It minimizes or ignores the fact that the medical interventions are distressful.

Two physicians, Dennis Massler and Mona Devanesan (1978), wrote about the sexual consequences of gynecological operations, "Gynecological procedures ought not to be dismissed with cursory explanations and a physician's half-hearted attempts to elicit patients' fears and feelings" (p. 153). They discussed, with great sophistication, the critical contribution of a woman's general appearance and the look, smell, and feel of her sexual organs to her sense of self. Noting that "being physically attractive and alluring to men is critically important to being feminine," they wrote:

A girl's genitals begin to take on special meanings which are modified and/or reinforced through the time of puberty, when menses occur and the first dramatic evidence that her uterus exists is manifested. The symbolic meanings of her buttocks, vagina, breasts, skin, uterus, clitoris, etc., exist on many levels. Some of the importance attached to these organs is related to their actual functions; some is related to the beliefs, biases and emotional transpositions which occur during the maturation process (p. 154).

Thus women view not only the vagina and the clitoris as sexual organs, but the uterus as well. Massler and Devanesan warned that gynecological procedures in which sexual organs are touched or altered have *symbolic* (emphasis the authors') value and may have negative consequences for the woman's sense of her own femininity and sexuality. For example, after a hysterectomy, some women feel horribly disfigured and defeminized.

Clinical experience leads us to believe that this same process is extended and amplified among infertile women. After less than a year of infertility, women become unusually sophisticated about their reproductive processes. They understand the role of their uterus, their cervical mucus, their fallopian tubes. All of these parts of their bodies, necessary for reproduction, begin to be seen and experienced as sexual/reproductive organs in their own right. Thus the loss of a fallopian tube because of an ectopic pregnancy is mourned in much the same way that the loss of a uterus is lamented.

Yet these real losses are minimized by comments made by medical personnel in an attempt to soothe the patient or "cheer her up." A patient who has lost a tube may be told "not to worry; you still have one healthy tube left, and that's all you need." A famous male specialist, in an attempt to be funny in breaking the news, said to a patient, "Congratulations, Charlene, you have my disease," when telling a patient that she had a condition that very likely would make pregnancy impossible. Each patient, no matter how calm and composed he or she appears, is vulnerable during infertility treatment. In this chapter, two cases, one lengthy and one brief, illustrate how a woman's denial of her true feelings of invasion during infertility treatment can lead to sexual dysfunction.

The Case of Susan: What Happens to the "Good" Infertility Patient

Susan, a lovely, bright, and talented forty-year-old Danish woman, came into treatment for her severely decreased sexual desire. She and her American husband, Adam, had enjoyed a good sex life for most of their marriage, and both were quite disturbed by the change in Susan's reaction to sex. Adam complained that Susan "spaced out" and "just didn't seem to get passionate anymore, the way she used to do."

Susan denied that there was any problem in her attraction to Adam or that she disliked anything about his sexual approach to her. Both of them agreed that the problem had developed over several years, especially the past few, while they were undergoing infertility treatment. Both of them wondered whether Susan's eight-year medical care for problems caused by endometriosis was involved in her changing feelings toward sex. In fact, Adam felt that she had held up "too well" in the face of a long, demanding treatment regime. During those years, she had had countless examinations, several surgeries, and three failed attempts at in vitro fertilization (IVF).

On exploration, it appeared that Susan and Adam might have a mild desire discrepancy. After the initial period of falling in love, Susan's high sex drive went down somewhat. Adam's desire, which Susan had assumed would diminish in the same way once the novelty wore off and the responsibilities grew, stayed high. This had been a slight problem, and Susan had tried to be available to Adam sexually when he wanted her.

When I questioned Susan in detail about all of the treatments she had received, it was clear that her sense of pleasure in her body had been disturbed. A beautiful woman, she reported hating to look at herself in the mirror since the infertility. She hated the scar from one of several surgeries on her fallopian tubes. She also revealed that she felt repulsed and upset when Adam performed oral sex on her and looked at her vagina, activities she had previously loved.

As she forced herself to recount the long course of her treatment, her face and her eyes filled with pain. When I asked if she had ever revealed to any of the medical personnel how much these procedures were taking out of her, she and her husband both commented that she had been the perfect patient: calm, self-possessed, cooperative, and rational.

A role-playing exercise that would address the issue was described as a potential intervention in future sessions: Susan would pretend to be in her physician's office on the examining table, but instead of being a good patient, she would refuse to let the physician pry her legs apart and would verbally express her true feelings: "NO! NO! NO!" Susan grimaced at the idea of the role play, and we all felt that we were onto something.

The best idea seemed to be for me to play the physician because we did not want Adam to get (further) aligned in Susan's mind with the invader. At this point, we decided to begin the therapy by individual work with Susan; Adam would join in periodically.

In order to take pressure off Susan, I suggested that Adam stop initiating sex altogether and that they forgo sex for a while, until getting the go-ahead to resume. This is a fairly standard intervention in sex therapy; its purpose is to give the patient who has come to dislike intercourse control over the couple's sexuality and a chance to get back in touch with her or his own sexual impulses. Adam agreed.

The treatment began.

Other than the sexual problem, Susan reported being happy with her life and having few other problems. She was pleased with her marriage of fourteen years and adored her adopted daughter, aged two. She did note on her intake questionnaire that, "When I am overwhelmed with responsibility, I get very routinized and less emotional."

Susan was the eldest of three children. Her parents were still married to each other, and both were alive. There was no kind of abuse in the family.

During history taking, an interesting pattern became apparent. One of Susan's parents had been very unstable and histrionic while she was growing up.

Even as a young girl, Susan seemed to have decided that it was very important to be strong and "unflappable." As she grew up, she had assumed the role of the most cooperative, responsible child in the family. To this day, she was the logical person on whom everyone counted. This picture of herself as always on an even keel, always the strong one, had become a treasured part of her sense of herself.

Periodically, I would ask Susan if she was ready to try the exercise. She would say that she wasn't willing. Frequently, she would express guilt over her sex-free life with Adam, and she voiced anxiety that he would leave her if we didn't get her sexual problem solved quickly.

As we struggled over the weeks trying to get Susan in touch with her vulnerability, she began to notice how much she did *not* want to have her sense of being a strong person nullified. Using a thesaurus, she and I explored the precise sense in which she needed to feel strong. Could she settle for feeling "energetic" rather than always unflappable?

Susan was sent home with the task of diagramming her sense of her personality, using the onion exercise (see Figure 3 in Chapter 3). What were the most central qualities? Which qualities were more on the "outskirts" of her personality? Was there a way in which she could picture herself as strong-most-of-the-time, but also sometimes upset?

Susan came back the next week with the diagram and some new insights. Through the exercise, she saw that she had relegated some previously treasured parts of her personality to the outskirts for the past ten years. She said that she now saw that she had been "screwed up and unhappy" for the past several years but had been denying it. At that point, she said she was ready to "work on the genital issue again."

And so, the hard work began. I wanted her to get back in touch with the unpleasant feelings she had had during the gynecological procedures. She said that, theoretically, it all made sense to her, but what was she going to do to change the bad feelings if she got in touch with them?

To alter the course and make it less threatening, I tried to get her in touch with good feelings about her body, suggesting that she imagine being at home, in a private time and space, lying partially unclothed and saying affirmative things about her vagina. Susan said that that didn't feel good. She couldn't imagine doing it.

Then I suggested that she imagine her vagina sitting in one of the office chairs and that she talk to it (the talking-chairs exercise in Chapter 4). Some patients may find this exercise too "far out." However, Susan cooperated readily. First, she said that she "didn't even want to think about her vagina, let alone talk to it." Then she stopped herself, and she again said that she wanted to give herself a push to do this work. But she said that that the exercise didn't feel right, that she didn't want her vagina "out there." When I asked her to tell me more, Susan said that she felt that she wanted to keep her vagina "buried deep inside somewhere." When I inquired into the reason, she drew a blank. I suggested that maybe she felt ashamed of her vagina, or that maybe she wanted to protect it. She said that shame didn't feel right, but that she did want to protect her vagina.

I proposed that she imagine that her vagina was buried safely, deep inside her, but that she, Susan, was the "palace guard" of her vagina and that we could talk to the guard. I began to ask the guard a series of questions about what was going on with the vagina, that she wanted to be buried so deep. The guard said that the vagina was "really, really tired and needed a long, long rest." The guard said that "the vagina had been on display for eight long years when she hadn't wanted to be, and then even after that, when she needed a rest, she had been made to have sex with Adam. So she just didn't feel like coming out right now."

I then talked to the vagina and said that she had indeed had a terrible time, being poked, prodded, and hurt, but that before that eight-year period, she had been a source of pleasure to Susan. Did she remember the fun she had had? The guard said that the vagina was out of touch with all of the fun she had ever had with Adam. However, said the guard, her vagina could remember fun she had had with her other boyfriend, before her husband.

Susan wondered aloud if her vagina would ever be able to feel happy again. I explained that what had happened was a kind of rape. After rape, people's sexual imagery has been disturbed and it can be difficult to enjoy sex again. But, I reassured Susan, women can do some things to help themselves feel good about being sexual again. I elaborated on the rape imagery a bit saying that it was as if Susan had been the adult and she had taken her child (the vagina) off to various places to be abused, all the while ignoring the child's pleas. Susan wept as she got in touch with the reality of what she had done to herself.

Later in the session, Susan wondered about the thoughtlessness of pursuing biological parenthood at such a high cost to herself. "How could I have done such a thing to myself?," she wanted to know. "Now that I know how much I love my daughter, I have no desire whatsoever for a biological child. Why didn't I just move on to adoption?"

I pointed out that adoption is a very upsetting concept for most people initially, and that Susan's inability to admit to herself or to show anyone else that she was hurting made everyone think that she was superwoman, that she could handle it. So no one suggested that she stop medical treatment and consider other alternatives! That session's time was almost up. She and I agreed that she would try to have some more conversations with her vagina during the week.

The week passed. Susan reported that she had not been able to have any talks with her vagina at home. But now Susan was willing to go into a state of deep relaxation to focus on this material. After she was very relaxed, I asked her if Vagina would come out and talk to us today. Susan reported that "Vagina is at the gateway, sort of behind bars, looking out. She still doesn't want to come out, but she isn't hidden so deep away."

I spoke directly to Vagina, asking how she felt. Vagina still wanted to stay inside. There was more discussion of how she didn't want anyone to "do anything" to her—not Adam, not anyone. I told Vagina that it was safe in the room, that all we wanted to do was talk. No one would force her to do anything. I asked Vagina if she knew what had happened to hurt her so. Vagina said that she did not know. At that point, I spoke to Susan, using her name, and asking her the same question: Did she know what had happened to hurt Vagina so badly?

Susan said, "Vagina wants to be hidden because she was forced open so much."

"What do you mean?" I asked.

Susan said that she must have done intrauterine inseminations twenty times. Each time, her vagina was "forced open" by the speculum, and she had had to lie there for long amounts of time while a catheter was threaded through the os of her cervix so that she could be inseminated with her husband's sperm.

"At times, when they put the sperm in, it hurt deep inside," Susan whispered. She said that she would "just lie there, vagina open with the speculum, and wait for the pain." She compared it to pain when the dentist was drilling: "You don't know when he will hit a nerve, and you just wait for the pain." Susan reported that, at the time, part of her knew that she was forcing her vagina open, forcing herself to stay still, to relax. Another part of her was "screaming to get up." But she ignored that part.

"I was split off from my vagina, and subjugating it," she said. "I would wait for long periods of time alone, with my vagina forced open. People, always someone different, would come in, withdraw the tube, withdraw the speculum. I would get up, dazed, and go pay the bill or whatever. At that point, I didn't want anything to do with my vagina, and my vagina didn't want anything to do with me. We were in two different worlds."

Susan was sobbing as she retold and reexperienced this traumatic part of her infertility treatment. After she cried some more, she talked about an incident that stood out in her mind as the most dramatically destructive single experience.

Susan had been having a good experience with IVF. The physician at the clinic she used had been quite skilled, and the procedure was "not too bad." But she recounted in great detail one IVF attempt in which a different physician had had trouble threading the catheter through her os. In the process, he was hurting her severely, and she was openly crying. In his frustration, the physician had loudly muttered something about there being "something wrong" with her cervix. As she was weeping with pain, Susan recalled that the nurses had tears in their eyes and were obviously upset. After the physician left the room, they comforted her and told her that this man was a "jerk," that he wasn't competent to do this procedure, and that she should complain. Retelling this incident, Susan again cried for several minutes.

After a few minutes more, Susan opened her eyes. She had been in a deeply relaxed, trancelike state for forty minutes. She was conscious of everything that she had said in the session. Again, she asked me how she could have done this to herself. I suggested that she apologize to her vagina for "subjugating it." This was hard for her to do, and she couldn't quite get the words out.

With her eyes open, sitting up, she said that she was actually doing better. After last week and after this exercise, she said, at least she could feel her vagina. Before that, she had felt "totally numb."

She had decided that she still did not want Adam to penetrate her, but she reported that during the previous week, they had had a "nice" sexual experience: They were kissing each other, and she was trying to give Adam an orgasm. In the process, she began to "grind" her vagina against him. This was very pleasurable, she said, because "Vagina was hidden deep inside, but at least I could feel her." As the session came to an end, she talked about still feeling wonderfully relaxed. She was sent home with written relaxation instructions and a homework assignment to keep feeling her vagina and to consider issuing her a formal apology.

When she came in for the next meeting, Susan said that she had had an extremely difficult week. She had felt "unhinged and vulnerable." The memories we had liberated had not gone back into hiding, and she was having flashbacks of the low points of her treatment and *feeling* things about it.

She described a sexual experience that she and Adam had had during the week. Even though genital contact had been discouraged, Susan had felt like making love, and they did:

> I was really enjoying myself and felt that I wanted him to enter me. At the same time, I was afraid that it wouldn't feel good. Adam was also afraid that it wouldn't be OK. I could imagine discussion between competing parts of myself. So I told Adam that I wanted to, and if it didn't feel good, we'd stop. So he entered me, and for a while, it felt really good, almost like old times. Then, it became clear that I wouldn't have an orgasm, and I began to feel that I didn't want him inside of me, and I had those old panicky feelings, that feeling of wanting Vagina hidden. So I asked Adam to come out from being inside me, and I talked myself out of the bad feelings, and we continued to make love without him in me and it was good.

We discussed this episode, and we both felt that it had been a good experience. Susan was glad the treatment had "given a voice to my sexuality" and asked if things would ever go back to the old way again. I told her I was optimistic about her sexuality returning to its formerly robust self, but I added that she might have to be careful to stay in touch with her own desires, not to begin a new pattern of routinely acquiescing to sex when Adam was interested and she was not.

The next meeting was two weeks later. Susan talked about having been much more vulnerable than she was used to being over the past several weeks. She didn't want to get deeply relaxed in the session; she simply wanted to stay sitting up and talk. We reviewed the incidents in her medical care that had upset her. She was obviously upset as she spoke, but she couldn't cry. She began to feel stuck and frustrated because she "couldn't get the feelings out."

I proposed that we use a doll to represent small, vulnerable Susan, and she agreed. She laid the doll down on a stool in front of her and propped its legs up and open, over a box of tissues (indicating an internal exam or procedure). Susan immediately and angrily took away the box of tissues, closed the doll's legs, and smoothed its dress down. I quickly rearranged the doll again in the vulnerable position. Susan again protected the doll, closing its legs and straightening its dress. At this point, she began to cry.

Susan cried as if her heart might break. When she was done, she calmed down and talked more about the infertility treatments she had received and how completely kept herself from admitting her pain. She felt satisfied and proud of herself. At last, she could confront her true feelings about the exams and procedures.

This work took place during seventeen weeks. By the eighteenth week, Susan was able to enjoy intercourse with her husband again, "just like old times." Interestingly, the fact that the psychotherapy had worked in a few months astounded her. Even though she knew that she had worked diligently, she didn't expect that the small number of times she had reexperienced her treatment trauma could repair her damaged sense of sexuality.

Comments

Women enter these long courses of medical treatment feeling a sort of impunity: either the treatment will work and they will have a biological baby and will be happy and fine, or they won't have a biological baby and, happy and fine, they will go on to decide how to resolve childlessness. Maybe it isn't this easy. Perhaps the treatment itself will leave emotional or sexual scars.

Susan was an intelligent, warm, strong woman who overvalued her strength. Her defenses against being weak worked too well. She repressed and contained all of her feelings of rage and sexual humiliation during the medical treatments, and the price was that her repression generalized to all of her sexual feelings. Psychotherapy focused on getting her to (re)experience her painful feelings, to accept them, and to integrate them into her sense of self, thus liberating her sexuality again.

We know that the core of female sexuality is not the vagina because it is the clitoris that triggers orgasm. Yet the vagina is seen by males and females alike as the specific sexual contact organ in the woman. Massler and Devanesan (1978) noted, "Since [the vagina] is generally the gate to specific sexual interaction, anything which results in pain, displeasure, embarrassment or concern centering around the introitus can have far-reaching effects" (p. 155). In this case, it was the vagina that had been wounded (along with the cervix), so the work centered on the vagina.

After the session with the vivid imagery about her vagina needing a rest, Susan realized the enormity of the (denied) damage that had been done to her sexual self-image. Susan spoke angrily on a number of occasions, saying, "I can't believe I was so driven to pursue biological parenthood for all those long years. Now that we have our daughter, I couldn't care less about genetic lineage. We can't wait to adopt again. We'd never go back and try more treatments. If I had only realized what all this was taking out of me, I would have given up and we would have had a child to love years sooner!"

Of course, the matter was never that simple. Susan had approached becoming pregnant in a methodical way, feeling sure that if she did all the steps in the process perfectly, she would be rewarded with a baby. She was determined to get what she wanted.

Because of the way she had composed herself, in her persona as the perfect, cooperative patient, no one on the medical staff could possibly have understood that she was in distress. "Good patients" such as Susan offer a welcome relief to medical staffs, who are exhausted from dealing with patients who are more demanding and who seem more fragile. This case teaches us that patients who are "too good" should set off medical staffs' inner alarm bells. These patients may be in trouble down the road.

Francesca: A Brief Sketch

Francesca was twenty-eight, a bright, dramatic, artistic married woman. Married to Gino for eight years, she came to sex therapy with several complaints, among them depression and a total lack in sexual interest after six years of infertility. She was the mother of one adopted daughter, Rose, aged two.

Francesca had severe endometriosis and had had surgeries and several failed attempts at IVF. She and Gino had adopted Rose privately, after four years of treatment failures.

Francesca had come from a family in which she had suffered emotional abuse. It had been impossible to please her parents, and she felt that she could never measure up to a brother who she felt was "Mr. Perfect."

Gino, her husband, was a very giving, even-tempered man who loved Francesca and valued her talents, intelligence, and energy. He was a giving father to Rose.

Francesca's adoration of Rose was clear, and she was a very creative and active mother. A perfectionist, she was exhausted from her attempts to do some artwork, keep her house perfectly clean, and be a good wife and mother. She loved her husband and felt lucky to have him. She felt guilty that she was depriving him of their sexual relationship.

Gino and his family loved Rose but still prayed that Francesca and Gino would have a biological child, especially a son. Francesca herself felt stigmatized because she had not been able to get pregnant. Part of her wanted to try for a biological child, but she felt so positive about adoption that she would have been pleased to adopt again.

Recently, she had begun to attempt pregnancy again. Her physical reaction to the fertility drugs was overwhelmingly negative. The last attempt at IVF had resulted in a miscarriage in the sixth week, totally devastating her. When she thought about going back to the IVF clinic again for the next try, "just the thought made me feel sick all over."

In therapy, we began to explore the sexual material. Francesca had much the same imagery as Susan. I put Francesca in a state of deep relaxation and asked her to say nice things to her body. She said that that was "difficult, if not impossible." She almost felt that she did not have a body."

"Could you say bad things to your body?"

"That would be much easier," said Francesca: "You're disgusting, useless, defective, fat."

I then asked Francesca to imagine drawing her body. She said that she pictured her body as a "shapeless blob." Could she remember when she felt better about her body? Francesca replied that it was a long time ago; she remembered that, as a teenager, she had felt quite beautiful.

I spent some time concentrating on Francesca's positive images of her body from the past, then switched to present-day imagery. She talked about her experience with medical treatment and got in touch with some vivid, distressing body imagery because of her endometriosis. Her insides were a "shapeless blob," with the internal organs stuck together.

Francesca cried and talked about "just wanting to be left alone these days, with no one even near me, no one touching me except for back rubs. How tired I am, the headaches, the backaches."

Francesca had been totally depleted by her miscarriage, but she felt she was expected to do another round of IVF. The pressure was intense. Her husband and in-laws wanted a biological child. Her own mother had said, "Well, if there is the technology, just do it." And her own perfectionism was a tremendous burden. Francesca spent much of the session crying about her exhaustion.

I commented that the choice of whether to pursue IVF again was ultimately hers because it was her body that was undergoing treatment. Although of course she needed to let her husband talk about his feelings, Francesca could respect her physical limits. Other people do not necessarily understand how draining and depleting pursuing medical treatment is.

When it was time to leave, I gave Francesca an assignment for next week, to draw her body the way she saw it now. Francesca said that she would. As she thought about the drawing on her way out the door, she said that she pictured her body as being drawn with distinct, thin lines on the top and a blurred bottom, "almost as if it had been done in charcoal and then rubbed away."

The next session, Francesca came in toting her sketchbook. She was excited about showing off her homework. It was a magnificent, detailed nude of an attractive Rubenesque woman. The woman's body was actually quite lovely; it looked round and feminine.

I talked about the attractiveness of the body. Francesca said that she, too, felt the body she had portrayed was comely, but she pointed out that there was some distortion in the drawing: the woman's midriff was collapsed to the point of being nonexistent, one arm twisted behind her back (indicating helplessness?).

What had happened to the drawing that she thought she would do, of the woman with the wispy, undefined lower half? Francesca said that after the last session, she had begun to feel better. Then, she had begun to think that she really did not want to do IVF. And as she felt that she wouldn't do IVF again, she felt much happier; This drawing was a good representation of how she now saw herself and her body.

After this session, Francesca's depression began to lift. Her rejection of her body abated, and she drew several more flattering self-portraits, in the process, forgiving her body for not producing a child.

In later sessions, we worked on her extreme perfectionism and on her belief that she wouldn't be loved by her husband, his family, or her family if she didn't produce a baby. She was driving herself so hard to be productive in every realm that she didn't have any energy left for sex.

We talked about how she needed to get rid of her internalized critical voice or she would certainly not be able to be the mother of two children and a sexual being besides. The week after this discussion, Francesca did a collage of pictures and words that portrayed her critical voice and then responded to it with words cut out of a magazine that said, "Enough is enough."

Next she talked honestly with her husband about how she dreaded continued medical treatment. He had not been aware of the sacrifices she was making in her attempt to give them a biological son. Gino turned out to be less attached to the idea of a biological son than Francesca had feared, and he agreed that they should stop trying. They decided to adopt a second child as soon as they could, and they put in an application to the agency within a few weeks.

Case Discussion and Recommendations

Who Should Decide When to Stop Treatment?

Pressure to pursue biological parenthood comes from everywhere, thanks to the media. Well-meaning parents, sibs, in-laws, and friends do not understand the symbolic meanings of undergoing treatment. Personnel in some clinics issue recommendations saying that patients who do not pursue a given procedure a certain number of times are "not giving it a fair chance" and will "regret it later" if they stop.

The pressure to keep going is internal, too. Women feel that if they don't use the technology, they are "sissies." Denials of the possible complications from the procedures and the process are everywhere. What should happen when the wife wants to stop treatment and her husband and family want her to continue?

Professionals from diverse orientations differ in their views. Many feel that, because having children is the couple's issue, the husband and the wife should have equal say in when to stop treatment. This is not my position.

Although the wife certainly needs to listen to the husband's feelings about wanting to pursue treatment further, when she experiences medical treatments as assaultive or rapelike, when the war is being fought in her body, then her wishes about when to stop should be primary.

Can Professionals Cushion the Blow of Infertility and Treatment?

Body image and sexual pleasure change with infertility, no matter how sensitively medical treatment is handled. "Isn't it amazing how closely tied reproduction and sexuality are?" Francesca commented one day, after she had spewed out such hateful words about her body: "disgusting, defective, useless." A body that can't reproduce little people is rejected in total, even though that "useless" body is quite able to feel sexual pleasure.

Prolonging the period during which the body is manipulated and invaded may well amplify the injury to the woman's sense of self, particularly her sexual self, if the outcome is unsuccessful. In her research, Cooper (1979) found that the longer the patient was infertile, the more she felt out of control of her life. Zoldbrod's descriptive study (1988) of women having inseminations, whether with their husband's or a donor's sperm, found that the greater the number of inseminations, the greater the emotional distress experienced.

Women who have functioned well sexually before infertility may recover rapidly when psychotherapy allows them to connect with their repressed negative experiences of their body or of patienthood. Certainly these two bright women, Susan and Francesca, did very well in an active, eclectic psychotherapy using imagery, hypnosis, psychodrama, and art therapy.

It isn't clear how well professionals can prepare patients for the wordless onslaught of self-contempt with which the "failures" in treatment will annihilate themselves. In one fascinating study, when the staff at an IVF clinic responsibly tried to prepare patients for the likelihood of failure, scientifically citing the statistical rate of success (less than 20 percent), patients still wildly overestimated their personal chances of success. Each couple believed that *they* would be the ones to beat the odds, succeed, and bring home a baby (Greenfield, Mazure, Hazeltine, & DeCherney, 1984).

Better preparation for vulnerable feelings during testing and treatment is possible. Mahlstedt (1985) suggested telling patients early that many others have experienced intense emotions during the testing and treatment process.

Might it not make sense to do this during even "routine," noninvasive procedures? Perhaps physicians should acknowledge that even a simple procedure like an internal exam may not feel like "business as usual" when the problem is infertility and the exam happens over and over again. After all, the metamessage of these examinations is "There is something wrong with your body." A simple comment like "It is difficult for you to do this over and over, isn't it?" can be powerfully coupled with a warm smile and some eye contact. This approach gives the patient permission to feel whatever she is feeling. If she is not disturbed, the comment will not cause problems. She can simply say that she's fine.

There are situations in which the medical interventions clearly make a bad situation worse. Susan, who had had no prior history of sexual abuse or rape, felt the invasive medical treatment as a kind of rape, but she repressed her experience. Was this a rare occurrence, or will psychotherapists be seeing more of such cases as the use of assisted reproductive technologies expands?

Psychologist Nancy Henley (1977, p. 13) cited research showing that women are more sensitive to nonverbal cues than men are, even though women may not be aware of what is leading them to feel a particular way in a given situation. There are nonverbal cues in the treatment situations that clearly indicate who has the power (the physician, often male), and who is inferior (the patient, usually female).

Henley stated in *Body Politics* (1977), "Superior or inferior spatial position . . . sitting or lying body posture . . . impassive or expressive demeanor . . . formal address versus first name . . . asking or answering personal questions . . . touching or being touched . . . these unnoticed details of an encounter are strong determiners of one person's power over another" (pp. 3–4).

The woman who is on the doctor's examining table, feet in stirrups, about to experience physical pain in the genital region at the hands of the physician, who is standing above her, is in a situation filled with the signs and signals of dominance, submission, and a subtle message of threat.

Reading this chapter, one of my colleagues shared with me that it had stirred up such memories of her own infertility treatment that she could not sleep the night after she read it. She, too, had had a rapelike experience. During a procedure, she had told her physician to stop because she was in such pain, and his only response was to continue to do what he was doing, only faster.

Physicians and nurses need to pay more attention to the symbolism, imagery, tone, and details of invasive medical treatment. This is a situation of great vulnerability for the patient, even if she doesn't recognize the fact. Patients who have a past history of sexual abuse, rape, or battering are in greater danger than Susan or Francesca were. (After a RESOLVE workshop about infertility treatment and sexuality, several patients stayed afterward to talk to me privately about how strongly their medical treatment had stirred up memories of their past rape experiences. One of them commented, "You're so right about all of this. When I was raped, it pretty much killed my husband's and my sexual relationship, but the infertility treatment really put the nails in the coffin!")

Medical staff might consciously think of cues they can give women patients that will make the situation feel safer, such as:

- Have another woman in the room during the procedure.
- Have conscious, engaged eye contact, and give a warm smile (which can be seen in the eyes even if the mouth is masked).
- Invite the woman to hold your hand.
- Acknowledge her feelings of helplessness.
- Take the formality out of the situation (one physician offered a patient under local anesthetic some chewing gum).
- If you can do it, tell the patient that you will stop if she tells you to stop. If you might not be able to stop at a certain point, don't promise that you will.
- Warn patients ahead of time about painful procedures. Do not minimize the pain.
- If you are in a situation such as donor insemination (DI), which isn't painful but can be humiliating, prepare the patient. Tell the patient that staff will change from month to month if this is true. Warn a patient undergoing DI that she may be alone in a cold room with her legs up and apart for some time, and suggest that she bring some "props" (e.g., a book, a tape recorder, or a photo) to make her feel more in control.

The assisted reproductive technologies are wonderful when they work. Infertile women the world over prize any intervention that allows them to bear a child. Women will continue to clamor to have "miracle babies" and will voluntarily undergo months and years of intrusive medical treatment. Hopefully, the increasing medical sophistication will be coupled with a growing attunement to the personal meanings of the interventions to the patients.

Part 4
Appendixes

Appendix 1: Multimodal Life History Inventory*

The purpose of this inventory is to obtain a comprehensive picture of your background. In psychotherapy records are necessary since they permit a more thorough dealing with one's problems. By completing these questions as fully and as accurately as you can, you will facilitate your therapeutic program. You are requested to answer these routine questions in your own time instead of using up your actual consulting time (please feel free to use extra sheets if you need additional answer space).

It is understandable that you might be concerned about what happens to the information about you because much or all of this information is highly personal. Case records are strictly confidential.

*Reprinted with permission from Research Press Multimodal Life History Inventory by Arnold A. Lazarus and Clifford N. Lazarus, Champaign, Illinois: Research Press, 1991.

Copies of the Multimodal Life History Inventory may be ordered from Research Press, 2612 North Mattis Avenue, Champaign, Illinois 61821.

GENERAL INFORMATION

Date: _____

Name: _____

Address: _____

Telephone numbers: Day_____ Evening_____

Age:_____ Occupation:_____ Sex: ___ M ___ F

Date of birth: _____ Place of birth: _____ Religion:_____

Height: _____ Weight:_____ Does your weight fluctuate? ___ Yes ___ No If yes, by how much? _____

Do you have a family physician? ___ Yes ___ No

Name of family physician: _____ Telephone number:_____

By whom were you referred?_____

Marital status (check one): ___ Single ___ Engaged ___ Married ___ Separated ___ Divorced

___ Widowed ___ Living with someone ___ Remarried: How many times? _____

Do you live in: ___ House ___ Room ___ Apartment ___ Other: _____

With whom do you live? (check all that apply): ___ Self ___ Parents ___ Spouse ___ Roommate

___ Child(ren) ___ Friend(s) ___ Others (specify): _____

What sort of work are you doing now? _____

Does your present work satisfy you? ___ Yes ___ No

If no, please explain: _____

_____

What kind of jobs have you held in the past? _____

_____

Have you been in therapy before or received any professional assistance for your problems? ___ Yes ___No

Have you ever been hospitalized for psychological/psychiatric problems? ___ Yes ___ No

If yes, when and where? _____

_____

Have you ever attempted suicide? ___ Yes ___ No

Does any member of your family suffer from an "emotional" or "mental disorder"? ___Yes ___ No

Has any relative attempted or committed suicide? ___ Yes ___ No

1

PERSONAL AND SOCIAL HISTORY

Father: Name: _____ Age: _____

Occupation: _____ Health: _____

If deceased, give his age at time of death: _____ How old were you at the time? _____

Cause of death: _____

Mother: Name: _____ Age: _____

Occupation: _____ Health: _____

If deceased, give her age at time of death: _____ How old were you at the time? _____

Cause of death: _____

Siblings: Age(s) of brother(s): _____   Age(s) of sister(s): _____

Any significant details about siblings: _____

_____

_____

If you were not brought up by your parents, who raised you and between what years?

_____

_____

Give a description of your father's (or father substitute's) personality and his attitude toward you (past and present):

_____

_____

_____

_____

_____

Give a description of your mother's (or mother substitute's) personality and her attitude toward you (past and present):

_____

_____

_____

_____

_____

2

In what ways were you disciplined or punished by your parents?

_____

_____

_____

_____

Give an impression of your home atmosphere (i.e., the home in which you grew up). Mention state of compatibility between parents and between children.

_____

_____

_____

_____

_____

_____

Were you able to confide in your parents? _____ Yes _____ No

Basically, did you feel loved and respected by your parents? _____ Yes _____ No

If you have a stepparent, give your age when your parent remarried: _____

Has anyone (parents, relatives, friends) ever interfered in your marriage, occupation, etc.? _____ Yes _____ No

If yes, please describe briefly: _____

_____

_____

Scholastic strengths: _____

Scholastic weaknesses: _____

What was the last grade completed (or highest degree)? _____

Check any of the following that applied during your childhood/adolescence:

_____ Happy childhood	_____ Not enough friends	_____ Sexually abused
_____ Unhappy childhood	_____ School problems	_____ Severely bullied or teased
_____ Emotional/behavior problems	_____ Financial problems	_____ Eating disorder
_____ Legal trouble	_____ Strong religious convictions	_____ Others: _____
_____ Death in family	_____ Drug use	_____
_____ Medical problems	_____ Used alcohol	_____
_____ Ignored	_____ Severely punished	_____

3

DESCRIPTION OF PRESENTING PROBLEMS

State in your own words the nature of your main problems: _____

_____

_____

_____

_____

_____

On the scale below, please estimate the severity of your problem(s):

____ Mildly upsetting   ____ Moderately upsetting   ____ Very severe   ____ Extremely severe   ____ Totally incapacitating

When did your problems begin? _____

_____

What seems to worsen your problems? _____

_____

What have you tried that has been helpful? _____

_____

How satisfied are you with your life as a whole these days?

            Not at all satisfied   1   2   3   4   5   6   7   Very satisfied

How would you rate your overall level of tension during the past month?

            Relaxed   1   2   3   4   5   6   7   Tense

EXPECTATIONS REGARDING THERAPY

In a few words, what do you think therapy is all about? _____

_____

_____

How long do you think your therapy should last? _____

_____

_____

What personal qualities do you think the ideal therapist should possess? _____

_____

_____

4

MODALITY ANALYSIS OF CURRENT PROBLEMS

The following section is designed to help you describe your current problems in greater detail and to identify problems that might otherwise go unnoticed. This will enable us to design a comprehensive treatment program and tailor it to your specific needs. The following section is organized according to the seven modalities of Behaviors, Feelings, Physical Sensations, Images, Thoughts, Interpersonal Relationships, and Biological Factors.

BEHAVIORS

Check any of the following behaviors that often apply to you:

___ Overeat	___ Loss of control	___ Phobic avoidance	___ Crying
___ Take drugs	___ Suicidal attempts	___ Spend too much money	___ Outbursts of temper
___ Unassertive	___ Compulsions	___ Can't keep a job	___ Others: _____
___ Odd behavior	___ Smoke	___ Insomnia	_____
___ Drink too much	___ Withdrawal	___ Take too many risks	_____
___ Work too hard	___ Nervous tics	___ Lazy	
___ Procrastination	___ Concentration difficulties	___ Eating problems	
___ Impulsive reactions	___ Sleep disturbance	___ Aggressive behavior	

What are some special talents or skills that you feel proud of? _____

_____

What would you like to start doing? _____

_____

What would you like to stop doing? _____

_____

How is your free time spent? _____

_____

What kind of hobbies or leisure activities do you enjoy or find relaxing? _____

_____

Do you have trouble relaxing or enjoying weekends and vacations?   ___Yes   ___ No

If yes, please explain: _____

_____

_____

If you could have any two wishes, what would they be? _____

_____

_____

FEELINGS

Check any of the following feelings that often apply to you:

___ Angry	___ Fearful	___ Happy	___ Hopeful	___ Bored	___ Optimistic
___ Annoyed	___ Panicky	___ Conflicted	___ Helpless	___ Restless	___ Tense
___ Sad	___ Energetic	___ Shameful	___ Relaxed	___ Lonely	___ Others: _____
___ Depressed	___ Envious	___ Regretful	___ Jealous	___ Contented	_____
___ Anxious	___ Guilty	___ Hopeless	___ Unhappy	___ Excited	_____

List your five main fears:

1. _____

2. _____

3. _____

4. _____

5. _____

What are some positive feelings you have experienced recently?_____

_____

_____

When are you most likely to lose control of your feelings? _____

_____

_____

Describe any situations that make you feel calm or relaxed: _____

_____

_____

PHYSICAL SENSATIONS

Check any of the following physical sensations that often apply to you:

___ Abdominal pain	___ Bowel disturbances	___ Hear things	___ Blackouts
___ Pain or burning with urination	___ Tingling	___ Watery eyes	___ Excessive sweating
___ Menstrual difficulties	___ Numbness	___ Flushes	___ Visual disturbances
___ Headaches	___ Stomach trouble	___ Nausea	___ Hearing problems
___ Dizziness	___ Tics	___ Skin problems	___ Others: _____
___ Palpitations	___ Fatigue	___ Dry mouth	_____
___ Muscle spasms	___ Twitches	___ Burning or itching skin	_____
___ Tension	___ Back pain	___ Chest pains	
___ Sexual disturbances	___ Tremors	___ Rapid heart beat	
___ Unable to relax	___ Fainting spells	___ Don't like to be touched	

6

What sensations are:

Pleasant for you? _____

Unpleasant for you? _____

IMAGES

Check any of the following that apply to you:

I picture myself:

____ Being happy   ____ Being talked about   ____ Being trapped

____ Being hurt   ____ Being aggressive   ____ Being laughed at

____ Not coping   ____ Being helpless   ____ Being promiscuous

____ Succeeding   ____ Hurting others   ____ Others: _____

____ Losing control   ____ Being in charge   _____

____ Being followed   ____ Failing   _____

I have:

____ Pleasant sexual images   ____ Seduction images

____ Unpleasant childhood images   ____ Images of being loved

____ Negative body image   ____ Others: _____

____ Unpleasant sexual images   _____

____ Lonely images   _____

Describe a very pleasant image, mental picture, or fantasy: _____

_____

_____

Describe a very unpleasant image, mental picture, or fantasy: _____

_____

_____

Describe your image of a completely "safe place": _____

_____

_____

Describe any persistent or disturbing images that interfere with your daily functioning: _____

_____

_____

How often do you have nightmares? _____

THOUGHTS

Check each of the following that you might use to describe yourself:

___ Intelligent	___ A nobody	___ Inadequate	___ Concentration difficulties	___ Lazy
___ Confident	___ Useless	___ Confused	___ Memory problems	___ Untrustworthy
___ Worthwhile	___ Evil	___ Ugly	___ Attractive	___ Dishonest
___ Ambitious	___ Crazy	___ Stupid	___ Can't make decisions	___ Others: ___
___ Sensitive	___ Morally degenerate	___ Naive	___ Suicidal ideas	_____
___ Loyal	___ Considerate	___ Honest	___ Persevering	_____
___ Trustworthy	___ Deviant	___ Incompetent	___ Good sense of humor	
___ Full of regrets	___ Unattractive	___ Horrible thoughts	___ Hard working	
___ Worthless	___ Unlovable	___ Conflicted	___ Undesirable	

What do you consider to be your craziest thought or idea? _____

_____

Are you bothered by thoughts that occur over and over again? ___Yes ___ No

If yes, what are these thoughts? _____

_____

What worries do you have that may negatively affect your mood or behavior? _____

_____

On each of the following items, please circle the number that most accurately reflects your opinions:

	Strongly disagree	Disagree	Neutral	Agree	Strongly agree
I should not make mistakes.	1	2	3	4	5
I should be good at everything I do.	1	2	3	4	5
When I do not know something, I should pretend that I do.	1	2	3	4	5
I should not disclose personal information.	1	2	3	4	5
I am a victim of circumstances.	1	2	3	4	5
My life is controlled by outside forces.	1	2	3	4	5
Other people are happier than I am.	1	2	3	4	5
It is very important to please other people.	1	2	3	4	5
Play it safe; don't take any risks.	1	2	3	4	5
I don't deserve to be happy.	1	2	3	4	5
If I ignore my problems, they will disappear.	1	2	3	4	5
It is my responsibility to make other people happy.	1	2	3	4	5
I should strive for perfection.	1	2	3	4	5
Basically, there are two ways of doing things—the right way and the wrong way.	1	2	3	4	5
I should never be upset.	1	2	3	4	5

8

INTERPERSONAL RELATIONSHIPS

Friendships

Do you make friends easily? ____ Yes ____ No   Do you keep them? ____ Yes ____ No

Did you date much during high school? ____ Yes ____ No   College? ____ Yes ____ No

Were you ever bullied or severely teased? ____ Yes ____ No

Describe any relationship that gives you:

Joy: _____

_____

Grief: _____

_____

Rate the degree to which you generally feel relaxed and comfortable in social situations:

    Very relaxed   1   2   3   4   5   6   7   Very anxious

Do you have one or more friends with whom you feel comfortable sharing your most private thoughts? ____ Yes ____ No

Marriage (or a committed relationship)

How long did you know your spouse before your engagement? _____

How long were you engaged before you got married? _____

How long have you been married? _____

What is your spouse's age? _____ His/her occupation? _____

Describe your spouse's personality: _____

_____

_____

What do you like most about your spouse? _____

_____

_____

What do you like least about your spouse? _____

_____

_____

What factors detract from your marital satisfaction? _____

_____

_____

On the scale below, please indicate how satisfied you are with your marriage:

| | Very dissatisfied | 1 | 2 | 3 | 4 | 5 | 6 | 7 | Very satisfied |

How do you get along with your partner's friends and family?

| | Very poorly | 1 | 2 | 3 | 4 | 5 | 6 | 7 | Very well |

How many children do you have? _____

Please give their names and ages: _____

_____

_____

Do any of your children present special problems? ____Yes ____ No

If yes, please describe: _____

_____

Any significant details about a previous marriage(s)?_____

_____

_____

Sexual Relationships

Describe your parents' attitude toward sex. Was sex discussed in your home? _____

_____

When and how did you derive your first knowledge of sex?_____

_____

_____

When did you first become aware of your own sexual impulses?_____

_____

_____

Have you ever experienced any anxiety or guilt arising out of sex or masturbation? ____Yes ____ No

If yes, please explain: _____

_____

Any relevant details regarding your first or subsequent sexual experiences? _____

_____

_____

10

Is your present sex life satisfactory? ___Yes ___ No

If no, please explain: _____

_____

_____

Provide information about any significant homosexual reactions or relationships: _____

_____

_____

Please note any sexual concerns not discussed above: _____

_____

_____

Other Relationships

Are there any problems in your relationships with people at work? ___Yes ___ No

If yes, please describe: _____

_____

Please complete the following:

One of the ways people hurt me is: _____

_____

I could shock you by: _____

_____

My spouse (or boyfriend/girlfriend) would describe me as: _____

_____

My best friend thinks I am: _____

_____

People who dislike me: _____

_____

Are you currently troubled by any past rejections or loss of a love relationship? ___Yes ___ No

If yes, please explain: _____

_____

_____

11

BIOLOGICAL FACTORS

Do you have any current concerns about your physical health? ____Yes ____ No

If yes, please specify: _____

_____

_____

_____

Please list any medications you are currently taking: _____

_____

_____

Do you eat three well-balanced meals each day? ____Yes ____ No

Do you get regular physical exercise? ____Yes ____ No

If yes, what type and how often? _____

_____

_____

Please list any significant medical problems that apply to you or to members of your family: _____

_____

_____

_____

Please describe any surgery you have had (give dates): _____

_____

_____

_____

Please describe any physical handicap(s) you have: _____

_____

_____

Menstrual History

Age at first period: _____ Were you informed? ____ Yes ____ No   Did it come as a shock? ____Yes ____ No

Are you regular? ____Yes ____ No   Duration: _____   Do you have pain? ____ Yes ____ No

Do your periods affect your moods? ____Yes ____ No   Date of last period: _____

12

Check any of the following that apply to you:

	Never	Rarely	Occasionally	Frequently	Daily
Muscle weakness					
Tranquilizers					
Diuretics					
Diet pills					
Marijuana					
Hormones					
Sleeping pills					
Aspirin					
Cocaine					
Pain killers					
Narcotics					
Stimulants					
Hallucinogens (e.g., LSD)					
Laxatives					
Cigarettes					
Tobacco (specify)					
Coffee					
Alcohol					
Birth control pills					
Vitamins					
Undereat					
Overeat					
Eat junk foods					
Diarrhea					
Constipation					
Gas					
Indigestion					
Nausea					
Vomiting					
Heartburn					
Dizziness					
Palpitations					
Fatigue					
Allergies					
High blood pressure				.	
Chest pain					
Shortness of breath					
Insomnia					
Sleep too much					
Fitful sleep					
Early morning awakening					
Earaches					
Headaches					
Backaches					
Bruise or bleed easily					
Weight problems					
Others:					

STRUCTURAL PROFILE

Directions: Rate yourself on the following dimensions on a seven-point scale with "1" being the lowest and "7" being the highest.

BEHAVIORS:
Some people may be described as "doers"—they are action oriented, they like to busy themselves, get things done, take on various projects. How much of a doer are you?

1   2   3   4   5   6   7

FEELINGS:
Some people are very emotional and may or may not express it. How emotional are you? How deeply do you feel things? How passionate are you?

1   2   3   4   5   6   7

PHYSICAL SENSATIONS:
Some people attach a lot of value to sensory experiences, such as sex, food, music, art, and other "sensory delights." Others are very much aware of minor aches, pains, and discomforts. How "tuned into" your sensations are you?

1   2   3   4   5   6   7

MENTAL IMAGES:
How much fantasy or daydreaming do you engage in? This is separate from thinking or planning. This is "thinking in pictures," visualizing real or imagined experiences, letting your mind roam. How much are you into imagery?

1   2   3   4   5   6   7

THOUGHTS:
Some people are very analytical and like to plan things. They like to reason things through. How much of a "thinker" and "planner" are you?

1   2   3   4   5   6   7

INTERPERSONAL RELATIONSHIPS:
How important are other people to you? This is your self-rating as a social being. How important are close friendships to you, the tendency to gravitate toward people, the desire for intimacy? The opposite of this is being a "loner."

1   2   3   4   5   6   7

BIOLOGICAL FACTORS:
Are you healthy and health conscious? Do you avoid bad habits like smoking, too much alcohol, drinking a lot of coffee, overeating, etc.? Do you exercise regularly, get enough sleep, avoid junk foods, and generally take care of your body?

1   2   3   4   5   6   7

14

Please describe any significant childhood (or other) memories and experiences you think your therapist should be aware of:

_____

_____

_____

_____

_____

_____

_____

_____

_____

_____

_____

_____

_____

_____

_____

_____

_____

_____

_____

_____

_____

_____

_____

_____

_____

_____

Appendix 2: Infertility-Specific Multimodal Questionnaire: Charting the Effects of Infertility on Your Life

The infertility that is troubling you has many different effects in your life. It will be helpful in your treatment for you to be as specific as possible in delineating these consequences. Please fill out this questionnaire and bring or send it back as soon as possible.

Behavior

Hint: Examples of behavior are frequent crying, working hard, paying attention to grooming, avoidance of people or situations, and fighting with your spouse.

What particular behaviors related to infertility do you have that you would

like to decrease? _____

_____

_____

Do you have any ideas about how to decrease these behaviors? _____

_____

_____

What particular behaviors would you like to increase? _____

_____

_____

How could you increase these behaviors? _____ _____

_____

_____

Feelings

What feelings do you have that you wish you didn't have? _____

_____

_____

What negative feelings would you like to reduce or eliminate? _____

_____

_____

What might help? _____

_____

_____

What positive feelings would you like to increase or amplify? _____

_____

_____

What might work? _____

_____

_____

Sensations

Hint: stomach trouble; floating, relaxed sensations; blurred vision; headache.

Among your physical senses, are there sensations that you are having now that you would like to decrease? _____

_____

_____

How might you do this? _____

_____

_____

What sensations would you like to increase right now? _____

_____

_____

How might you do that? _____

_____

_____

What mental images, pictures or "flashes" are you having these days which trouble you, so that you would like to erase them? _____

_____

_____

What mental pictures or images soothe you, so that you would like to promote them? _____

_____

_____

Beliefs, Thoughts, and Values

Examples of beliefs: Belief that I did something to cause my infertility; belief that this will be resolved in one way or another.

Are there any thoughts, beliefs, or values that get in the way of your

happiness? _____

_____

_____

Are there any beliefs you have about the infertility that you wish you didn't

have? _____

_____

_____

Are there any beliefs or thoughts about infertility that actually make you

feel worse? _____

_____

_____

Do you have any thoughts, beliefs, or values that make you feel better?

_____

_____

Are there any beliefs you have about the infertility that make you feel

better? _____

_____

_____

Interpersonal

In your dealings with other people, what gets in the way of close, personal, loving, and mutually satisfying interactions? _____

_____

_____

Can you think of anything you can do to change this? _____

_____

_____

Are there any specific people or specific kinds of interactions that make you feel better these days? _____

_____

_____

Interpersonal: Marital

How often do you fight about the infertility?

Often _____   Sometimes _____   Rarely _____

How would you describe the fights? Is there one characteristic dynamic?

Without discussing your answer with your spouse, how would you describe

the dynamic? _____

_____

_____

If you fight, have you tried anything to stop the fights? What? How has it worked, or not worked, and why? _____

_____

_____

For you, what do you think is the most difficult part of dealing with your spouse's reaction to the infertility? _____

_____

_____

In your opinion, what parts of *your* reaction to the infertility are most difficult for your spouse to handle? _____

_____

_____

Please use a blank sheet to tell me anything else you believe to be significant about your relationship to your spouse. _____

Health

Are there any things you are doing to your body that are not good for you? Under what conditions do you use drugs (alcohol, nicotine, coffee)? _____

_____

_____

Are there any ways in which you could be kinder to your body now?

_____

_____

Name _____

Date _____

Appendix 3: Worksheet for Regaining Bodily Pleasure

Often the experience of infertility makes it difficult to feel good about your own body. This worksheet will help you to find sources of pleasure in your body that you have forgotten. As you answer the questions, forget about how you feel now and think about what the answers would have been before you found out about the fertility problem. Both partners should complete this worksheet. When you are done, trade the worksheets and talk about your answers. Which of them could be included in your life now?

Name _____

My favorite scenery is looking at _____

_____

_____ .

It makes me feel good to look at _____

_____

_____ .

My partner and I especially like to look at _____

_____ together.

My favorite smells are _____

_____

_____ .

Sensual things that I have enjoyed throughout my whole life include ____

_____

_____ .

My favorite sensual things to do with my partner are ____

_____

_____ .

I have always liked to touch ____

_____

_____ .

I particularly like the touch of ____

_____ against my skin.

My favorite music is ____

_____

_____ .

Other than music, some sounds that have always pleased me are ____

_____

_____ .

The most wonderful and sensual experience I have ever had outdoors in

nature was ____

_____

_____ .

Foods that I find particularly wonderful are _____

_____

_____ .

Appendix 4: Infertility Prayers

Prayer For Someone Who Is Leaning Toward Adoption or Who Is About to Adopt

Oh, Creator, please give us the strength and courage to pursue adoption. Help us to find a child who truly needs us. Let our hearts be filled with the pleasure of knowing that we will have a child to love, at last. Help us to love this special child with all our hearts.

Adoption takes courage, Creator. Help us always to be in touch with our child's special need to know his (her) biological roots. Help us to be open to our child's changing questions about his (her) origin as he (she) grows. Keep us from being threatened by such questions, from being afraid.

Creator, we know that somewhere, at certain times, the mother who grew our child inside her body is filled with sadness and emptiness. She misses her child and wonders if her child is safe and very well loved. Let her know how grateful we are to her and bless her in her life. If she wants to see her child, let her find us, and help us to welcome her visit without fear.

Creator, we have traveled a hard path in our quest for a biological child. We have become depleted and sad. Help heal all of our past sadness and fill us full of loving energy. Allow us to be our best selves. Help us to love each other as man and woman, as husband and wife, so that our bond is strengthened. And out of the strength of our new selves and our strengthened union, help us to create a wonderful, loving home for our new child.

by A.Z. 10-90

Prayer For a Person Who Chooses to Have No Children, Rather Than Adopt

Creator, if I am not to be a parent at all, I pray that you will take away my deep sorrow, fill the emptiness in me, and give me the courage to find my calling in the world. I beg you to heal my relationships. Allow me to fully love my husband (wife), my family, my friends, myself. Help me to forgive all who have said hurtful words or done hurtful deeds to me, for they did not understand. If, in my anger, frustration or disappointment, I have hurt others, let me ask them for forgiveness and help them to forgive me. Lead me to see the beauty and feel the pleasure that is available to me in my own body again, and help my body to become strong yet relaxed. Please allow me to feel joy again, to take pleasure in a beautiful, sunlit meadow, the drama of the desert, the crashing of the waves on the beach, the majesty of the mountains, and in music, art, books, and all of the wonderful pleasures of this world. Help me to wish well to pregnant women.

Please give me the inner peace to smile again when I see babies and small children, and the strength to reach out to them. Enable me to participate fully in the world again, to be a citizen and a worker. Please help me to do good in the world, to have the strength, the courage, and the determination to act as your agent, to be, in significant ways, a creator on the stage of life.

Appendix 5: Unusual Resources

Continuing Adoption Support

Adopted Child Newsletter
c/o Lois Melina
P.O. Box 9362
Moscow, Idaho 83843

Healing Rituals for Grief

A Jewish ritual service for ending treatment and giving up the dream of a biological child is available frm Bonnie and Laurie Baron. It is available as part of a book entitled *A Ceremonies Sampler: New Rites, Celebrations, and Observances of Jewish Women,* from The Women's Institute for Continuing Jewish Education, 4126 Executive Drive, LaJolla, California 92037 (619) 442-2666. $9.95 plus $2.00 postage. For further information, call (619) 461-4120 or write the Barons at 7494 Rainswept Lane, San Diego, California 92119.

Some local RTS Bereavement Services groups run periodic candlelight services to memorialize children lost to miscarriages. To find the local group near you and ask about these services, call (608) 791-4747.

Self-Help Imagery Booklet for Patients

Getting around the Boulder in the Road: Using Imagery to Cope with Fertility Problems is a twenty-three-page reader-friendly self-help manual that presents the behavioral interventions described in this book to the lay audience. It has been favorably reviewed in *Fertility News, The Family Psychologist, Shattered Dreams, SHARE* newsletter, and *RESOLVE's National Newsletter.* It can be ordered for $6.50 (within the United States) or $8.00 (outside the United States) from Aline P. Zoldbrod, The Center for Reproductive Problems, 12 Rumford

Road, Lexington, Massachusetts 02173. Bulk rates are available. For information, write or call (617) 863-1877.

Calming Card for Pregnant Patients Anxious about Miscarriage

Suggestions and diagrams explaining the anxiety process and how to keep calm during precious pregnancies are available to patients. The Calming Card is written so that it is easy to understand, and it is printed on a sturdy plasticized card that will fit inside a woman's purse. Each card is $4.00. plus $1.00 shipping and handling. Outside the United States, shipping and handling are $2.00 for one to three cards. Write for bulk rates, which are lower. Order from Aline P. Zoldbrod, 12 Rumford Road, Lexington, Massachusetts 02173.

References

Abbey, A., Andrews, F., & Halman, J. (1991). Gender's role in responses to infertility. *Psychology of Women Quarterly, 15*(2), 295–316.

Abbey, L., Halman, L., & Andrews, F. M. (1992, January). Psychosocial, treatment, and demographic predictors of the stress associated with infertility. *Fertility and Sterility, 57*(1), 122–128.

Adler, T. (1989, October). Emotional life of teens different for boys, girls. *American Psychological Association Monitor,* pp., 13.

American Fertility Society. (1991). *Recurrent miscarriage: A guide for patients.* Birmingham, AL: American Fertility Society.

American Psychological Association. (1975). Report of the task force on sex bias and ex-role sterotyping in psychotherapeutic practice. *American Psychologist, 30,* 1169–1175.

Atkinson. R. (1988, October). Respectful, dutiful teenagers. *Psychology Today,* pp. 22–26.

Barlow, D., & Craske, M. (1989). *Mastery of your anxiety and panic.* Albany, NY: Graywind.

Beck, A., Rush, J., et al. (1979). *Cognitive therapy of depression.* New York: Guilford.

Beck, A. (1988). Love is never enough. New York: Harper & Row

Becker, G. (1990). *Healing the infertile family.* New York: Bantam.

Bell, J. S. (1981). Psychological problems among patients attending an infertility clinic. *Journal of Psychosomatic Research, 25,* 1–3.

Berezin, N. (1982). *After a loss in pregnancy.* New York: Simon & Schuster.

Berke, J. H. (1987). Shame and envy. In D. Nathanson (Ed.), *The many faces of shame* (pp. 318–334). New York: Guilford.

Bernstein, J., Potts, N., & Mattox, J. H. (1985). Assessment of psychological dysfunction associated with infertility. *Journal of Obstetric, Gynecological and Neonatal Nursing, 14,* 635–665.

Bierkins, P. (1975, March). Marital hostility, blaming and communications problems: Childlessness from the psychological point of view. *Bulletin of the Menninger Clinic,* pp. 177–182.

Birnbaum, M., & Eskin, B. A. (1973). Psychosexual aspects of endocrine disorders. *Medical Aspects of Human Sexuality, 7*(1), 134–136, 138–139, 146–199.

Bombadieri, M. 1981 The baby decision. How to make the most important choice of your life. New York: Rawson.

Borg, S., & Lasker, J. (1981). *When pregnancy fails: Families coping with miscarriage, stillbirth, and infant death.* Boston: Beacon.

Borysenko, J. (1987). *Minding the body, mending the mind*. Reading, MA: Addison-Wesley.

Bowlby, J. (1980a). *Loss: Separation and depression*. New York: Basic Books.

Bowlby, J. (1980b). *Sadness and depression*. New York: Basic Books.

Bresnick, E., & Taymor, M. L. (1979). The role of counseling in infertility. *Fertility and Sterility, 32*, 154–156.

Brown, G. K., & Nicassio, P. M. (1987). Development of a questionnaire for the assessment of active and passive coping strategies in chronic pain patients. *Pain, 31*, 53–64.

Bullock, J. L. (1974). Iatrogenic impotence in an infertility clinic: illustrative cases. *American Journal of Obstetrics and Gynecology, 120*, 476–485.

Burish, T. G., & Lyles, J. N. (1979). Effectiveness of relaxation training in reducing the aversiveness of chemotherapy in the treatment of cancer. *Journal of Behavior Therapy and Experimental Psychology, 10*, 357–361.

Burns, D. (1980). *Feeling good*. New York: New American Library.

Cameron, R., & Meichenbaum, D. (1982). The nature of effective coping and the treatment of stress-related problems: A cognitive-behavorial perspective. In L. Goldberger & S. Breznitz (Eds.), *The handbook of stress* (pp. 695–710). New York: Free Press.

Caplan, L. (1990). *An open adoption*. New York: Farrar, Straus & Giroux.

Carter, J., & Carter, M. (1989). *Sweet grapes*. Indianapolis: Perspectives.

Ciabattari, J. (1989, December). Will the 90's be the age of envy? *Psychology Today*, pp. 47–50.

Cohen, B. (1986). *The Snow White syndrome: All about envy*. New York: Macmillan.

Cole, D. (1988, December). Grief's lessons: His and hers. *Psychology Today*, pp. 60–61.

Cook, E. (1987). Characteristics of the biopsychosocial crisis of infertility. *Journal of Counselling Development, 65*, 465–469.

Cooper, S. (1979). *Female infertility: Its effect on self esteem, body image, locus of control, and behavior*. Ed.D. dissertation, Boston University School of Education.

Craske, M., & Barlow, D. (1990). *Therapists' guide for the mastery of your anxiety and panic program*. Albany, NY: Graywind.

Croog, S., Lipson, A., & Levine, S. (1972). Helping patterns in severe illnesses: The roles of kin network, non family resources and institutions. *Journal of Marriage and the Family, 34*, 32–41.

Dachman, K., & Lyons, J. (1990). *You can relieve pain*. New York: Harper Perennial.

Daniels, K. R. (1989). Psychosocial factors for couples awaiting in vitro fertilization. *Social Work in Health Care, 14*, 81–98.

Daniluk, J. C. (1988). Infertility: Intrapersonal and interpersonal impact. *Fertility and Sterility, 32*, 982–990.

Daniluk, J.C., Leader, A., & Taylor, P.J. (1985). Infertility: Clinical and psychological aspects. *Psychiatric Annals, 14*, 461–467.

De Angelis, T. (1991, July). When going gets tough, the hopeful keep going. American Psychological Association. *Monitor*, p. 18.

Debrovner, C., & Shubin-Stein, R. E. (1975, January). Sexual problems associated with infertility. *Medical Aspects of Human Sexuality, 9*, 140–150.

Debrovner, C., & Shubin Stein, R. (1976, March). Sexual problems associated with infertility. *Medical Aspects of Human Sexuality,* pp. 161–162.

Denber, H. C. January 1978. Psychiatric Aspects of Infertility, *Journal of Reproductive Medicine,* 20, 1, 23–29.

Dennerstein, L., & Morse, C. (1985). Psychological issues in IVF. *Clinical Obstetrics and Gynecology,* 12(4), 835–846.

Derogatis, L. (1976). Psychological assessment of sexual disorders. In J. Meyer (Ed.), *Clinical management of sexual disorders* (pp. 35–73). Baltimore: Williams & Wilkins.

Derogatis, L. (1977). Distinctions between male and female invested partners in sexual disorders. American Journal of Psychiatry, 134(4), 385–390.

Domar, A., & Seibel, M. (1990). The emotional aspects of infertility. In M. Seibel (Ed.), *Infertility: A comprehensive text.* East Norwalk, CO: (Appleton & Lange) pp. 23–35.

Domar, A., Seibel, M., & Benson, H. (1990, February). The mind/body program for infertility: A new behavorial treatment approach for women with infertility. *Fertility and Sterility,* 53(2), 246–249.

Dorfman, W. (1969). Psychosomatics, psychopharmacology, psychotherapy and sterility. *Journal of Reproductive Medicine,* 3(4), 39–41.

Douglas, J., & Atwell, F. (1988). *Love, intimacy and sex.* Los Angeles: Sage.

Drake, T., & Grunert, G. (1979). A cyclic pattern of sexual dysfunction in the infertility investigation. *Fertility and Sterility,* 32, 542–545.

Drake, T. & Tredway, D. (1978, July). Spontaneous pregnancy during the infertility evaluation. *Fertility and Sterility,* 29, 36–38.

Eichler, L. S. (1973). *Feminine narcissism.* Ph.D. dissertation, Boston University Graduate School.

Eimer, B. (1988). The chronic pain patient. *Medical Psychotherapy,* 1, 23–40.

Elstein, M. (1975, August). The effect of infertility on psychosexual function. *British Medical Journal,* 3, 296–299.

Fagan, P., Schmidt, C., et al. (1986). Sexual functioning and psychologic evaluation of in vitro fertilization couples. *Fertility and Sterility,* 46(4), 668–672.

Feldman-Summers, S., Gordon, P. E., & Meagher, J. R. (1979). The impact of rape on sexual satisfaction. *Journal of Abnormal Psychology,* 88(1), 101–105.

Fincham, F., et al. (1985). Attribution processes in distressed and non-distressed marriages. *Journal of Abnormal Psychology,* 94, 183–190.

Fisher, S. (1989). *Sexual images of the self: The psychology of erotic sensations and illusion.* Hillsdale, NJ: Erlbaum.

Fletcher, F. C., & Evans, M. I. (1983). Maternal bonding in early fetal ultrasound examinations. *New England Journal of Medicine, 308,* 392–393.

Freeman, E. W., Boxer, A. S., Rickels, K., Tureck, R., & Mastroianni, L. J. (1985). Psychological evaluation and support in a program of in vitro fertilization and embryo transfer. *Fertility and Sterility,* 43, 48–53.

Freeman, A., & DeWolf, R. (1989). *Woulda, coulda, shoulda: Overcoming regrets, mistakes, and missed opportunities.* New York: Silver Arrow Books, William Morrow.

Freeman, A., Garcia, C., & Rickels, K. (1983). Behavorial and emotional factors: Comparisons of anovulatory infertile women with fertile and other infertile women. *Fertility and Sterility,* 40(2), 195–210.

Friedman, R. M. D., & Gradstein, B. (1982). *Surviving pregnancy loss.* Boston: Little, Brown.

Gagnon, J., Rosen, R. C., & Lieblum, S. R. (1982) Cognitive and social aspects of sexual dysfunction: Sexual scripts in sex therapy. *Journal of Sex and Marital Therapy, 8,* 44–56.

Galbraith, G. G. (1969). The Mosher sex-guilt scale and the Thorne sex inventory: Intercorrelations. *Journal of Clinical Psychology, 24,* 292–294.

Gergen, M. M. (1990, December). Finished at 40: Women's development within the patriarchy. *Psychology of Women Quarterly, 14*(4), 471–493.

Given, J. E., Jones, G., & McMillen, D. (1985). A comparison of personality characteristics between in vitro patients and other infertility patients. *Journal of In Vitro Fertilization and Embryo Transfer, 2,* 49–54.

Glazer, E. (1990), The Long Awaited Stork, Lexington, MA: Lexington Books.

Glazer, E., & Cooper, S. (1988). *Without child: Experiencing and resolving infertility.* Lexington, MA: Lexington Books.

Goldberger, L., & Breznitz, S. (Ed). (1982). *Handbook of stress.* New York: Free Press.

Good, M. D. (1989, April). Disabling practitioners: Hazards of learning to be a doctor in American medical education. *American Journal of Orthopsychiatry, 59*(2), 303–309.

Greenfield, D., Mazure, C., Hazeltine, F., & DeCherney, A. (1984, Winter). The role of the social worker in the in vitro fertilization program. *Social Work in Health Care, 10*(2), 71–79.

Greer, G. (1984). *Sex and destiny: The politics of human fertility.* New York: Harper & Row.

Greil, A. L., Leitko, T. A., & Porter, K. L. (1988). Infertility: His and hers. *Gender and Society, 2,* 172–199.

Hamburg B., & Killilea, M. J. (1979). Relationship of social support, stress, illness, and the use of health services: Background paper for healthy people. In *Surgeon General's report on health promotion and disease prevention.* Washington, DC: U.S. Government Printing Office.

Harrison, R., O'Moore, R., & McSweeney, J. (1979). Stress, prolactin and infertility. *Lancet,* p. 209.

Harrison, R., O'Moore, R., & McSweeney, J. (1981). Stress profiles in normal infertile couples: Pharmacological and psychological approaches to therapy. In B. Insler & G. Bettendorf (Eds.), *Advances in diagnosis and treatment of infertility.* North Holland: Elsevier.

Hartley, R. E. (1959). Sex-role pressure in the socialization of the male child. *Psychological Reports, 5,* 457–468.

Hartley, R. E. (1974). Sex role pressures and the socialization of the male child. In J. Pleck & J. Sawyer (Eds.), *Men and masculinity* (pp. 7–14). Englewood Cliffs, NJ: Prentice-Hall.

Heatherington, L., & Allen, G. J. (1984). Sex and relational communication patterns in counseling. *Journal of Counseling Psychology, 3.*

Hees-Stauthamer, J. (1985). *The first pregnancy: An integrating principle in female psychology.* Ann Arbor, MI: UMI Research Press.

Henley, N. (1977). Body politics: Power, sex and nonverbal communication. Englewood Cliffs: Prentice-Hall.

Holtzworth-Monroe, A., & Jacobson, N. (1985). Causal attributions of married couples. *Journal of Personality and Social Psychology, 48,* 1398–1412.

Horowitz, M. J. (1978). Control of visual imagery and therapeutic intervention. In J. Singer & K. Pope (Eds.), *The power of human imagination.* New York: Plenum.

Horowitz, M. J. (1982). Stress response syndromes and their treatment. In L. Goldberger & S. Breznitz (Eds.), *Handbook of stress* (pp. 711–732). New York: Free Press.

Horowitz, M. J., Wilner, N., Marmar, C., & Krupnick, J. (1980). Pathological grief and the activation of latent self-images. *American Journal of Psychiatry, 137,* 1137–1162.

Humphrey, M. 1977. Sex differences in attitude toward parenthood. *Human Relations, 30,* 737–749.

Ipsaro, A. J. (1986). Male client-male therapist: Issues in a therapeutic alliance. *Psychotherapy, 23,* 257–272.

Jacobson, N., et al. (1985). Attributional processes in distressed and non-distressed married couples. *Cognitive Therapy and Research, 9,* 35–50.

Jacobson, N. & Margolin, G. (1979). Marital therapy: Strategies based on social learning and behavior exchange principles. New York: Brunner Mazel.

Jaffe, D. T., & Bresler, D. E. (1980). Guided imagery: Healing through the mind's eye. In J. Shorr, (Ed.), *Imagery: Its many dimensions and applications.* New York: Plenum.

Jamison, P., Franzini, L., & Kaplan, R. (1979, Winter). Some assumed characteristics of voluntarily childfree women and men. *Psychology of Women Quarterly, 4*(2), 266–273.

Janda, L. H., O'Grady, KE, Nichelous, J., Harsher, D Denny, C, & Denner, K. (1981). Effects of sex guilt on interpersonal pleasuring. *Journal of Personality and Social Psychology, 40,* 201–209.

Janoff-Bulman, R., & Frieze, I. H. (Ed). (1983, 2 November). A theoretical perspective for understanding reactions to victimization. *Journal of Social Issues, 39*(2), pp. 1–18.

Johnston, P. (1984). *An adopter's advocate.* Fort Wayne, IN: Perspectives.

Jordan, J., Kaplan, A., et al. (1991). *Women's growth in connection.* New York: Guilford.

Jourard, S. M. (1971). *The transparent self.* New York: Van Nostrand.

Kabat-Zinn, J. (1990). *Full catastrophe living: Using the wisdom of your body and mind to face stress, pain and illness.* New York: Delacorte.

Kasl, S., Gore, S., & Cobb, S. (1975). The experience of losing a job: Reported changes in health systems and illness behaviors. *Psychosomatic Medicine, 37,* 106–121.

Kaufman, G. (1985). *Shame: The power of caring.* Cambridge, MA: Shenckman.

Kaufman, S. A. (1969). The impact of infertility on the marital and sexual relationship. *Fertility and Sterility, 20,* 380–383.

Kedem, P., Mikulincer, M., et al. (1990). Psychological aspects of male infertility. *British Journal of Medical Psychology, 63,* 73–80.

Keye, W. (1984). Psychosexual responses to infertility. *Clinical Obstetrics and Gynecology, 27*(3), 760–766.

Keye, W., & Deneris, A. (1983). Female sexual activity, satisfaction and function in infertile women. *Infertility, 5,* 275.

Kirk, D. H. (1981). *Adoptive kinship: A modern institution in need of reform.* Toronto: Butterworths.

Kirk, D. H. (1981). *Shared fate*. London: Free Press of Glencoe.

Kirk, H. D. (1963). Nonfecund people as parents—Some social and psychological considerations. *Fertility and Sterility, 14*, 310–319.

Kirksey, J. (1987). The impact of pregnancy loss on subsequent pregnancy. In J. Woods & J. Esposito (Eds.), *Pregnancy loss: Medical, therapeutic and practical considerations* (pp. 248–268). Baltimore: Williams & Wilkins.

Klein, M. (1957). *Envy and gratitude and other works, 1946–63*. London: Hogarth.

Klein, R. D. (Ed.). (1989). Infertility: Women speak out about their experiences in reproductive medicine. London: Pandora.

Klock, S. C., & Maier, D. (1991, September). Psychological factors related to donor insemination. *Fertility and Sterility, 56*(3), 489–494.

Kopitzke, E., Berg, B., et al. (1991). Physical and emotional stress associated with components of the infertility investigation: Perspectives of professionals and patients. *Fertility and Sterility, 55*, 1137–1143.

Lalos, A., Lalos, O., Jacobsson, L., & von Schoultz, B. (1985a). A psychosocial characterization of infertile couples before surgical treatment of the female. *Journal of Psychosomatic Obstetrics and Gynecology, 4*, 83–93.

Lalos, A., Lalos, O., Jacobsson, L., & von Schoultz, B. (1985b). the psychosocial impact of infertility two years after completed surgical treatment. *Acta Obstetricia at Gynecologica Scandinavica, 64*(7), 599–604.

Lazarus, A. A. (1969). Relationship therapy: Often necessary, but usually insufficient. *The Counseling Psychologist, 1*, 25–27.

Lazarus, A. A. (1981). *The practice of multimodal therapy: Systematic comprehensive and effective psychotherapy*. Baltimore, MD: Johns Hopkins University Press.

Lazarus, R. (1966). *Psychological stress and the coping process*. New York: McGraw-Hill.

Lazarus, R. S., & Folkman, S. (1984). *Stress, appraisal and coping*. New York: Springer.

Lerner, M. J. (1970). The desire for justice and reactions to victims. In J. Macauley & L. Berkowitz (Ed.), *Altruism and helping behavior*. New York: Academic.

Leugar, R. (1986). Imagery techniques in cognitive behavior therapy. In A. Sheikh (Ed.), *Anthology of imagery techniques* (pp. 61–83). Milwaukee: American Imagery Institute. (Can be ordered from American Imagery Institute, P.O. Box, Milwaukee, WI 13453.)

Levant, R. F. (1990), (Fall). Psychological services designed for men: A psychoeducational approach. *Psychotherapy, 27*(3), 309–314.

Levant, R., & Kelly, J. (1989). *Between father and child: How to be the kind of father you want to be*. New York: Viking.

Levine, S. (1984). An essay on the nature of sexual desire. *Journal of Sex and Marital Therapy, 10*, 83–96.

Levy-Schiff, R., Bar, O., & Har-Even, D. (1990, April). Psychological adjustment of adoptive parents-to-be. *American Journal of Orthopsychiatry, 60*(2), 258–267.

Lieberman, M. A. (1982). The effects of social supports on responses to stress. In L Goldberger & S Bresnitz (Eds.), *The handbook of stress* (pp. 764–785). Free Press, NY

Lieblum, S. (1988). Intimacy and the new reproductive options. *Women and Therapy, 7*(2–3), 131–143.

Liebmann-Smith, J. (1987). *In pursuit of pregnancy*. New York: Newmarket.

Limbo, R., & Wheeler, S. (1986). *When a baby dies*. La Crosse, WI: Resolve through Sharing.

Litwak, E., & Szelenyi, I. (1969). Primary group structures and their function: Kin, neighbors and friends. *American Sociological Review, 34,* 465–581.

Lowenthal, M. F., Thurnher, M., & Chiraboga, D. (1975). *Four stages of life: A comparitive study of women and men facing transitions.* San Francisco: Jossey-Bass.

MacNab, T. (1984). *Infertility and men: A study of change and adaptive choices in the lives of involuntarily childless men.* Unpublished Ph.D. dissertation, Fielding Institute, Berkeley, California.

Mahlstedt, P. P. (1985). The psychological component of infertility. *Fertility and Sterility, 43,* 335–346.

Markus, H., & Nurius, P. (1986). Possible selves. *American Psychologist, 41,* 954–969.

Massler, D., & Devanesan, M. (1978). Sexual consequences of gynecological operations. In A. Comfort (Ed.), *Sexual consequences of disability* (pp. 153–182). Philadelphia: George Stickley.

May, R. (1980). *Sex and fantasy.* New York: Norton.

Mazor, M. (1978). The problem of infertility. In M Notman & C Nadelson (Eds.), *The woman patient* (Vol. 1, pp. 137–160). New York: Plenum.

Mazor, M. (1979). Barren couples. *Psychology Today, 22,* 101–112.

Mazor, M. (1980a, May), Emotional reactions to infertility. Paper presented at the 133rd annual meeting of the American Psychiatric Association, San Francisco.

Mazor, M. (1980b). Psychosexual problems of the infertile couple. *Medical Aspects of Human Sexuality, 14,* 32–50.

Mazor, M. (1984). Emotional reactions to infertility. In M. Mazor & H. Simons (Eds.), *Infertility: Medical, emotional, and social considerations* (pp. 23–35). New York: Human Sciences.

McBride, A. (1973). *The growth and development of mothers.* New York: Harper & Row.

McGrade, J. J., & Tolor, A. (1981). The reaction to infertility and the infertility investigation: A comparison of the responses of men and women. *Infertility, 4,* 7–27.

Meichenbaum, D. (1977). *Cognitive-behavior modification: An integrative approach.* New York: Plenum.

Meichenbaum, D. (1978). Why does using imagery in psychotherapy lead to change. In J. Singer & K. Pope (Eds.), *The power of human imagination.* New York: Plenum.

Meichenbaum, D., & Cameron, R. (1972). *Stress inoculation: A skills training approach to anxiety management.* Manuscript, University of Waterloo, Canada.

Meichenbaum, D., & Jaremko, M. (1983). *Stress reduction and prevention.* New York: Plenum.

Melina, L. (1990, March). Adoption rituals needed to enhance sense of "family." *Adopted Child, 9*(3),.

Menning, B. (1977). *Infertility: A guide for the childless couple.* Englewood Cliffs, NJ: Prentice-Hall.

Menning, B. (1981). Donor insemination: The psychosocial issues. *Contemporary Obstetrics/Gynecology, 10,* 155–172.

Michael, J. (1985). *Motherless child.* New York: Norton.

Mikesell, S. (1990, Fall). Therapist effectiveness in the face of client shame. *Family Psychologist, 6*(4), 23.

Milne, L. S., & Rich, O. J. (1981). Cognitive and affective aspects of the responses of pregnant women to sonography. *Maternal Child Nursing Journal, 10,* 15–39.

Mintz, L., & O'Neil, J. (1990 March–April). Gender roles, sex and the process of psychotherapy: Many questions and few answers. *Journal of Counseling and Development, 68,* 381–387.

Moos, R. H., & Tsu, D. (1977). The crisis of physical illness: An overview. In R. Moos (Ed.), *Coping with physical illness.* New York: Plenum.

Mosher, D. L. (1966). The development and multitrait-multimethod matrix analysis of three measures of three aspects of guilt. *Journal of Consulting Psychology, 36,* 25–29.

Mosher, D. L., & Cross, H. J. (1971). Sex guilt and premarital sexual experience of college students. *Journal of Consulting and Clinical Psychology, 36,* 27–32.

Mosher, W., & Pratt, W. (1990). *Fecundity and infertility in the United States, 1965–1988* (Advance Data –192). Washington, DC: National Center for Health Statistics.

Mosley, P. (1976). Psychophysiologic infertility: An overview. *Clinical Obstetrics and Gynecology, 19*(2), 407–417.

Nachtigall, R. D., Becker, G., & Wozny, M. (1992, January). The effects of gender-specific diagnosis on men's and women's responses to infertility. *Fertility and Sterility, 57*(1), 113–121.

Noller, P. (1980). Misunderstandings in marital communication: Study of nonverbal communication. *Journal of Personality and Social Psychology, 39,* 1135–1148.

Offit, A. (1981). *Night thoughts: Reflections of a sex therapist.* New York: Congdon-Lettes.

O'Moore, A., O'Moore, R., Harrison, G., & Carruthers, M. (1983). Psychosomatic aspects in idiopathic infertility: Effects of treatment with autogenic training. *Journal of Psychosomatic Research, 27,* 145–151.

Osherson, S. (1986). *Finding our fathers: How a man's life is shaped by his relationship with his father.* New York: Fawcett Columbine.

Owens, D. (1982). The desire to father: Reproductive ideologies and involuntarily childless men. In L. McKee & M. O'Brien (Eds.), *The father figure.* London, New York: Tavistock.

Pachuta, D. (no date). Evaluation and treatment of pain. In A. Skeikh & D. Pachuta (Eds.), *Guided imagery: Workshop training manual* (pp. 383–397). Milwaukee: American Imagery Institute.

Panuthos, C., & Romeo, C. (1984). *Ended beginnings: Healing childbearing losses.* New York: Warner Books.

Peppers, L., & Knapp, R. (1980a). Maternal reactions to involuntary fetal/infant death. *Psychiatry, 43,* 155–159.

Peppers, L., & Knapp, R. (1980b). *Motherhood and mourning: Perinatal death.* New York: Praeger.

Pleck, J., & Sawyer, J. (Eds.). (1974). *Men and masculinity.* Englewood Cliffs, NJ: Prentice-Hall.

Plouffe, L. and McDonough, P. (1982). Recurrent pregnancy loss. Arlington, Massachusetts: RESOLVE (fact sheet).

Quarentelli, E. L. (1960). A note on the protective function of the family in disaster. *Journal of Marriage and Family Living, 22,* 263–264.

Reinharz, S. (1988). What's missing in miscarriage. *Journal of Community Psychology, 16*, 84–103.

Richardson, A. (1969). *Mental imagery.* New York: Springer.

Robinson, S. (1985). *Having a baby without a man: A woman's guide to alternative insemination.* Boston: Simon & Schuster.

Rodrigues, B., Bermudez, L., Ponce de Leon, E., & Castor, L. (1983). The relationship between infertility and anxiety: Some preliminary findings. Paper presented at the Second World Congress of Behavior Therapy, Washington, DC.

Rook, K. S., & Hammen, C. (1977). A cognitive perspective on the experience of sexual arousal. *Journal of Social Issues, 33*(2), 7–29.

Rosen, R., & Lieblum, S. (1987). Current approaches to the evaluation of sexual desire disorders. *Journal of Sex Research, 23*(2), 141–162.

Rosenfeld, D., & Mitchell, E. (1979). Treating the emotional aspects of infertility: Counseling services in an infertility clinic. *American Journal of Obstetrics and Gynecology, 135*(2), 177–180.

Ross, J. (1979). Reflections on the adult crisis of fatherhood and its developmental reverberations. In T. B. Karasu and C. W. Socarides (Eds.) On Sexuality: Psychoanalytic observations. New York: International Universities Press.

Rubin, L. (1985). *Just friends.* New York: Harper & Row.

Russo, N. (1976). The motherhood mandate. *Journal of Social Issues, 32*, 143–153.

Ryan, W. (1971). *Blaming the victim.* New York: Vantage.

Salzer, L. (1986). *Infertility: How couples can cope.* Boston: G. K. Hall.

Sandelowski, M., & Pollock, C. (1986). Women's experiences of infertility. *Images, 18*(4), 140–144.

Scher, M., Stevens, M., Good, G., & Eichenfield, G. (Ed.). (1987). *Handbook of counseling and psychotherapy with men.* Newbury Park, CA: Sage.

Schultz, D. (1978). Imagery and the control of depression. In J. Singer & K. Pope (Eds.), *The power of human imagination.* New York: Plenum.

Schwartz, L. L. (1991). *Alternatives to infertility: Is surrogacy the answer?* New York: Brunner/Mazel.

Seibel, M. M., & Graves, W. L. (1980). The psychological implications of spontaneous abortions. *Journal of Psychosomatic Research, 25*, 161–175.

Seibel, M. M., & Taymor, M. L. (1980). *Emotional aspects of infertility.* Unpublished paper, Division of Reproductive Medicine, Boston.

Sheikh, A. (Ed). (1986). *Anthology of imagery techniques.* Milwaukee: American Imagery Institute.

Sheikh, A., & Jordan, C. (1983). Clinical uses of mental imagery. In A. Sheikh (Ed.), Imagery: Current theory, research and application. New York: Wiley.

Sheikh, A., Sheikh, K., & Moleski, L. M. (1985). Improving imaging abilities. In *Imagery in education.* New York: Baywood.

Shorr, J. E. (1978). Clinical uses of categories of therapeutic imagery. In J. Singer & K. Pope (Eds.), *The power of human imagination.* New York: Plenum.

Silver, R., Boon, C., & Stones, M. (1983). Searching for meaning in misfortune: Making sense of incest. *Journal of Social Issues, 39*, 81–102.

Simons, H. P. (1988). *Resolve, Inc.: Advocacy within a mutual support organization.* Dissertation, Brandeis University. UMI dissertation information service order –8819281.

Singer, J. L. (1974). *Imagery and daydream methods in psychotherapy and behavior modification.* New York: Academic.

Singer, J. L., & Pope, K. S. (1978). The use of imagery and fantasy techniques in psychotherapy. In Singer JL & Pope KS (Eds.), *The power of human imagination*. New York: Plenum.

Singer, J. L. & Switzer, E. (1980). *Mind play: The creative uses of imagery*. Englewood Cliffs, NJ: Prentice-Hall.

Snarey, J. (1988, March). Men without children. *Psychology Today*, pp. 61–62.

Stanton, A., & Dunkel-Schetter, C. (1991). *Infertility: Perspectives from stress and coping research*. New York: Plenum.

Stroebel, C. (1982). *The quieting reflex*. New York: Putnam.

Sturgis, S. H., Taymor, M., & Morris, T. A. (1957). Routine psychiatric interviews in a sterility investigation. *Fertility and Sterility, 8,* 521–528.

Tannen, D. (1990). *You just don't understand: Women and men in conversation*. New York: William Morrow.

Tatelbaum, J. (1984). *The courage to grieve*. New York: Perennial Library, Harper & Row.

Taylor, S. E. (1983). Adjustment to threatening events: A theory of cognitive adaptation. *American Psychologist, 38,* 1161–1173.

Taylor, S. E. (1990). Health psychology: The science and the field. *American Psychologist, 45,* 40–50.

Taylor, S. E., & Brown, J. D. (1988). Illusion and well-being: A social psychological perspective on mental health. *Psychological Bulletin, 103,* 193–210.

Taylor, S. E., & Clark, L. F. (1986). Does information improve adjustment to noxious events? In M. Saks & L. Saxe (Eds.), *Advances in applied social psychology* (Vol. 3, pp. 1–28). Hillsdale, NJ: Erlbaum.

Taylor, S. E., Lichtman, R. R., & Wood, J. V. (1984). Attributions, beliefs about control, and adjustment to breast cancer. *Journal of Personality and Social Psychology, 46,* 489–502.

Taylor, S. E., Wood, J. V., & Lichtman, R. R. (1983). It could be worse: Selective evaluation as a response to victimization. *Journal of Social Issues, 30*(2), 19–40.

Ulanov, A. B. (1983). *Cinderella and her sisters: The envied and the envying*. Philadephia Westminster Press.

Van Keep, P. A., & Schmidt-Elmendorff, H. (1975). Involuntary childlessness. *Journal of Biosocial Science, 7,* 37–48.

Walker, H. E. (1978). Sexual problems and infertility. *Psychosomatics, 19*(8), 477–479, 483–484.

Wellman, B. (1976b). *Urban connections*. Toronto: University of Toronto, Center for Urban and Community Studies.

Wellman, B. (1976a). Community ties and support systems: From intimacy to support. In L. Bourne, R. McKinnon, & J. Simmons (Eds.), *The form of cities in central Canada*. Toronto: University of Toronto Press.

Wilson, R. (1986). *Don't panic*. New York: Harper & Row.

Wolpe, J. (1958). *Psychotherapy by reciprocal inhibition*. Stanford, CA: Stanford University Press.

Woods, J., & Esposito, J. (Eds.). (1987). *Pregnancy loss: Medical, therapeutic and practical considerations*. Baltimore, MD: Williams & Wilkins.

Woollett, A. (1985). Childlessness: Strategies for coping with infertility. *International Journal of Behavorial Development, 8,* 473–482.

Wright, J., (1991, 1 January). Psychosocial distress and infertility: Men and women respond differently. *Fertility and Sterility, 55,* 100–108.

Young, M. (1980). Body image and female's sexual behavior. *Perception and Motor Skills, 50,* 425–426.

Zilbergeld, B. (1978). *Male sexuality.* New York: Bantam.

Zilbergeld, B., & Lazarus, A. A. (1987). *Mind power: Getting what you want through mental training.* Boston: Little, Brown.

Zoldbrod, A. (1988). The emotional distress of the artificial insemination patient. *Medical Psychotherapy, 1,* 161–172.

Zoldbrod, A. P. (1990). *Getting around the boulder in the road: Using imagery to cope with fertility problems.* Lexington, MA. [Order from 12 Rumford Road, Lexington, MA 02173; $6.50 in U.S., $8.00 outside U.S.; Mass residents add 5% sales tax.)

Zoldbrod, A. P. (1991, 19 August). Men's reactions to infertility. Paper presented at the Ninety-ninth Annual Convention of the American Psychological Association: Symposium on men and parenting over the life cycle, San Francisco.

Index

About the Author

Aline P. Zoldbrod, Ph.D., is a licensed psychologist and certified sex therapist in private practice in the Boston area. A seasoned practitioner with over 20 years of experience, she is known for her engaged and highly interactive style. She works with individuals, couples, families, and groups.

Besides working with issues of sexuality, infertility, and miscarriage, she treats people for many other problems, including addiction; post-traumatic stress disorder; the sequellae of physical, emotional, and sexual abuse; medical problems; depression; grief; and the strains of adjusting to developmental crises. A expert in wife abuse, she consults to clinics and teaches continuing education courses, training professionals on how to recognize and treat family violence. She also is a specialist in the behavioral treatment of panic and anxiety.

She has served on the national Board of Directors of RESOLVE since 1984, serving on the Clinical Committee, the Personnel Committee, and as the current Chair of the Minority Outreach Committee. Dr. Zoldbrod also is one of the consulting editors for the Human Sexuality Information and Advisory Service (HSX), a sex education and information service available to the 725,000 subscribers of the Compu-Serve computer network.

Besides this book, she is the author of several articles on infertility as well as the self help booklet *Getting Around the Boulder in the Road: Using Imagery to Cope with Fertility Problems*. She currently is working on a new book about couples and sexuality.

A dynamic speaker, she has had many speaking and training engagements in the areas of stress control, infertility, aging, and family violence. Nationally, her approach to working with infertile individuals and couples has been featured at several conferences, and she has been quoted in the *Boston Globe* and the *New York Times* on fertility problems.

If you are interested in having Dr. Zoldbrod do training or consultation for your organization or group, she can be contacted at 617-863-1877. Dr. Zoldbrod lives in Lexington, Massachusetts with her husband and two children.